HUBRIS

HUBRIS

A Brief Political History
of the

NIGERIAN ARMY

Akintunde A. Akinkunmi

AMVPS

Published by

AMV Publishing

P.O. Box 661
Princeton, NJ 08542-0661
Tel: 609-227-0220; Fax: 609-7164770
emails: publisher@amvpublishingservices.com &
customerservice@amvpublishingservices.com
worldwide web: www.amvpublishingservices.com

Hubris: A Brief Political History of the Nigerian Army

Book & Cover Design: AMV Origination & Design Division

Library of Congress Control Number: 2017959129

ISBNs: 978-0-9984796-7-5 (Paperback); 978-0-9984796-8-2 (e-Book)

Photos marked with asterisk (***) are courtesy of *The Punch* Newspapers of
Nigeria.

DEDICATION

This book is dedicated to the memory of the officers and men of the Nigerian Army (and of its' sister Services) who lost their lives in the upheavals between 1966 and 1999.

Contents

LIST OF ABBREVIATIONS

ABN	Association for a Better Nigeria
AD	Alliance for Democracy
ADC	Aide de Camp
AFCA	Armed Forces Consultative Assembly
AFRC	Armed Forces Ruling Council
AG	Action Group
APP	All Peoples Party
BOI	Board of Inquiry
CA	Constituent Assembly
CDC	Constitution Drafting Committee
CDCC	Constitution Debate Coordinating Committee
CDS	Chief of Defence Staff
CGS	Chief of the General Staff
CMS	Church Missionary Society
CNC	Committee of National Consensus
CO	Commanding Officer
CRC	Constitution Review Committee
CSM	Company Sergeant Major
DFRRI	Directorate of Food, Roads and Rural Infrastructure
DPA	Distributable Pool Account
DPN	Democratic Party of Nigeria
FEDECO	Federal Electoral Commission
FESTAC	World Black and African Festival of Arts and Culture
GCE	General Certificate of Education
GDM	Grassroots Democratic Movement
GNPP	Great Nigerian Peoples Party
GOC	General Officer Commanding
HQ	Headquarters
IBB	Ibrahim Badamasi Babangida
ICRC	International Committee of the Red Cross
IMF	International Monetary Fund
INEC	Independent National Election Commission
ING	Interim National Government
IS	Internal Security
MAMSER	Mass Mobilisation for Economic Reconstruction, Social Justice and Self Reliance
MCDO	Marine Commando
NA	Nigerian Army
NADECO	National Democratic Coalition

NANS	National Association of Nigerian Students
NARD	National Association of Resident Doctors
NBA	Nigerian Bar Association
NCNC	National Council of Nigerian Citizens
NCO	Non Commissioned Officer
NCPN	National Centre Party of Nigeria
NDA	Nigerian Defence Academy
NDSC	National Defence and Security Council
NECON	National Election Commission
NEPU	Northern Elements Progressive Union
NIPSS	National Institute for Policy and Strategic Studies
NLC	Nigerian Labour Congress
NMA	Nigerian Medical Association
NMTC	Nigerian Military Training College
NNA	Nigerian National Alliance
NNDP	Nigerian National Democratic Party
NPC	Northern Peoples Congress
NPMC	Nigerian Produce Marketing Company
NPN	National Party of Nigeria
NPP	Nigerian Peoples Party
NR	Nigerian Regiment
NRC	National Republican Convention
NSO	National Security Organisation
NUPENG	National Union of Petroleum and Natural Gas Workers
NYSC	National Youth Service Corps
OAU	Organisation of African Unity
OCS	Officer Cadet School
OFN	Operation Feed the Nation
OIC	Organisation of the Islamic Conference
PDP	Peoples Democratic Party
PENGASSAN	Petroleum and Natural Gas Senior Staff Association
PRC	Provisional Ruling Council
PRP	Peoples Redemption Party
QONR	Queens Own Nigerian Regiment
RCDS	Royal College of Defence Studies
Recce	Reconnaissance
RMAS	Royal Military Academy Sandhurst
RNA	Royal Nigerian Army
ROSTS	Regular Officers Special Training School
RSM	Regimental Sergeant Major
RWAFF	Royal West African Frontier Force
SAP	Structural Adjustment Programme

SDP	Social Democratic Party
SIP	Special Investigation Panel
SMC	Supreme Military Council
SMT	Special Military Tribunal
SNCO	Senior Noncommissioned Officer
TIC	Transition Implementation Committee
UAC	United African Company
UMBC	United Middle Belt Congress
UN	United Nations
UNIFIL	United Nations Interim Force in Lebanon
UNPC	United Nigerian Peoples Convention
UPE	Universal Primary Education
UPGA	United Progressives Grand Alliance
UPN	Unity Party of Nigeria
WAI	War Against Indiscipline

CHRONOLOGY OF NIGERIAN MILITARY LEADERS (1966-1999)

1. Major-General Johnson Aguiyi-Ironsi (16 Jan 1966 - 29 Jul 1966)
2. General Yakubu Gowon (01 Aug 1966 - 29 Jul 1975)
3. General Murtala Muhammed (29 Jul 1975 - 13 Feb 1976)
4. General Olusegun Obasanjo (14 Feb 1976 - 01 Oct 1979)
5. Major-General Muhammadu Buhari (31 Dec 1983 - 27 Aug 1985)
6. General Ibrahim Badamasi Babangida (27 Aug 1985-27 Aug 1993)
7. General Sani Abacha (17 Nov 1993 - 08 June 1998)
8. General Abdulsalam Abubakar (09 Jun 1998-29 May 1999)

Foreword

Vice-Admiral (rtd.) GTA Adekeye, CFR mni

It gives me great pleasure to write this foreword to Dr. Akinkunmi's book, *Hubris: A Brief Political History of the Nigerian Army*.

I have known Dr. Akinkunmi for several years now. His easy and expressive communication style, combined with his punctuality and urbane wisdom immediately made it easy for me to relate with him, but none of this is perhaps surprising in a man who is both a doctor and a lawyer, and has reached high rank in the British Army. He has demonstrated, in my interactions with him, and in this book, a sound knowledge of military operations and a good grasp of the development trajectory of the Nigerian Armed Forces, and especially of the Army's forays into politics. In these days when the Nigerian nation has stopped the teaching of history in schools, with the attendant danger of a whole generation of our younger citizens being blind to the turbulent development of our democracy, his rendition of this history in this book is a valuable asset, and is a delight to read.

This book takes the reader through the unedifying origin of the Army as a punitive and repressive organ of the colonial government, which made the Army as an institution alien to the population. One is enabled to follow the development of the Army through two world wars and the run-up to independence, during which time the Army was a replica on Nigerian soil of the British Army's apolitical nature. Deployments on peacekeeping operations at home and abroad did not appear to have shifted the Army from its apolitical stance, and it was able to resist the attempt by President Azikiwe to involve the Army in politics after the controversial 1964 Federal elections.

Dr. Akinkunmi takes us through the events of January and July 1966, but the real value of this book lies in its analysis of the various military regimes over the next three decades or so, highlighting their strengths, successes and failures as the Army's top and middle echelons exhibited a dog-eat-dog syndrome, toppling one another, ostensibly to eliminate corruption whilst actually fertilizing it. Dr. Akinkunmi's background as a psychiatrist is likely to have been an asset in his discussion of the personalities involved in the upheavals during this time. This book is a compendium of the development and subsequent decline of the Nigerian Army as a consequence of its involvement in the politics of Nigeria, and I heartily commend this book to anyone desirous of a deeper understanding of the Army and the politics of Nigeria.

December, 2017

(Vice-Admiral (rtd.) GTA Adekeye was Chief of Naval Staff, Nigerian Navy 2005-2008)

Lt. General Ipoola A. Akinrinade, CFR FSS

Akintunde Akinkunmi has carefully chosen the word "Hubris" as the title of this Brief History of the Nigerian Army as the contents will reveal how the Army originated, developed, acquitted itself around Africa, earned a good reputation before it got mired in Nigeria's politics and came to grief.

The colonial origin had tilted its composition in favour of Northern Nigeria and its colonial creed had not endeared it to the South, which the author captured as the theme that determined its outlook and activities before and after Nigeria attained independence in 1960.

The author had a concise, but still vivid and accurate description of pre and post independence political setting, activities of the political classes, the delicate relationships between them, and above all, their varying outlooks with regards to the future of the country. It appears however, that had there been sufficient understanding, goodwill and less of sectional agenda, especially by the Northern politicians, the civil war could have been averted. Who knows? Perhaps If Gowon had been allowed to implement, howbeit with some slight agreed modifications, the September 1966 report of the ad hoc Committee and the Aburi accord that followed thereafter, the course of Nigerian history might have been different. I do not share entirely Akinkunmi's fear that the agreement could have left Northern Nigeria without a navy, as I do not think a land locked nation has need for a Navy nor the resultant regional armies could have been nothing more than "glorified regional militias" as the regions had functioning regional governments backed by the political classes. The agreement did not amount to a complete disintegration of the country, at worst, it portended a loose federation.

The events that led to the civil war, the prosecution of the war with all its ugly carnage as the extension of the various pogroms before it, were dealt with succinctly. The ragtag label attached to the war machine, the incompetence of the leadership and the inability of the central command to come to grips with firm control of the operations are accurate observations by the author. The unwillingness of the Northern leadership to demobilize after the war and the lasting effect of that dereliction, lingers on till the present as the author noted.

The work has traced with deadly accuracy the various military interventions, numbering seven; the underlying reasons, the course of those coup d'états and the disastrous results of each one. The author read correctly, to my mind, the nature, character, competence and motives of the executors of each of the coup d'états. He has a good trace of the lives of most of the senior officers involved, their backgrounds and career trajectories. He did no less on the various military heads of state in his narrative.

Akinkunmi decided to write a brief history of the Nigerian Army putting it in the context of the institution's foray into the country's politics. In the concise work, he addresses both aspects exhaustively, accurately, and methodically. His language is simple as if he knew a work like this would be of immense value to the young, who, for undisclosed reasons, have been deprived of the study of history in the current official school curriculums. Perhaps, I hazard, that it could be devastating to link the pogrom of the 1960s to the on going carnage being perpetrated by the Fulani herdsmen in the Middle-Belt and southern parts of the country.

This is a welcome addition to literature currently available on the Nigerian Army. The book will be attractive to the generality of those interested in examining why Nigeria, in spite of all its natural advantages, has remained a dysfunctional country. I recommend it to all segments of the reading public.

January 2018

(Lt. General (rtd.) Ipoola A. Akinrinade was Nigeria's Chief of Army Staff, (1979-1980) and Chief of Defense Staff (1980-1981) during the Second Republic)

Air Vice Marshall (rtd.) A. D. Bello, GCON CFR

Dr. Akinkunmi took on a noble task when he decided to write on a brief political history of the Nigerian Army, a very important institution in the evolution of the modern Nigerian state. Seeing how the Army's long association with the country, especially its leadership has determined the developmental strides or otherwise of the country, I consider the book an important contribution to scholarship.

In the early years of its establishment, not only was the army free from the political meddlesomeness of leading politicians, it enjoyed the undivided respect of all. And when the conditions of service of the officers were improved and made comparable with those in the public service, interests and commission into the army grew. And the institution strictly maintained its constitutional duty of defense of the territorial integrity of the country, chalking up remarkable feats in international peace missions when invited to do so.

While the author did his bit to interrogate the relationship between the army's evolution and its relationship with political development in Nigeria, and the kind of impact this association may have had separately and jointly on the spirit of the army and government in Nigeria, I believe it must always be stressed that scholarship of the subject must be undergirded by a sense of balance and fairness. For example, when General Gowon introduced the phenomenon of states creation in the days leading to the Civil War, it was a decision made following due consultation and consideration of its likely effect on the tense atmosphere in the country at the time, which eventually proved fortuitous. Therefore, to place the creation of states on that occasion and treat it in much less the same way as subsequent attempts at states creation did not take the principle of balance and fairness into account.

In another vein, the author's treatment of the number of troops of the Nigerian army just before the Civil War and after the War would have gone full cycle had he included the historical fact of restructuring of the army, which led to a significant reduction in the number of officers and men, following the exercise carried out by the army, in the mid-70s, under the leadership of General T Y Danjuma, as Chief of Army Staff.

While the army must carry the can for whatever gaps and failures it is alleged to have introduced into the Nigerian society, the purpose of scholarship is not helped if investigators avoid the almost corrupting roles of politicians, who held nocturnal meetings with soldiers, sold all kinds of ideas to them, then distanced themselves from these soldiers, when the public chose to lionize them. Surely, it would make for interesting reading to know the roles leading politicians played in the various military coups and subsequent governments that were formed in Nigeria.

The author's treatment of the Civil War, especially the extant factors and immediate causes, and the roles of the principal actors, is concise and in line with the generally accepted narrative but more details about the gallantry or otherwise of specific officers would surely have raised the strength of the work. Perhaps, because the author set out to do a 'brief' historical account, he did not engage in deep analyses of the respective merits and demerits of the dominant decisions taken by the successive military regimes, despite his demonstrated expertise and thoroughness.

Speaking of thoroughness, and since the book is about being presented, I am of the view that mention should be made of the stabilizing role the army has made since the return to democracy in 1999. We have had two former soldiers as presidents, and countless officers as one political leader or another. And thanks to the army, we have significantly managed the recent threat of terrorism in the country.

November 28, 2017

(Air Vice Marshal (rtd.) A.D. Bello, was Chief of Air Staff 1980-1983)

***

Acknowledgements

This book represents the culmination of a virtually lifelong fascination with all things military (and particularly the Nigerian Army) and with the history of the Nigerian State. That fascination has led, in part, to more than a quarter of a century of service (and counting) in the British Army, but it has also spurred several years of seeking out information and knowledge on these subjects of interest; the acquisition of that knowledge has in turn brought home the need to share it widely with the several generations of Nigerians that very sadly remain ignorant of the history of their country.

A chance conversation in 2014 with Air Vice Marshal (rtd) Abdullahi Dominic Bello, Chief of the Air Staff in Nigeria between 1980 and 1983, and a fount of knowledge and wisdom, provided the spark that triggered my putting pen to paper – I am deeply grateful to Oga Abdul for that, and for his graciously consenting to write the foreword.

I am also deeply grateful to two former Service Chiefs — Lieutenant General (rtd) Alani Akinrinade CFR, Chief of Army Staff from 1979 to 1980 as well as Chief of the Defence Staff from 1980 to 1981, and Vice Admiral (rtd) Ganiyu Tunde Adekeye CFR, Chief of Naval Staff from 2005 to 2008, for kindly agreeing to review and comment on the manuscript. Sirs, you have both been an inspiration to me in my own (slightly less stellar) military career

I am grateful also for the very professional help of my publisher, Damola Ifaturoti of AMV Publishing in the U.S. — Taffy, many thanks indeed.

Several friends and family members, too numerous to list here, provided encouragement and support throughout the long gestation period of this book — I am deeply grateful to you all.

Any errors are, of course, my responsibility.

Akintunde Akinkunmi
London, April 2017

Introduction

A purely contemporary view of any problem is necessarily a limited and even distorted view. Every situation has its roots in the past...the past survives into the present; the present is indeed the past undergoing modification.[1]
— **S. Phillipson and S.O. Adebo**

The Nigerian Army is an institution that has played a pivotal role in the affairs of the Federal Republic of Nigeria. For more than half of the fifty-seven years since Independence, Nigeria was directly ruled by a Military Government, largely composed of army officers, and always headed by one. It is impossible to explore any facet of modern Nigerian history or society without the military (and in particular the Army) looming significantly. Whilst several authors have documented the history of Nigeria (and significantly less many of its Army), rarely, if ever, has the impact of the politics of Nigeria on the Army, and vice-versa, formed the *exclusive* subject of study. This volume is an endeavor to plug that gap.

The interplay between the Army and the politics of Nigeria antedates the formal existence of both country and Army. In order to properly explore the interaction between Nigerian politics and the Nigerian Army, it is necessary to start by examining the evolution of both Army and country. The period leading up to the Army's first overt entry into the politics of Nigeria is then looked at, firstly in the pre-Independence years, and then in the years immediately following independence. The effects of the Nigerianisation of the Army, especially of the officer corps, and of the policy decisions made following the passing of control over the Army from the British to the Nigerian Governments are considered. The political circumstances surrounding the Army's first overt entry into politics

— the January 1966 coup — and the political performance of the subsequent first military regime are discussed, as a precursor to the second coup in July 1966.

Previous brothers-in-arms found themselves on opposing sides in the bloody civil war that followed. The impact of the Army's direct involvement in politics on the military performance of both sides in the Civil War is explored. The rapid and large expansion of the Army during the war had consequences both for the military conduct of the war and for the post-war political performance of the military government. After a nine-year interregnum, in July 1975 Nigeria returned to the era of coups, with at least eight attempted and successful coups, some of them bloody, over the next quarter century before the return to civilian rule in 1999. Other writers have explored the coups in some detail; that is beyond the remit of the present study, save for how the genesis, participants and execution of the coups impacted upon the military governments that followed each of them. The personalities leading the resultant military governments, and the policies of those governments, are explored, in an attempt to discern their legacy on the political development of Nigeria, and on the Nigerian Army as an institution. It is, for example, instructive to note that of the four civilian presidents of Nigeria since the return to civilian rule in 1999, two are retired generals who were both former military heads of state.

The analyses in this book will present evidence, direct and circumstantial, in order to reach conclusions that will provoke discussion, agreement and dissent. If, in so doing, this volume adds to the ability of Nigerians to better understand their history whilst retaining the ability to disagree without falling out, it will have served its purpose.

Notes: Introduction

1. S. Phillipson and S. O. Adebo. *The Nigerianisation of the Civil Service*, in A. H. M. Kirk-Greene, *Crisis and Conflict in Nigeria* (Lagos: Oxford University Press, 1954), Vol. 1, p. 5.

CHAPTER 1

In the Beginning

Personally, I am thoroughly of the opinion that the force should consist as far as may be of Hausas, who by universal consensus of opinion are the best fighting men and the most amenable to discipline.

— Lord Lugard

The Nigerian Army as we know it today is completely unrecognizable from its early, humble beginnings. Currently embroiled in a ferocious counter insurgency campaign in the Northeast of the country, and having previously fought an equally bloody Civil War in the South of the country in the late 1960s, it can, with some justification, lay claim to being a tool for preserving the territorial integrity and the security of the Nigerian nation. This, however, is far from having always been the case.

The sundry forces that evolved into what we now know as the Nigerian Army were anything but designed to protect and defend the inhabitants of the country that later became known as Nigeria. On the contrary, these forces were designed to subjugate and cow the inhabitants into submission to the will of the British colonial authorities acting through a number of surrogates. The best known of these surrogate forces were Glover's Hausas, a motley collection of runaway slaves and other miscreants from what is now Northern Nigeria who attached themselves to Lieutenant John Glover, RN, during that officer's journey overland from Jebba, where his ship, the *Day Spring*, was wrecked during an 1863 experimental voyage to Lagos on the River Niger. These individuals, initially fewer than twenty in number, grew to become several hundred strong, and were mainly used thereafter to protect British trade routes into and out of Lagos, and to mount punitive raids into the surrounding hinterland, for example, in Ijebu in 1892 and Oyo in 1895. Similar use was made of other militias such as the Oil Rivers Irregulars raised in the East in 1885 (with punitive raids to Brass in 1894 and Benin in 1897), and the Royal Niger Constabulary Company raised in the North by Sir George Goldie in 1886 (with punitive raids to Nupe in 1896 and Ilorin in 1897).[1] These forces were also used to subdue the Ashanti rebellion in 1900, and to subdue Sultan Attahiru Ahmad of Sokoto in 1903 (resulting in the formal annexation of the whole of what is now Northern Nigeria).

All these forces were eventually consolidated into what became known as the Nigeria Regiment of the West African Frontier Force (WAFF), under the command of Lieutenant Colonel Lugard. If there were any doubt as to the purpose for establishing this force, such doubts are quickly dispelled by a reading of the July 1897 telegram in which the command of this force is offered to Lugard:

> From the Secretary of State for Colonies to High Commissioner, Cape Town. London, July 30 1897. It is the intention of H.M.'s Government to raise without delay a West African Force of two thousand or three thousand men to occupy important places in the Hinterland of Gold Coast and Niger territories which are within the British sphere of influence and which otherwise may be occupied by the French. [Author's emphasis]. Forward this information by letter in the most sure and secret manner, if possible in cipher, to Major Lugard, and in the name of H.M.'s Government offer him the command of this force at a salary of one thousand, five hundred pounds and with the title of Commissioner and Commandant of the forces with the local rank of Lieutenant-Colonel.[2]

It seems clear that the purpose of this force, far from being to protect the populace, was to protect British colonial interests from being usurped by the competing French.

The formation of the Nigeria Regiment of the WAFF occurred shortly before the outbreak of hostilities in the First World War. It comprised, at the outbreak of the war, of four infantry battalions and one mounted infantry battalion, with units stationed at Kaduna, Lokoja, Calabar, Lagos; and Kano. The outbreak of war prompted a recruiting drive, and, given the thrust of the present work, Lugard's views on this subject are worth quoting:

Personally, I am thoroughly of the opinion that the force should consist as far as may be of Hausas, who by universal consensus of opinion are the best fighting men and the most amenable to discipline.[3]

In this context, it is hardly surprising that it became official policy that only one language, Hausa, was to be used in the instruction of local recruits. This approach to recruitment was not unique to Nigeria. The former Chief of General Staff of the British Army, General Richard Dannatt, in his book *Boots on the Ground: Britain and Her Army Since 1945*, describes the British approach to recruitment in India thus:

...Senior commanders who held to "martial race" theories were biased in favour of certain ethnic groups, particularly the Sikhs.... many (Indian) nationalist politicians...regarded the army as "the sword of the Raj", the instrument not of India's defence but of continuing British rule...the British had conquered and held India by the use of Indian military manpower.[4]

Wherever they came from, these troops saw action in the conquest of German Kamerun (today's Cameroon) and in Tanganyika in German East Africa (today's Tanzania); this commitment overseas did not preclude their simultaneous use in suppressing the rebellion by the people of Abeokuta against Lugard's imposition of indirect rule upon them.[5] The First World War produced up a remarkable individual named Chari Maigumeri. A Kanuri from Maiduguri, he joined the German Kamerun Force in 1913, before the outbreak of the war, at a time when tribal and ethnic links, rather than national borders, mattered. He was captured by troops of the Nigerian Regiment in 1915, but not before he had been awarded the Iron Cross by the Germans for gallantry in action. Upon his release from captivity in 1917, he responded to a call for volunteers to join the Nigeria Regiment, and subsequently he served in German East Africa, this time fighting against the Germans. His service in the Nigerian Regiment extended up to and beyond the Second World War, where he again saw action in East Africa and was decorated for gallantry, this time with the Military Medal. He was also awarded the British Empire Medal in the King's Birthday Honours List in 1944. He attended the coronation ceremonies of both King George VI and Queen Elizabeth II, as well as the funeral of the former, all as a representative of the Nigeria Regiment. Upon his retirement in 1953, Maigumeri was made an Honorary Captain in the Nigeria Regiment.

The interwar years saw the Nigeria Regiment shrink to its prewar establishment of four infantry battalions, and it was mainly involved in low-level operations. However, the one significant incident during this period was the so-called *yakin mata* or Women's War of 1929-30, when the imposition of taxes provoked furious riots by women traders in Eastern Nigeria. With the outbreak of the Second World War in 1939, the Nigerian Regiment again required significant expansion, which meant another recruitment drive. Although there were some incidents of forced conscription, such as that which occurred after a protest by schoolboys at King's College in Lagos,[6] the majority of the new entrants were willing volunteers, though not necessarily well-informed ones.

The Nigeria Regiment saw action against the Italians in Abyssinia (now Ethiopia) and in Somalia in 1940-41; the First, Second and Third Battalions of the regiment constituted the Twenty-third (West Africa) Brigade, which, along with the Twenty-first (East Africa) Brigade, made up the Eleventh (African) Division. The Fourth, Sixth, Seventh and Twelfth Battalions of the regiment constituted the Third (West African) Brigade, which, with other formations from the Gold Coast (now Ghana), Sierra Leone, and the Gambia made up the Eighty-first (West Africa) Division, which saw action against the Japanese in Burma in 1943-44. A second division, Eighty-second (West Africa) Division, was later raised. The names of several places where hard-fought battles took place have passed into the modern-day lexicon of the Nigerian Army as barracks and cantonment names — Dodan, Letmauk, and Arakan being just a few examples.

Those troops who had joined the Nigeria Regiment as a result of the war (i.e., most of them) were demobilized upon their return to Nigeria at the war's end. They were paid gratuities, which depended on rank, and efforts were made to secure employment for them in and outside of government service. The regiment was reduced to five Infantry battalions and supporting units such as an artillery battery and medical, transport, signals, and electrical and mechanical engineers, and it was mainly employed over the next decade in training and ceremonial duties. The one exception was in 1948, when large-scale civil disturbances broke out in the Gold Coast, and three battalions of the Regiment were flown in to help restore order; they were all back in Nigeria by the following year.[7]

The troops returning from the Second World War brought with them more than the fighting experience. They mixed with troops from other parts of the Commonwealth, particularly India, where nationalist agitation for independence was more advanced than they were used to at home. They also realized that Caucasians generally, and the British in particular, were not the omnipotent and invincible beings they had been brought up to believe. They returned to a country where nationalist agitation by the intelligentsia (political groups, journalists, students, etc.) was on the rise. Despite the fact that soldiers in general commanded very little prestige in society (see below), the intelligentsia nonetheless made common cause with the returnees as far as this particular issue was concerned.

The general disdain for servicemen in Nigeria was long-standing, and had no particular geographical focus. For example, as far back as the nineteenth century, the men of the Niger Coast Constabulary were referred to as the Forty Thieves. In 1962 the Sardauna of Sokoto described the origins of the military in Nigeria thus:

> When the British came to the North, they started recruiting their army of soldiers by getting slaves who ran away from their masters, labourers from the markets and so on, and had them enlisted by force....We did not like the soldiers; they were our own people and had conquered us for strangers...[8]

In the East, the people's view of the army was described in 1963 by Major Tony Eze in the *Nigerian Army Magazine* as follows:

> The army was a place for the illiterates and criminals whose duties were to kill and be generally brutal. The activities of some soldiers in the villages and markets during the last war only confirmed their opinions.

And in the West, the view was summed up by Chief Longe in the course of a Senate debate in 1965:

> I remember during the last war some soldiers were brought to my area at Ede...most of them committed atrocities.[10]

This level of disdain for service personnel did not escape the attention of visiting expatriates. A letter to the *West African Pilot* newspaper in 1956 complained that:

> I have visited many countries in my life, but in none have I seen soldiers being treated with such discourtesy as I have in Nigeria and especially here in Lagos...what I see in Lagos is abuse, insult and derision...[11]

Politicians whose fate would be inexorably tied to that of the army were not left out either. Chief S. L. Akintola, who, as premier of the West, would be killed in the January 1966 coup, requested during a 1955 parliamentary debate that military units be moved out of Lagos, because "the proximity of some of these army headquarters to the areas where civilians live is most embarrassing to us...." The following year, Mr. Louis Ojukwu, the father of the future leader of the attempted breakaway of the Republic of Biafra that triggered the bloody Civil War, declared in the same House that "...nobody likes to live with soldiers. We like them; they are our brothers; but at the same time we would like them to be far from us."[12]

So just how did an institution that was held in such widespread disdain by politicians and populace alike come to exert such a profound and enduring impact on the politics of Nigeria, and in turn was just as much impacted upon by politics? N.J. Miners who has explored in some detail the received wisdom in the run up to independence, concludes that the army as an institution was aloof from politics in every sense, and that the prospects of it becoming involved as a major player on the political scene were vanishingly small for a number of reasons. First, it was small in size; at independence, the entirety of the Nigerian military (including the fledgling navy) numbered no more than 7500, which, for a country with a population of at least 45 million, was miniscule (by comparison, Argentina at the time had a population half the size of Nigeria's, and an army of 120,000).[13] Second, given the army's relative lack of prestige as discussed earlier, it was seen as a mercenary force employed in the subjugation of the indigenous people and not as an object of national pride; nor was it seen as having been involved in the struggle for independence. A third reason was the relative lack of African officers: in 1951, there were only thirteen officers in the four

West African colonies of Nigeria, the Gold Coast, Sierra Leone, and the Gambia; in January 1956, there were only fifteen Nigerian officers in the Nigeria Regiment. There were therefore precious few officers who might be inclined toward intervention in politics; even if they were, the organization of such an intervention in an army in which the Officer Corps and the Warrant Officers and Senior NCOs were overwhelmingly white Britons would take some doing.

Or so it was thought. All of these factors would change with the approach of independence.

NOTES

1. Miners, NJ. *The Nigerian Army: 1956-1966*, Methuen & Co., 1971, pp. 12-13; Nigerian Army Education Corps and School. *History of the Nigerian Army: 1863-1992*. Nigerian Army HQ, 1992, pp. 21-26.

2. NAECS pp. 29-30.

3. Ibid, p. 38.

4. Dannatt, General The Lord Richard. *Boots on the Ground: Britain and Her Army Since 1945*. Profile Books 2016, pp. 36-37.

5. Miners p13.

6. Enahoro, Chief Anthony. *Fugitive Offender: An Autobiography*. Casell, 1965 pp. 68-70.

7. NAECS pp. 98-100.

8. Miners p. 29.

9. Ibid p. 30.

10. Ibid.

11. Ibid.

12. Ibid p. 31.

13. Ibid pp. 2-4.

CHAPTER 2
The Political Background

We introduced a quota system in the army, thus preventing the possible fear that the Army would sometimes become unreliable....But now....this country's safety is assured.

– Ibrahim Tako Galadima, Minister of State (Army), May 1965

The British colonial authorities gave little serious thought to handing over of power to Nigerians prior to 1950. When the process began, it was generally acknowledged that, in addition to the political process, there would also be a need to start promoting Nigerians into senior positions in the public services that had hitherto been the exclusive preserve of white Britons. A committee appointed by the Governor-General, Sir John Macpherson, and headed by the Chief Secretary, Hugh Foot (and included Dr. Nnamdi Azikiwe and Alhaji Muhammadu Ribadu as members), laid down the rules by which Nigerianisation would proceed:[1] no non-Nigerian would be recruited when a qualified and suitable Nigerian was available,[2] there would be no discrimination in favour of Nigerians for promotion, and standards would not be lowered. These remained the basis of official government policy for the next decade.

It is worth noting that the army was not covered by this arrangement because it was not regarded as part of the Nigerian public service. Upon the outbreak of war in 1939, the colonial government in Nigeria had placed the Nigeria Regiment under the authority of the Army Council in London, and this continued after the war ended. This meant that the army in Nigeria came under the budget of the UK and received very limited contribution from the Nigerian taxpayer; this in turn meant that the Nigerian government (both Executive and Legislative branches) had very little say in how the military budget was spent; he who pays the piper dictates the tune. (This situation prompted an exasperated and entirely justified — complaint from one legislator in Parliament in March 1955 that "...the Nigeria Regiment is no more nor less than the British Army stationed in this country, subject to the Army Council of the British War Office....Is the Nigeria Regiment just Nigerian only in name?"[3] In 1956, the Nigeria Regiment consisted of some two hundred and fifty officers, and six thousand four hundred from other ranks, of which there were only fifteen Nigerian officers, but more than three hundred British warrant officers and SNCOs. The majority of the British Officers were newly commissioned doing their two-year compulsory national service; whilst the rest were regulars, on secondment from their regiments and corps in the British Army to West Africa Command, with headquarters in Accra, Ghana, under whose operational command the Nigeria Regiment fell. Although the paucity of Nigerian officers was slowly becoming an issue, what was more aggravating at the time to nationalist opinion was the vast gulf in pay and conditions between British SNCOs and their Nigerian counterparts. They were messed separately and some schools were provided exclusively for the children of white servicemen only. N.J. Miners gives an example:

> ....an African RSM drawing full allowances received less than 20 pounds a month, travelled second class on the railway and had to pay for his wife to travel with him. But a British sergeant whose wife was with him in Nigeria was paid more than 20 pounds a week, travelled first class and had leave allowances paid for his wife and children".[4]

It is debatable whether the fact that the British taxpayer, and not the Nigerian one, was funding the army at this time justified such overt discrimination.

The pattern of recruitment Lugard laid down at the time of the establishment of the WAFF continued in the interwar years, i.e., virtually all army recruits were from the North. The Second World War called for a significant expansion of the RWAFF, requiring large numbers of tradesmen such as clerks, storemen, signallers, drivers, and mechanics. The exigencies of that war meant there were no white men available to fill these roles, and the fact that such roles required some degree of formal education meant that the majority of the tradesmen thus recruited were southerners, since that was where the bulk of the educated population was to be found. The resulting schism between northern infantrymen and southern tradesmen continued after the war, and assumed a greater significance after control of the army passed to Nigerians at independence.

As stated earlier, there was no parallel process of Nigerianisation of the officer Corps of the army as there was in the senior echelons of the public service. Throughout the Second World War, only one West African, Lieutenant Seth Anthony of the Gold Coast, was commissioned. The first Nigerian officer, Lieutenant Ugboma, was not commissioned until 1948. He was a serving NCO at the time of his short-service commission, and the same applied to the next half-dozen commissioned officers (Lieutenants Bassey, Sey, Aguiyi-Ironsi, and Ademulegun in 1949; and Lieutenant Shodeinde and Wellington in 1950 and 1952 respectively). The first regular officers were not commissioned until 1953, when Second Lieutenants Maimalari and Umar Lawan passed out of the Royal Military Academy Sandhurst (RMAS).

It is interesting to note the requirements laid down for a candidate (serving SNCOs and warrant officers) for a short-service commission when appearing before a selection board: he (and they were all male) must be between the ages of twenty-five and thirty, a British subject, of a high medical category, and have passes in English and three other subjects at GCE O-Level. It is hardly surprising that the first half-dozen officers commissioned were all from southern Nigeria, where such educational qualifications were more likely to be found. If successful at the board, the candidate then had to successfully navigate a sixteen-week course at either Mons or Eaton Hall Officer Cadet Schools in Aldershot and Chester respectively.

It is therefore surprising to note that the first five regular officers to pass out of RMAS were all northerners, given that region's acknowledged relative lack of educational establishments; it is even more surprising when one notes the number of hurdles they had to overcome in order to reach their goal. These were ostensibly to ensure that the necessary standards were kept up, and that the finished product would stand up to scrutiny; in fact, the standards were much more stringent than those required of a British cadet for a regular commission. The Nigerian had to pass the following levels:

1.   A general written examination
2.   Medical examination
3.   Interview at District Headquarters
4.   Interview at Army Headquarters
5.   Six-month recruit course at Teshie in the Gold Coast
6.   Final selection Board at Teshie
7.   Four-month officer cadet course at Eaton Hall or at Mons
8.   Regular Commissions Selection Board
9.   Eighteen-month course at RMAS

It was not unknown for Nigerian candidates to fall at any of these hurdles, up to and including the penultimate one, the Regular Commissions Selection Board. By contrast, the British candidate did not have to pass two selection boards, nor did he have to attend a recruit course or the officer cadet course at Eaton Hall before proceeding to RMAS. It is difficult to escape the conclusion that the colonial authorities were in no hurry to produce Nigerian officers for the army.[5]

In the meantime, there were significant changes on the political front. The Richards Constitution of 1946 had introduced *regionalism* into Nigerian politics. Ostensibly created to promote Nigerian unity whilst catering to the diverse elements that made up Nigeria, it was seen as being attractive to the colonial authorities because it would help to assuage nationalist agitation whilst ensuring that the Legislative Council at the centre would not become too large and unwieldy. It came under fierce attack from nationalists who claimed, with some justification, that the argument that the Constitution increased the participation of Nigerians in their government was a fallacy, since the governor appointed the majority of the members of the council, and the few elected members were restricted to Lagos and Calabar.

Given the prevailing dissatisfaction with the Richards Constitution, a review was inevitable, and, following extended consultations and a constitutional conference in 1950, the Macpherson Constitution came into being in 1951. This document hard-wired Regionalism into the country's DNA, providing, as it did, for a federal system, and for transforming the regions from administrative to political entities. It created a unicameral Federal legislature, and a mixture of uni- and bicameral legislatures at the regional level. It did not, however, provide for regional self-government, and this quickly became a flashpoint amongst the political class, the West and East being keen to move quickly toward independence, and the North less so. Things came to a head when, in 1953, Chief Anthony Enahoro of the Action Group moved a motion in Parliament for independence in 1956; the Northern Peoples' Congress moved a countermotion, substituting the phrase "as soon as practicable" for a firm date of 1956. This was unacceptable to the agitators for independence, an uproar ensued and Northern members were jeered and heckled as they left the House. As a result, riots broke out and there was a threat to secede by the North. Although this threat was almost certainly an empty one (it is virtually certain that the colonial authorities would have had no hesitation in suppressing such an uprising, if need be, by deploying the army from the UK in some force), it triggered another constitutional conference in 1953, which led to the adoption of the Lyttelton Constitution of 1954. This granted more autonomy to the regions, and, more importantly from the point of view of the West and the East, it granted self-government to those regions that desired it. What it did not do was settle the agitation of the minorities in each of the regions, nor did it douse the increasing agitation for the creation of more regions or states, both of which would become significant issues after independence.

A key factor in the operation of these constitutions was the basis upon which elections would be held into the various legislatures — the census. The census of 1952 was controversial. The results gave the North the majority of the population (18 million vs. 14.5 million for the South), which meant that the North held more seats in Parliament than the other two regions combined. This in-built electoral majority provoked accusations from southern politicians that the colonial authorities had deliberately inflated the North's census figures in order to ensure that the Northerners would remain in power after independence, as they were seen to be more reliable protectors of British interests going forward than the more radical Southerners. Whatever the merits or otherwise of this point of view, the fact was that at the federal elections of both 1954 and 1959 (both conducted by the British colonial authorities), the Northern Peoples' Congress (NPC) won the largest number of seats but not a majority: the pre-independence election of 1959 resulted in 148 seats for the NPC, 89 for the Eastern National Council of Nigerian Citizens (NCNC) and its allies, the Northern Elements Progressive Union (NEPU); and 75 for the Action Group (AG), and its allies, the United Middle Belt Congress (UMBC). It will be seen that an alliance between the NCNC and the AG would have created a majority, but these two southern parties were unable to agree on collaborating in a coalition; the result was an NPC/NCNC coalition government. The NCNC appears to have chosen to form a coalition with the NPC rather than with the AG in part because of the long-standing antipathy between the leaders of both parties, and in part because of a cynical calculation by the NCNC that it could leverage on its presence in government to destroy the AG and therefore become the dominant party of the South. Once in power, the NPC, given its built-in parliamentary majority and its access to the powers of patronage, was in a very strong position; and it seemed virtually impossible to bring about a change in government by constitutional methods for as long as it controlled the greatest number of seats, the NPC government was almost invulnerable. It was fully awake to this fact, and therefore stoutly resisted any and all measures that might undermine this position, for example, different census results or amendments to the Constitution that might put it at a disadvantage. In these circumstances, there appeared to be only three courses of action to about a change in government — a popular revolution, an executive action, or a coup d'état.

All three options would eventually be put to the test in Nigeria. The leader of the federal opposition, Chief Awolowo, was tried and convicted in 1962 on charges of treasonable felony, on the grounds that he had allegedly fomented an armed insurrection in the country. Following the controversial federal elections of December 1964, the President of the Republic, Dr. Azikiwe, had for several days refused to invite the Prime Minister, Sir Abubakar Tafawa Balewa, to form a government because of the widespread irregularities that accompanied the elections; and he had attempted, on the basis of his titular role as Commander-in-Chief of the Armed Forces, to order the heads of the armed services and the police to support his plans to appoint a caretaker government and conduct fresh elections. Led by Major-General Welby-Everard, the Army GOC, the service chiefs firmly rebuffed Azikiwe's gambit. And finally, in January 1966, Nigeria experienced the first of several coups d'état. It seems fairly obvious that the success or failure of any, and probably all, of these courses of action would require control over the levers of coercive power, which, for all practical purposes, meant having and controlling a reliable army, and to a lesser extent, a police force. And therein lies the genesis of the fateful (for both sides) interplay between politics and the army.

The 1957 Constitutional Conference mandated that control of Nigeria's armed forces would pass from the UK government to the government of Nigeria in April 1958 as part of the run-up to independence, and that the Nigerian government would also assume the full costs of the upkeep of its forces. This watershed was significant in that decisions about how the army was recruited, equipped, trained, and utilized were now made entirely by Nigerian politicians. It was even more significant because the army's previous exclusion from the Nigerianisation policy was brought to an end, since it was now fully funded by the Nigerian taxpayer, and the insulating buffer between the War Office in London and the Nigerian government in Lagos was removed.

As stated earlier, there were 15 Nigerian officers in January 1956, out of a total of 250. Of these 15 Nigerians, the following 9 officers were former NCOs initially on short-service commissions: Wellington Bassey, Johnson Aguiyi-Ironsi, Sam Ademulegun, Ralph Shodeinde, Babafemi Ogundipe, Adeyinka Adebayo, Conrad Nwawo, Adekunle Fajuyi, and Ime Imo. The other 6 officers were trained at RMAS and were on regular commissions from the start: Zakariya Maimalari, Umar Lawan, Kur Muhammed, Abogo Largema, Yakubu Pam, and George Kurubo. In total, there were 6 from the West, 5 from the North, and 4 from the East. (Nwawo was from the Midwest, which was at the time still part of the Western Region.) By the time control of the army passed into Nigerian hands, there were a total of 32 Nigerian officers, and that number had increased to 61 at the time of independence in October 1960.

In order to explain this rate of increase, it is first necessary to explore the reasons why there had been so few Nigerian officers in the first place. The attitudes of the War Office in London regarding setting high standards for entry have been mentioned already, as have the army's lack of prestige and low reputation amongst the Nigerian population. A significant aggravating factor was the impact the policy of Nigerianisation in the public service had on the already wide gulf between army officers and their peers in the public service. As Miners puts it:

In the 1950s, almost any graduate could find employment in the pullulating Federal and Regional public services and the new government corporations. Once appointed, the graduate immediately qualified for a salary advance of up to 800 pounds to buy a car. This advance had to be paid back over five years. But each month the graduate received a "Car Basic Allowance" of 13 pounds, free of tax, which was more than enough to cover the repayments. In addition, he was entitled to a mileage allowance when he used the car on Government business. Thus, in effect, a newly appointed senior service officer was given a free car. He also qualified for a loan to build himself a house, if he did not live in Government quarters.[6]

The Nigerian army officer, prior to April 1958, saw none of this, as the British War Office in London was not in the habit of giving housing loans or free cars to its officers. Nor could the Nigerian officer, whether trained at RMAS, Mons, or Eaton Hall, put any letters after his name, in the way a graduate could, which was a "big deal" in colonial Nigeria. In addition, prospects for rapid promotion for the army officer, when compared with his peers in the public services, were distinctly gloomy. Whereas a Nigerian graduate appointed to the public services in the early 1950s could potentially reach a "superscale" position at the top of the tree within a decade, a Nigerian army officer's promotion progression followed the normal British Army ladder of two years from Second Lieutenant to Lieutenant; four years from Lieutenant to Captain, and seven years from Captain to Major. Finally, the question of financial reward was crucial. Although Nigerian officers had received a pay increase in 1956, which put a newly commissioned subaltern at roughly the same basic pay as a graduate working in the public services (and the subaltern could pass out of RMAS within three years of obtaining his school certificate, as well as be paid during training as opposed to having to find school fees for A-Levels and university), the other factors tended to negate this effect. To compound matters, until August 1957, advertisements for potential officers for the army made no mention of pay on commissioning; the first advert that did so resulted in a three-fold increase in the number of applications received.[7]

The transfer of control of the army from British to Nigerian control in April 1958 remedied some of these issues. Whilst RMAS could not grant degrees in order to satisfy Nigerian aspirations, the Nigerian government could and did extend the Nigerianisation policy to include the army, and helped to ease officer recruitment by making two key decisions. First, the restriction that only serving soldiers were sent to Mons and Eaton Hall for short-service commissions was lifted, allowing direct entry officers fresh out of school to be sent directly to Mons (Eaton Hall closed and was merged with Mons in 1958). This meant that the rate of commissioning direct entry officers increased from the maximum six per year, which was the number of places at RMAS allocated to Nigerian cadets. Second, the government instituted the right to a car advance and a "Car Basic Allowance" for Nigerian officers, and also improved cadet pension arrangements, bringing them more in line with their counterparts in the public services, and making service as an army officer more attractive to potential recruits. In addition to these two key decisions, other measures which increased the numbers of Nigerian officers included, from 1960, the granting of executive and quartermaster commissions to existing SNCOs and warrant officers over the age of thirty largely in the workshops, pay, records, signals, education and stores branches of the Army, and the granting of direct commissions to professionally qualified officers such as doctors, nurses, clergymen, and accountants. The vast majority (83 percent) of those granted these types of commissions were southerners. Prior to independence, only two graduates were given combatant commissions: Emeka Ojukwu in 1958 and Olufemi Olutoye in 1960. They were followed by Oluwole Rotimi and Emmanuel Ifeajuna in 1961 and Adewale Ademoyega in 1962, after which no other graduates were granted combatant commissions. This was for two reasons. First, the government, unnerved by student demonstrations against the Anglo-Nigerian Defence Pact, did not wish to offer potential revolutionaries a home in the combatant arms of the army. Second, there was opposition within the army itself, given the fact that these graduates had their seniority backdated thirty months to compensate for time spent at university. This was a very sensitive subject at a time when the army was rapidly being Nigerianised, and indeed was arguably, at least in part, the basis of the antipathy between Yakubu Gowon (commissioned in 1956) and Emeka Ojukwu (commissioned two years later but with backdated seniority), the absence of which might have led to a peaceful resolution of the differences that eventually culminated in a bloody civil war.[8]

All these measures played a part in not only increasing the number of Nigerian officers; they also impacted the regional distribution of the army's officer corps. Whereas in January 1956, only four out of fifteen officers were Easterners (27 percent), at independence in 1960 they made up two-thirds of the officer corps; by contrast, the number of Westerners had declined from six out of fifteen (40 percent) to 17.5 percent at independence. The North contributed one-third of the officer corps in January 1956; this number had declined to 14 percent at independence. There had therefore been a significant increase in the proportion of Easterners at the expense of both the West and the North.[9] Why was this so? A number of reasons can be advanced. First, serving soldiers, who were candidates for short-service commissions, needed high educational qualifications, and were therefore more likely to be found in the technical areas, where Easterners predominated; Easterners also, by virtue of high educational attainment (a propensity for military service that far exceeded that of the similarly highly educated Westerners), made up the majority of direct-entry applicants for short-service commissions. Secondly, the comparatively greater propensity for military service in the East was partly the result of two southern secondary schools developing a military tradition similar to that of Government College, Zaria (from where virtually all the Northern RMAS-commissioned officers came). These schools were the Government Colleges at Ughelli and Umuahia, which produced the likes of David Ejoor, George Kurubo, Mike Okwechime, and Alex Madiebo. Third, the Western Region had traditionally been a poor recruiting area for the army, despite having a comparatively well-educated population; they preferred the public services instead, and the changes made following transition to Nigerian control in 1958 did little to alter this.

Following the transition to Nigerian control, regional quotas were first instituted in 1959 for the recruitment of soldiers (not officers) into the army; henceforth, the North would provide 50 percent of the rank and file, and the West and East 25 percent each. This measure was not regarded as controversial at the time, and indeed tended to discriminate against the North, which had traditionally provided the bulk of the rank and file. The East had no difficulty in filling its quota, but the West continued to struggle (despite the fact that the majority of its soldiers came from the Midwest, which at the time still formed part of the Western Region).

Quotas for officer recruitment were not introduced until after independence, in 1961. It is perhaps no coincidence that, with the exception of the brief interregnum between October 1960 and August 1961, all the defence ministerial portfolios between independence and the first coup in January 1966 were held by Northern politicians (Ribadu and Inuwa Wada as ministers, and Obande and Galadima as ministers of state); the permanent secretaries in the Ministry of Defence were also Northerners (Atta and Sule Kolo). This facilitated the introduction of quotas (and other measures to increase the number and proportion of Northern officers). The ostensible reason for the new quota system was to ensure that the composition of the army's officer corps reflected and was fully representative of the nation that it served; for some, it was interpreted as an attempt by the NPC government, and by the Northern ministers and civil servants running the Ministry of Defence, to ensure the loyalty of the Army. On 1 May 1965, the Minister of State for the Army informed the Senate that:

We introduced a quota system in the Army, thus preventing the possible fear that the Army would sometimes become unreliable.... But now....this country's safety is assured.

He could not have been more wrong.

A number of other measures were put in place, starting in September 1959. Prior to this, the educational requirement for potential officers was four O-Level credits, including English; this was now reduced to four O-Level passes, and the maximum age for enlistment was increased from twenty-two to twenty-five for direct entrants, i.e., those not already serving in the ranks. In May 1961, the educational requirement was further reduced to permit the recruitment of candidates with a Teachers' Grade II or a Royal Society of Arts Stage II certificate. The Nigerian Military Training College (NMTC) was set up to replace the course at Teshie in the Gold Coast following Ghanaian independence, and each of its first four courses, which ran from April 1960 to March 1962, had a maximum loading of twenty-five places, with an average pass rate of 60 per cent. Starting in April 1962, it increased the number of places available on each course initially to forty-eight, and then to sixty-four, with virtually a 100 percent pass rate. More importantly, the

NPC-led government was now in a position to decree in April 1961 for the NMTC (in a way it could not have done for Teshie or RMAS) that henceforth 50 percent of *all* cadets must be from the North, and that this would apply both to initial selection and to the final pass list, *whatever the order of merit*.[10] (author's emphasis). This meant that it was now possible for a Northern cadet to make the final pass list above a Southerner who may have been above him in the order of merit, but not the other way round.

The changes in the army after it passed to Nigerian control also included an increase in its size, and a corresponding increase in its budget. By 1965, the army was 10,500 strong, and the budget for the armed forces had jumped from 5.5 million pounds for the period 1955-1962 to a projected 30 million pounds for the period 1962-1968, of which 19.5 million pounds had already been spent by April 1966.[11] This figure included costs for building and refurbishing barracks, equipment for two artillery batteries, two Recce Squadrons, a federal guards company; aircraft and other equipment for the fledgling air force, warships for the navy, and a new ordnance factory. The expansion in army officer training meant that the traditional training establishments in the UK (RMAS and Mons OCS) could no longer offer places in the required numbers, and cadets were sent to different places such as Canada, India, Ethiopia, the USA, Australia, and Pakistan, thus diluting the hitherto exclusively British flavour of officer training. Similar diversity was soon seen as far as the sourcing of equipment was concerned; machine guns from West Germany, artillery field guns from Italy, mortars from Sweden, the ordinance factory contract and the training team for the new air force from West Germany — and not from the traditional UK sources.

For reasons discussed above, the army was seen in the 1950s, especially in the South, as a low-paying, low-prestige career, one having limited promotion prospects when compared with the public services. All of this had been reversed by the 1960s. At independence, the pay of a newly commissioned subaltern was 768 Pounds per annum, compared to 720 pounds for a university graduate; the graduate would have taken at least five years from leaving school to getting his degree, in the course of which he would have needed to come up with school and university fees; the fresh subaltern, on the other hand, could pass through the NMTC course, and Mons OCS, within eighteen months of leaving school, throughout which he had no fees to pay — indeed, he was paid throughout his training.[12] The army had steadily gained in prestige as independence approached, and its exploits overseas in the Congo and in Tanganyika (see below) simply increased that prestige. Compared with the police, the army had a much better reputation as being free from corruption and for honesty, and it was also much better regarded when it came to dealing with civil disturbances, as it was sometimes called upon to do (see below).

When Nigeria became a Republic in 1963, the army's ceremonial dress — the old RWAFF dress consisting of a red fez, zouave jacket, red cummerbund, and khaki shorts, memorably described by one officer as "being fit only for performing monkeys", was significantly changed. In 1961, the then governor-general, and now president of the new Republic, Dr. Azikiwe, had noted that, "the fact that the uniform was designed originally for the colonial army of occupation makes it imperative for a complete departure from the past to take place."[13] The new uniform now consisted of a green long-sleeved jacket and trousers and a peaked cap. An eagle replaced the crown on the badges of rank for majors and above, and the monogram of Queen Elizabeth on officers' swords was replaced by Nigeria's Coat of Arms. At the same time, "the title 'Queen's Own' was dropped from the names of the battalions, and 'Royal' from the title of the Army."[14] By the end of 1963 all the battalion commanders were Nigerian, and by the end of the following year all the staff appointments at Brigade and Army Headquarters were in Nigerian hands, with the exception of the last GOC, Major-General Welby-Everard, who left in February 1965 and was replaced by Major-General Aguyi-Ironsi.

Between 1960 and 1964, the army was almost continuously employed on peacekeeping operations abroad. Prior to these engagements, the army was deployed in October 1959 to the Southern Cameroons, which was at that time part of Nigeria. Trouble arose between the French colonial authorities and a political party, that was popular amongst members of the Bamileke tribe, which straddled the Nigerian and Cameroonian border; when the political party was proscribed, the tribesmen took up arms, and would frequently cross over to their tribal kinsmen on the Nigerian side after operating on the French side. In response, the Nigerian government deployed several battalions of the Queen's Own Nigerian Regiment (QONR), as the army was then known, to keep the peace; they did so effectively until Nigeria became an independent nation in October 1960, and Southern Cameroons became a British Trust Territory, pending the determination of its future via a plebiscite, whereupon the QONR returned to Nigeria and its peacekeeping role abroad was taken over by a British battalion.

Meanwhile, in the Congo, the Belgian colonial authorities hastily granted independence on 30 June 1960 to a government under the leadership of Patrice Lumumba, a left-leaning politician. Five days later, the Force Publique, a combined gendarmerie/military troop, mutinied against its (almost totally) white Belgian officers, prompting Lumumba to seek assistance from the United Nations. The Nigerian government announced that it would contribute a battalion strength force, and Major Aguiyi-Ironsi, then second-in-command of 1QONR in Enugu, was promoted acting Lieutenant-Colonel and given command of 5QONR then in Kaduna, which left for the Congo in mid-November 1960. By this time, the UN Secretary-General had asked for more troops, and 4QONR in Ibadan was sent to join 5QONR, under the command of a British officer, Lieutenant-Colonel Price; another British officer, Brigadier Ward, was also deployed to set up a Brigade HQ to command the two Nigerian battalions. By the end of November 1960, there were 1350 Nigerian troops in the Congo.[15]

The performance of the deployed troops was mixed. There was widespread acknowledgment that their performance was excellent in most instances, and several of the deployed Nigerian officers and soldiers were recognized with awards: Lieutenant-Colonel Aguyi-Ironsi, Major Hilary Njoku, and twelve soldiers were awarded medals for gallantry by the Austrian government for their role in rescuing a kidnapped Austrian ambulance unit; Majors Fajuyi and Nwawo were awarded the Military Cross, and Company Sergeant Major Jibrin Gulani, the Military Medal. British Officers were also honoured, with Lieutenant-Colonel Price and Major Lawson receiving the Distinguished Service Order, and Lieutenant Matthews, the Military Cross. However, there were splits between Nigerian and British officers, resulting in discipline problems, with some officers on both sides being posted out and several soldiers being reduced in rank or sent home with sentences of detention for insubordination.[16] These problems, however, did not affect the Nigerian public holding their soldiers in great esteem for the help provided by their army to their brethren elsewhere in Africa, in Nigeria's new, self-appointed role as the "Giant of Africa". Each of the five battalions served at least two tours of duty in the Congo between November 1960 and June 1964, with Aguyi-Ironsi ending up as the UN Force Commander while the acting rank of Major General for the last six months of operations.

No sooner was the Congo operation over than the army was on its travels again, this time to Tanganyika. In January 1964, two battalions of the Tanganyikan Army had mutinied. The insurrection was brought under control only when the Prime Minister, Julius Nyerere, sought the assistance of British troops. Following this, Nyerere ordered the disbandment of his entire army, with the exception of a few officers, and sought to create a new army from members of the youth wing of the ruling party, the Tanganyikan African National Union. The government sought the assistance of Nigeria, and the Third Battalion of the Nigerian Army (3NA) — Nigeria was by this time a Republic) under the command of Lieutenant-Colonel Pam was chosen. The unit flew out to Dar-es-Salaam in the first week of April 1964, and remained in theatre until recovery back to Nigeria at the end of September 1964.

Although the army had been put on standby for internal security (IS) operations in the period between 1950 and 1958, i.e., during the transition to independence but *before* control passed to the Nigerian government (for example, at the times of the Kano riots in 1953, or the riots in Ibadan in 1958 following the death of Alhaji Adegoke Adelabu, former Minister of Natural Resources and Social Services), it was never actually deployed in this role until *after* it came under Nigerian control. The suspicion that the army's deployment in these circumstances was, at least in part, a partisan political act is stoked by an examination of the circumstances of its deployments. It has been noted that the people of the Tiv Division of Benue Province,

...had long been the main center of opposition to the NPC Government of the Northern Region. In the 1959 Federal elections 85% of the voters there had supported candidates of the UMBC, an ally of the Action Group. Since then, they had remained impervious to the normal methods of persuasion used by parties in power — that is, the manipulation of tax assessments, patronage and the local courts to the disadvantage of those who persisted in supporting the opposition.[17]

Unsurprisingly, riots broke out, and the army was deployed for a few weeks in April 1960, August 1961, and February 1964 to support the police. More serious and extensive riots broke out in July 1964, with political parties blaming each other — the NPC government of the North claimed that its own coalition partners at the Federal level, the NCNC, which controlled the government of the East, was instigating and funding the unrest; whilst the UMBC "put the blame on arbitrary taxation and victimization by clan heads who were trying to force them to support the NPC." Despite the escalating violence, with possibly several hundred fatalities, the NPC federal government declined to intervene with the army until it became clear that the approaching federal parliamentary elections scheduled for December 1964 could not be held in this area until order was restored. Eventually, on 18 November 1964, the Prime Minister ordered the army to intervene: "to take immediate steps to ensure a return to normal life in the area." Under the command of Lieutenant-Colonel Pam, the 3NA which had only recently returned from Tanganyika, was deployed, together with the Recce Squadron in Kaduna. The troops rapidly brought the situation under control, partly because the UMBC leadership welcomed them as being more impartial than the police. The elections went ahead uneventfully, although the troops remained in the area at least until the middle of 1965.

The federal government's willingness to repeatedly deploy the army in the Tiv area was in marked contrast to its reluctance to intervene in the Western Region crisis of 1962 and, more importantly, in the mayhem that accompanied the blatantly rigged Western regional elections of October 1965, which led to death and destruction on a scale that dwarfed anything that occurred in the Tiv area. The 1962 crisis can be summarized as a divergence of opinion between Chief Obafemi Awolowo, leader of the Action Group and leader of the opposition at the Federal level, and Chief S. L. Akintola, who had taken over from Awolowo as premier of the Western Region when the latter moved to Lagos. Akintola was of the view that the Action Group should abandon its attempts to seek electoral gains outside the West, make its peace with the NPC-led federal government, and seek to enter the coalition on the most favourable terms available to it; Awolowo was resolutely opposed to this. Matters came to a head in May 1962, when at the instigation of Awolowo, a majority of the AG members of the Western Region Assembly signed a petition requesting the Regional Governor to dismiss Akintola from the premiership, and instead to appoint Alhaji Adegbenro, an ally of Awolowo. Akintola refused to accept his dismissal, and when the matter came up in the Assembly for a vote, his followers created an uproar in the chamber, after which the police, acting on the orders of the federal Prime Minister, cleared the chamber with tear gas and then sealed it, preventing a vote being taken. On this relatively trivial basis, the federal government declared a state of emergency, suspended the regional government, and appointed an ally of the Prime Minister as administrator; the AG leaders, including Awolowo, were put under restriction. When the state of emergency was lifted in January 1963, rather than conducting fresh elections, Akintola, by now a firm ally of the NPC, was reappointed premier at the head of a coalition of carpet-crossing AG members and the NCNC members of the Western Assembly; hitherto the latter group had constituted the opposition. In the meantime, Awolowo and several leaders of the AG had been put on trial for treasonable felony, accused of planning to stage a revolution (see chapter 1) and were convicted and sentenced to long terms of imprisonment. Whilst this outcome was highly satisfactory to the NPC, the NCNC and Akintola (who soon formed a new party, the Nigerian National Democratic Party (NNDP), and formally joined the federal government in coalition), it sowed the seeds of the simmering discontent, which, quite literally, burst into flame at the time of the Western regional elections in October 1965.

Prior to this, however, was the small matter of the federal parliamentary elections due in December 1964. The battle lines were drawn between the NPC and NNDP (who formed the NNA) on the one hand, and the rump of the AG, the UMBC and the NCNC on the other, who formed the UPGA (United Progressive Grand Alliance). The campaign was characterised by significant amounts of thuggery across the entire country, but the real flashpoint arose when NPC officials in the North forcibly prevented UPGA candidates from filing their nomination papers, which secured the unopposed return of sixty-seven NPC candidates. The UPGA leaders promptly demanded that the election be postponed. When the Electoral Commission (three of whose six members subsequently resigned) declined to do so, the UPGA announced that it was boycotting the election. Notwithstanding this, voting went ahead as scheduled on 30 December, albeit not in the East or in Lagos, and only in a limited way in the West and the Midwest (which had been carved out of the Western Region in 1963 after the crisis there the previous year). When results were declared on New Year's Day 1965, it was clear that the NPC had "won" in a landslide, and had enough seats to command a majority on its own, even without the help of its NNDP allies. The President, Dr. Nnamdi Azikiwe, declined to summon the Prime Minister, Sir Abubakar Tafawa Balewa, and ask him to form a government; it seems Azikiwe was, initially at least, swayed by the UPGA view that, given the irregularities attending the election, he was not obliged to accept the results, and, instead, would "assume 'executive powers', nominate a 'caretaker government' under a Prime Minister of his own choice (i.e., a member of UPGA) and hold a fresh election."[18] The trouble with this reasoning was that it seemed that Azikiwe had no such powers under the Constitution, and although he had been so advised by an impressive array of legal luminaries, including the chief justices of the federation and the Eastern Region, as well as the Federal Attorney-General (respectively Sir Adetokunbo Ademola, Sir Louis Mbanefo, and Mr. G.C.M. Onyiuke). Azikiwe, still determined at this stage to avoid reappointing Abubakar, next summoned the heads of the armed services and the police, and informed them that as a result of the crisis he proposed to take control of the government, and asked for their support in this venture as their Commander in Chief. Major-General Welby-Everard of the army, Commodore Akinwale Wey of the navy, and Inspector-General Louis Edet of the police all listened politely, then rebuffed Azikiwe's request, and declined to accept orders from him. In the circumstances, Azikiwe had no option but to yield and summon Abubakar, asking him to form a new government. Abubakar did so, and went as far as finding portfolios within the new government for the NCNC as well as the NNDP; the AG remained excluded.

The stage was now set for the Western Region elections of 1965. The AG believed that the elections offered them an opportunity to get rid of Akintola's discredited NNDP government, whilst the NCNC, notwithstanding its craven betrayal of its erstwhile AG allies in the UPGA to return to the ruling federal coalition, hoped that by unseating the NNDP in the West, it would control all three Southern Regions and make life so difficult for the NPC federal government that it might force fresh elections where it would stand a reasonable chance of at last taking control in the centre. The NPC, alive to all this, was determined to ensure that Akintola's NNDP remain in power. What followed was, even by Nigeria's own prior low standards, quite remarkable. The trick of preventing opposition candidates from filing their nomination papers and subsequently declaring ruling party candidates returned unopposed — used effectively in the North the previous year — was reprised. Those electoral officers who had the temerity to accept nomination papers from opposition candidates were subsequently sacked. Where opposition candidates were allowed to stand, ballot boxes were stuffed with ballots in favour of NNDP candidates, and poll results were not declared after the count was completed, so that entirely made-up results could be announced from the regional capital. The declared final "result" showed that the NNDP had won seventy-three of the ninety-four seats contested. If the NPC and the NNDP hoped that, after the initial demonstrations against this result, the AG would accept the outcome, and be "compensated" by offers of portfolios in a coalition government under Chief Akintola, they were very much mistaken. The AG and its supporters, furious at this brazen demonstration of election rigging, responded with an orgy of violence hitherto unseen anywhere in Nigeria. The NNDP politicians, their supporters, and their collaborators (including some traditional rulers) were subjected to a wave of murder and arson; several abandoned their homes and businesses in outlying parts of the region, and fled for safety to their regional capital, Ibadan or in Lagos. Journeying through the region became a game of Russian roulette, as bands of thugs utilized the chaos to assault and rob travellers. People from the North who had traded and lived in the West for years now became identified with the NPC government that was viewed as propping up Akintola, and ethnic conflict between the Yorubas and the Hausas now added to the mayhem. And yet, the Prime Minister, who had been quick to declare a state of emergency three years earlier as a result of a much smaller and less severe squabble in the House of Assembly, did nothing, using the somewhat lame pretext that the declaration of a state of emergency was the function of parliament and not the Prime Minister. Clearly, this was nonsense, as the NPC had the votes in the House to make such a declaration, if it so wished, even over the objections of NNDP members. As Miners points out, "the real point was that Sir Abubakar could not command this majority against the wishes of the president of the party, the Sardauna", who was determined at all costs to keep Akintola in power in the West.[19]

While history does not formally record the views of all the middle ranking Nigerian officers who were witnesses to the political shenanigans described above, one cannot help but wonder whether the fact that several officers (Christian Anuforo, Ademoyega, and Timothy Onwuatuegwu), who subsequently played central roles in the January 1966 coup had either been deployed on internal security duties in the Tiv region or had had vantage points at either Army or Brigade headquarters from which to view the interactions between members of the army's higher hierarchy and the politicians (Ifeajuna, Humphrey Chukwuka, Donatus Okafor, Chukwuma Nzeogwu).

Whilst it is uncontested that the army's overt entrance into the politics of Nigeria did not take place until January 1966, there have been several suggestions that such an entrance was first contemplated more than a year earlier; at the time of the federal election crisis in December 1964/January 1965. At least one of the suggestions needs to be taken with a bit more than the proverbial pinch of salt, and that is the account given by the federal government following the July 1966 coup, and during the period of tension leading up to the outbreak of the Civil War the following year. According to this account, the exact same fourteen officers whom the federal government subsequently accused of complicity in the January 1966 coup were supposedly involved in a plot "designed to take place at Enugu during the shooting competition of the army which is normally attended by all the senior officers of the army. The plan leaked, most senior officers kept away and the plan was temporarily abandoned."[20] This account fails to explain why no action was taken against any of the officers involved, particularly against those occupying key positions, for example, Ifeajuna at HQ Second Brigade as Brigade Major or Okafor at the Federal Guard as Commander, both of whom remained in post. Another version of this alleged plot comes from no less than General Yakubu Gowon himself, who told an interviewer during the war that he had been approached at the time of the federal election crisis by Lieutenant-Colonels Ojukwu and Victor Banjo with a proposal that they form a triumvirate and take over the running of the country. In weighing the merits or otherwise of this account, it should be noted that by this time Gowon and Ojukwu had spectacularly fallen out with each other and were at the heads of opposing forces in the Civil War, and that Banjo was dead, having been executed by Ojukwu.

Carl von Clausewitz famously described war as the continuation of politics by other means; it should therefore come as no surprise to anyone that armies — which are after all the principal tool for waging war — should be closely entwined in politics, and from this perspective the Nigerian Army is no different. Where it may possibly lay claim to being different, however, is the *extent* to which it became so embroiled in the politics of Nigeria, in the course of which it both fundamentally changed the nature of and the development of Nigeria's politics, and was in turn fundamentally changed by that involvement. It is clear that from its inception, the motley militia forces, which evolved into the Nigerian Army, were established for an overtly *political* purpose, i.e., to secure the subjugation of the native population to the colonial authorities. Its subsequent employment up to the middle of the twentieth century never deviated from that original aim; thereafter, once in the hands of the new Nigerian government as independence approached, its composition, organisation and employment all too often seemed to be dedicated to little more than ensuring the continuation of that government in power. Eventually, and some might perhaps say inevitably, it became *the* Government.

NOTES

1. Miners p. 33.
2. Ibid.
3. Ibid pp. 17-18.
4. Ibid p. 21.
5. Ibid p. 35.
6. Ibid pp. 42-43.
7. Ibid p. 45.
8. Ibid p. 114.
9. Ibid p. 51.

10. Ibid p. 116.
11. Ibid pp. 94-95.
12. Ibid p. 112.
13. Ibid p. 103.
14. Ibid.
15. Ibid pp. 74-75.
16. Ibid 79-80.
17. Ibid p. 90.
18. Ibid p. 142.
19. Ibid p. 52.
20. Ibid p. 147.

CHAPTER 3

The Overt Entry into Politics

Our enemies are the political profiteers, the swindlers, the men in high and low places that seek bribes and demand ten percent, those that seek to keep the country divided permanently so they can remain in office as Ministers or VIPs at least, the tribalists, the nepotists, those that make the country look big for nothing before international circles, those that have corrupted our society and put the Nigerian political calendar back by their words and their deeds.

— Major Chukwuma Nzeogwu, January 1966

In the early hours of Saturday, 15 January 1966, the sounds of small and heavy weapons fire broke the stillness of the night air in Lagos, Ibadan, and Kaduna. When the smoke cleared, it became clear (over several days) that there had been a cataclysmic upheaval in the affairs of Nigeria. The prime minister and the federal finance minister, the premiers of the Northern and Western regions, and several senior army officers were either dead or missing and later confirmed dead. The situation as to who was running the country remained unclear. Eventually, late in the evening of Sunday, 16 January, Dr. Nwafor Orizu, the President of the Senate (and Acting President, of the Federation in the absence from the country of the President, Dr. Azikiwe), made a radio broadcast to announce that the federal cabinet had decided to hand over power to the armed forces. Shortly afterwards, the army GOC, Major General Aguyi-Ironsi announced the formation by decree of the federal military government, designating himself at its head as the supreme commander.

Several explanations have been offered as to why the coup occurred at that time, particularly why it was carried out by the particular people involved, who else might have been involved or in the know, and why it turned out the way it did. Some explanations are more credible than others. The accounts given by the protagonist federal and Eastern regional governments after the events of July

1966 and in the buildup to the outbreak of the Civil War deserve in particular to be treated with caution.[1] But even these nakedly partisan accounts cannot be dismissed out of hand as totally lacking in merit or credibility. Other accounts, such as the report on the investigation by the Special Branch of the Nigerian Police into the coup (based as it was on the interrogations of those arrested for their participation), carry a greater degree of credibility, as do the scholarly works by writers such as Miners, Kirk-Greene, Luckham, Omoigui, and Siollun.

Whatever school of thought one belongs to, some events provoke a broad degree of consensus. First, there was widespread disillusionment in the country, especially amongst the intelligentsia, with the Nigerian political ruling class at the time of the January 1966 coup. That sense of disillusionment arose out of the patent failures of the ruling class to provide security for the population at the same time as they were conspicuously (and contemptuously) flaunting their venality. Second, many army officers, who, unlike the majority of the population, possessed the means to do something about the situation, shared that sense of disillusionment. Third, the events surrounding the federal parliamentary elections of 1964 and the Western regional elections of October 1965, described above, so deepened the sense of despair amongst some sections of the population (mainly in the South), that a change of government by democratic means was not within reach in the foreseeable future. Fourth, it must have been obvious to those members of the army who cared to think about it, and who had been involved in the crises and internal security operations of 1964-65, that the survival or failure of the existing political order depended on them, for the flurry of coups elsewhere in Africa — in Congo Kinshasa, Dahomey (now Benin Republic), Central African Republic, and Upper Volta (now Burkina Faso) between November 1965 and early January 1966 – must have fertilized thoughts of military intervention.[2]

Although the coup has now become synonymous with Major Patrick Chukwuma Nzeogwu, he was not, as widely imagined, one of the original instigators of the plot. Commissioned in 1959 from RMAS, he was at the time of the coup the chief instructor at the NMTC in Kaduna. The plot was first hatched around August 1965 by Major Emmanuel Ifeajuna (Mons 1961), Major. Donatus Okafor (Mons 1959), and Captain Ogbo Oji (Mons 1961). Ifeajuna, at the time of the coup, was the Brigade Major at Second Brigade in Apapa whilst Okafor was the commander of the Federal Guards Company in Lagos. These core plotters subsequently recruited Majors Humphrey Chukwuka (RMAS 1960) and Christian Anuforo (RMAS 1961), both of Army HQ Lagos, as well as Nzeogwu, who in turn recruited Major Tim Onwuatuegwu (RMAS 1961), his colleague at NMTC. Others who later joined the plot included Major Adewale Ademoyega (Mons 1962), and Captains Ben Gbulie (RMAS 1962) and Emmanuel Nwobosi (RMAS 1963). Nzeogwu, along with Onwuatuegwu and Gbulie, took responsibility for the coup in Kaduna, and were responsible for the demise of the Northern Premier, the Sardauna of Sokoto, Brigadier Ademulegun (Commander, First Brigade) and his wife; and for that of Colonel Shodeinde (Commander, NMTC). Several politicians were arrested, and the coup, in Kaduna at least, was completely successful. Ifeajuna was in charge of operations in Lagos, whilst Nwobosi was responsible for operations in Ibadan. Nzeogwu, in a subsequent radio broadcast announcing the coup in the name of the Supreme Council of the Revolution of the Nigerian Armed Forces said:

> Our enemies are the political profiteers, the swindlers, the men in high and low places that seek bribes and demand ten percent, those that seek to keep the country divided permanently so they can remain in office as Ministers or VIPs at least, the tribalists, the nepotists, those that make the country look big for nothing before international circles, those that have corrupted our society and put the Nigerian political calendar back by their words and their deeds.[3]

He announced the imposition of martial law across the Northern Region, and also the range of offences that would be punishable by a sentence of death.

Nzeogwu's colleagues elsewhere in the country were not so successful. On the night of 14-15 January, the plotters held a meeting in Lagos at the home of Major Ifeajuna, after a cocktail party hosted by Brigadier Maimalari at his home, which several of the plotters had attended. In the early hours, they fanned out to execute their allotted tasks. In fairly short order, the conspirators, who included Anuforo, Okafor, Chukwuka, and Ademoyega, had arrested the Prime Minister, Sir Abubakar Tafawa-Balewa, and Festus Okotie-Eboh, the Finance Minister. They assassinated Brigadier Maimalari, Colonel

Kur Mohammed (who was acting as Chief of Staff at Army HQ in the absence of Colonel Adebayo), Lieutenant-Colonels Arthur Unegbe (Quartermaster-General), Pam (Adjutant-General) and Largema (CO Fourth Battalion based in Ibadan, but who was in Lagos that weekend). Sir Abubakar and Okotie-Eboh were subsequently shot dead. The plotters also managed to take over key installations such as Police HQ, the Nigerian Broadcasting Corporation and the telephone exchange (although the exchange was occupied, it was not disabled, which greatly assisted those who rose up in opposition to the coup). Despite this carnage, the coup in Lagos failed, because the plotters had failed to eliminate the GOC, Ironsi, who used his authority (and a still-functioning telephone exchange) to rally the opposition. By daybreak, Ironsi was in control in Lagos.

Operations in Ibadan were led by Captain Emmanuel Nwobosi (RMAS 1963), although he was actually based at the Abeokuta Garrison. He and his team succeeded in effecting the arrest of the Deputy Premier of the Western Region, Chief Remi Fani-Kayode, and in assassinating the Premier, Chief Akintola, before returning to Lagos, where they were arrested and their prisoner, Fani-Kayode, was freed. There was very little coup activity in Enugu, the Eastern Region capital (troops of the First Battalion stationed there briefly cordoned off the house of the Regional Premier, Dr. Michael Okpara, who happened to be hosting the visiting Cypriot President, Archbishop Makarios). There was no activity at all in Benin, the capital of the Midwest, where no troops were stationed.

A tense standoff now ensued between Ironsi in Lagos (where the rest of the army had rallied around him), and Nzeogwu in Kaduna. The announcement late on the evening of 16 January that the Federal cabinet had handed power over to Ironsi, and the subsequent declaration of the setting up of the new federal military government appears to have been the game changer. Even faced with the extraordinary events of the previous few days, in which the plotters had murdered several of their senior officers, an army officer's default setting is familiarity with and deference to a chain of command, and Nzeogwu now, after negotiations, submitted to Ironsi's authority. He announced that he had agreed to do so after Ironsi's acceptance that, amongst other things, "those whom we fought to remove would not be returned to office."[4] Whilst this turned out to be the case, the other "conditions", such as guarantees of safety and freedom from prosecution for himself and his associates, were clearly never actualised, as, after the hand over on 18 January to Major Hassan Katsina, erstwhile Commander of First Recce Squadron, whom Ironsi had by this time appointed Military Governor of the Northern Region, Nzeogwu was flown to Lagos in the company of Lieutenant-Colonel Conrad Nwawo and was soon detained along with his fellow conspirators.

Why did the coup take place at that time and in that manner? There were suspicions towards the end of 1965, apparently shared by some of the plotters, that the federal government was about to deploy the army in great strength in the West, ostensibly to deal with the increasing violence, but in reality to ensure the continuance of Akintola and the Nigeria National Democratic Party (NNDP) in power, and in addition, to use the pretext of a deliberately instigated (by the government) uprising by minorities in the Eastern Region to declare a state of emergency there and thus ensure that the ruling party, the NPC, was in a position to directly control the affairs of three of the country's four regions. Miners succinctly described the potential situation in the West consequent upon the rumoured use of the army:

> Clearly a concentrated military effort would be required to bring the situation under control, and the Army would be forced to suppress, and probably kill, their fellow-countrymen who were protesting against the refusal of the government to allow them to exercise their right to vote Chief Akintola's discredited regime out of office.[5]

In order to facilitate all this, according to this scenario, Ironsi was to be removed as head of the army, as was Police Inspector-General Edet, and both replaced by officers, such as Ademulegun for the army and Kam Selem for the police, who were more sympathetic to government interests. The Sardauna and Akintola were alleged to be involved in this plot, as was Lieutenant-Colonel Largema.[6] The fact that Akintola and Largema flew from Ibadan to Kaduna on 14 January to meet with the Sardauna upon his return from Mecca, and that Brig Ademulegun was also present at that meeting, simply served to fuel those suspicions. The coup may therefore have taken place at a time that would preempt any such action. Indeed, this is exactly what Nzeogwu himself asserted in an interview with Tai Solarin, published in the *Nigerian Tribune* on 2 July 1967, shortly before the outbreak of the Civil War and Nzeogwu's subsequent death:

> When therefore the significance of the state of emergency due to be proclaimed on January 17 was made known to us, it became inevitable that the operation of January 15 must necessarily take place before the dawn of January 17.[7]

The plotters asserted at the time, and afterwards, that they wished to put an end to a regime that they saw as corrupt. As Nzeogwu stated in his speech on Kaduna Radio on 15 January, 1967 that they were targeting "political profiteers" and those "in high and low places who seek bribes and demand ten percent." He and his colleagues promised that, as a result of their actions, their countrymen would "no more be ashamed to be Nigerian". Two days later, he told a reporter from the *New Nigerian* newspaper in Kaduna that "elections are always rigged. It is impossible to vote out a Nigerian Minister." And, in another interview, he stated, as the goal of the conspirators: "We wanted to get rid of rotten and corrupt ministers, political parties, trade unions and the whole clumsy apparatus of the federal system. We wanted to gun down all the bigwigs in our way."[8]

Unlike their successors in the deadly game of coup-making, it seems unlikely that the plotters were motivated either by personal gain (from the point of view of assuming power themselves), or out of pique at being disadvantaged professionally. Whilst it was true that the meteoric rates of promotion in place during the rapid Nigerianisation of the army between 1960 and 1965 was coming to an end, and that the rates of promotion going forward would be much slower, it was also true that, as a group, the acknowledged conspirators had not been disadvantaged in comparison with their peers as far as promotions were concerned. Not one of the officers acknowledged to have been involved in the coup had been superseded in the army list by another officer who had previously been his junior. Of the seven majors involved (Nzeogwu, Ifeajuna, Okafor, Anuforo, Chukwuka, Ademoyega, and Onwuatuegwu), the first four were substantive in rank, while the latter 3 held acting rank; but none of them could complain about this, since none of their contemporaries had been substantively promoted. Of the seven majors, only two, Anuforo and Onwuatuegwu, had been commissioned from RMAS, at the same time as the four Northern officers, i.e., Iliya Bisalla, Muhammed Shuwa, Ibrahim Haruna, and Murtala Muhammed. Only Anuforo was a substantive major; the rest were acting majors.[9]

Of all the possible motivations for the coup, the single most controversial is the idea that it was provoked by tribalism, and that the coup was staged as part of a drive by the Igbos to take over and dominate the country. This perception arises largely out of the fact that the conspirators were disproportionately Igbo-speaking, and that the victims of the coup were disproportionately non-Igbo-speaking; indeed, the fact that Northern officers and politicians were the largest single group of casualties played a major role in the genesis of the July 1966 coup (see below). It would be helpful to examine separately, and in some more depth, this particular theory.

The planning and execution of a coup is a high-risk business. Discovery or failure will more likely than not to lead to a rapid, painful, and quite possibly permanent termination to one's career and continued existence. It is therefore obvious that the plotters should seek to minimize the risk of either occurrence, and the best way of doing so is to enter into a conspiracy only with those whom one can trust, and with those who are in a position to contribute to the success of the proposed venture — in other words, with those of one's fellow officers whom one feels are of like mind. The central plotters in this coup, and who were critical to its success, were all majors and captains (whether substantive, acting or temporary), and Easterners formed by far the majority of this group in the army at the time. Twenty-three of the thirty-two substantive majors at the time of the coup were Easterners, as were fifteen of the fifty-four substantive captains, and the Easterners made up three quarters of the majors and lieutenant-colonels in the army.[10] It therefore is obvious that simply on the basis of their numbers in the middle ranks of the officer corps, that one might expect Igbo officers to play a leading role in any conspiracy. However, as Luckham has pointed out, it is possible to demonstrate that the ethnic composition of the conspirators "exceeded chance expectations."[11] He also demonstrates that this association between ethnicity and participation in the coup is greater for RMAS graduates, and is most marked in the group of officers who entered RMAS in 1959, all four Igbo officers who entered the academy in that year (Chukwuka, Udeaja, Anuforo, and Onwuatuegwu) were involved in the January plot; whereas none of the non-Igbos who entered that the same year (Adegoke, Adekunle, Esuene, Bisalla, Ikwue, Shuwa, Haruna, and Murtala Muhammed) were involved, although, as will be seen, some of them participated in subsequent coups. Several of the plotters who attended RMAS overlapped in terms of their course years; the group also included two (Ifeajuna and Ademoyega) of the six graduates holding combatant commissions in the army at that time. Of the four remaining graduates, two (Ojukwu and Banjo) were regarded by the plotters as being unlikely to oppose them, even if they would not actively participate. Of all the plotters, only Okafor had been commissioned after spending several years in the ranks; the others were, as has been pointed out, either graduates or commissioned after leaving school, and could therefore be reasonably expected to share the "enthusiasm for radical changes in society that was common among Nigerian students in the South."[12] Indeed, both Ademoyega and Nzeogwu confirmed this in subsequent books and interviews.[13] Finally, Luckham refers to Lenin in describing the organizational requirements of revolutionary groups as including secrecy, ease of communication, and group cohesion. It is therefore not surprising, given all the points above, that the conspirators took on the appearance of an Igbo-centric clique, even if they were not all Igbos, and more than likely were motivated by revolutionary zeal as opposed to tribal considerations.

The issue of the tribal origins of the victims of the coup also needs some scrutiny. Amongst the politicians, the Prime Minister and the Premiers of the North and West, as well as the Federal Finance Minister were killed (Sir Abubakar and the Sardauna were from the North, Akintola from the West and Okotie-Eboh from the Midwest). None of these were of Igbo-speaking origin. The premiers of the East and the Midwest, both Igbo-speakers, escaped unharmed, although, as has been pointed out earlier, there was barely any coup activity in the East, and none at all in the Midwest (where there were no troops stationed). As far as the soldiers were concerned, seven were killed: two Brigade Commanders (Ademulegun and Maimalari), three staff officers at Army HQ, (Kur Muhammed, Pam, and Unegbe), one NMTC Commandant (Shodeinde), and one Battalion CO (Largema). Of these seven soldiers, four were Northerners (Maimalari, Kur Muhammed, Pam, and Largema); two were Westerners (Ademulegun and Shodeinde), and one, a Midwesterner (Unegbe), the only Igbo-speaker, killed. Of the twenty-one officers of the rank of Lieutenant-

Colonel and above, none of the seven Easterners (Ironsi, Bassey, Imo, Njoku, Effiong, Ojukwu, and Kurubo) were killed. Two of the three Midwesterners (Ejoor and Nwawo) survived, as did four of the six Westerners (Ogundipe, Adebayo, Fajuyi, and Banjo). On the other hand, of the five Northerners, only Gowon survived. This apparent lopsidedness in the pattern of killings is not, however, as straightforward as it seems. It must be appreciated that the total of *all* those troops who took part in the coup, whether officers or other ranks, numbered no more than 200 in an army of 10,000-plus officers and other ranks. The number and range of targets (installations such as telephone exchanges, broadcasting facilities, Army and Police HQs, which all needed to be manned), as well as prisoners, (who also required guarding as long as they were alive), and the need for simultaneous action in at least two different places (Lagos and Kaduna as the centres of gravity politically and militarily) meant that the plotters were, *ab initio*, seriously overextended. The cold logic was that dispensing with the need to guard prisoners, i.e., by killing them, could ease the conspirators' task. From the plotters' perspective, this had the benefit that those in positions of authority who could rally opposition to the coup (the senior officers and some of the politicians) were permanently removed from the equation; it also meant, at least as far as the politicians were concerned, that whatever the outcome of the coup, the old government could not remain in power in the same form. Since those who fitted the bill in this regard, whether militarily or politically, were overwhelmingly Northerners and Westerners, it is hardly surprising that they were the majority of the casualties. Sir Abubakar was the Prime Minister and the Sardauna was the acknowledged leader of the ruling party, whose will could be easily imposed on surviving NPC ministers even if the Prime Minister was taken out. Ademulegun and Maimalari commanded the army's two fighting brigades. As Commandant of the NMTC, Shodeinde had access to troops he could rally in opposition to the coup. (Indeed, the soldiers who executed the coup in Kaduna came mainly from the NMTC.) The Army HQ staff officers could also rally opposition to the coup by virtue of their positions, and the same applied to Largema as CO of the Fourth Battalion. Largema also had the disadvantage of being closely identified with the discredited government by the plotters, as had Ademulegun. As Nzeogwu himself said subsequently:

We wanted to gun down all the bigwigs in our way. This was the only way. We could not afford to let them live if this was to work. We got some, but not all. General Ironsi was to have been shot. But we were not ruthless enough. As a result, he and the other compromisers were able to supplant us.[14]

It is also important to note that several senior officers were away from the country or from their posts at the time of the coup, and therefore were both out of reach of the plotters and of limited relevance in the context of the coup. Brigadier Ogundipe and Colonel Adebayo were out of the country; Lieutenant-Colonel Fajuyi, who had recently taken over command of the Abeokuta garrison, was on leave in his home town; Lieutenant-Colonel Ejoor, who was to take over from Fajuyi as CO First Battalion in Enugu, had not yet reported for duty; nor had Lieutenant-Colonel Gowon taken over command of the strategically placed Second Battalion in Ikeja. Further afield, Lieutenant-Colonel Kurubo, CO of the Third Battalion in Kaduna, was in Lagos for the weekend.

None of this, however, explains why the biggest fish of all, Ironsi, escaped. As it turned out, his survival was the main reason why the coup failed, for he was responsible for rallying opposition to the coup, first in Lagos and then in the rest of the country apart from Kaduna, where Nzeogwu initially remained in control. There has been much speculation that Ironsi was tipped off about the plot, and that this was the explanation for his survival, but this appears on the face of it to make little sense. If indeed Ironsi was tipped off, this could only have been done by someone privy to the plot, most likely one of the conspirators; but they would surely have realized that this would more likely than not to ensure the plot's failure. If the leaker of the plot was acting as a government stool pigeon, then why were the conspirators not rounded up before they put their plan into action, especially since in that case the authorities would also have known of the plotters' deadly intentions? And if he was spared on tribal grounds, because he was an Igbo, why did the plotters show little hesitation in killing Unegbe, also an Igbo, albeit one from the Midwest? It is necessary at this point to debunk the oft-asserted and profoundly foolish myth that Unegbe, as the Quartermaster-General, was killed for refusing to surrender the keys of the Armoury. This view implies gross ignorance of the role and duties of Quartermasters-General, which do not include, as a general rule, sleeping with armoury keys under their pillows. Nor does it explain the logical inconsistency that, in order to kill Unegbe and all the other victims, the conspirators were *already* armed. Unegbe, like all the other victims, was killed because of his ability, by virtue of the post he held, to rally opposition to the coup.

Returning to the subject of Ironsi's escape, as has been stated above, Nzeogwu clearly asserts that Ironsi was to have been eliminated. It may well have been that the plotters in the South made the mistake of starting to kill Ironsi's staff before they had eliminated the general himself. The undisputed fact that Ironsi put so much energy into ensuring the failure of the coup does not suggest that he was privy to it; but it also cannot be disputed that he was the ultimate beneficiary of the coup in that he, and not the authors of the coup, took power after it. Nzeogwu asserted afterwards that:

> Neither myself nor any of the other lads was in the least interested in governing the country. We were soldiers and not politicians. We had earmarked from the list known to every soldier in this operation who would be what. Chief Obafemi Awolowo was, for example, to be released from jail immediately and to be made the Executive Provisional President of Nigeria. We were going to make civilians of proven honesty and efficiency who would be thoroughly handpicked to do all the governing.[15]

Perhaps the failure of the coup, seeing that the conspirators were unable to implement their post-coup plans, was responsible for the subsequent perception that it was motivated by a desire for Igbo domination of the federation.

NOTES

1. Miners p. 260.

2. Luckham, Robin. *The Nigerian Military: A Sociological Analysis of Authority and Revolt: 1960-1967*. Cambridge University Press 1971 p. 17-19.

3. Ibid p. 123.

4. Miners p. 166, Luckham p. 27.

5. Miners p. 178.

6. Luckham pp. 19-20.

7. Ibid p. 41.

8. Miners p. 177.

9. Miners pp. 173-174; Luckham pp. 344-345.

10. Miners p. 123, 169; Luckham p. 47.

11. Luckham, ibid.

12. Miners p. 170.

13. Luckham p. 40; Ademoyega, Adewale. *Why We Struck: The Story of the First Nigerian Coup*. Evans Brothers, 1981, p. 33.

14. Luckham pp. 32-33.

15. Ibid pp. 284-285.

CHAPTER 4

The First Military Government

The best Generals are those who arrive at the results of planning without
being tied to plans

— Winston Churchill, 1930

Johnson Thomas Umunakwe Aguiyi-Ironsi had by February 1965 reached the pinnacle of an army career that began in the ranks some twenty-three years before, in 1942. He started out as a clerk in the Ordnance Stores (a fact which contributed to the contempt in which he was held by some of his own officers later on — Nzeogwu, in his final interview before his own death, dismissed Ironsi by stating that, "He joined the Army as a tally clerk and was a clerk most of the time."[1] Luckham recounts an incident in which a junior officer, on being admonished to pay attention to Ironsi's comments at an army dinner was heard to mumble 'General Idiot' at him under his breath.[2] Following a commission in 1949, Ironsi transferred to the infantry in 1951 after being court-martialed (and acquitted) on a charge of theft from the Ordnance Stores. Prior to being appointed as General Officer Commanding (GOC) the Nigerian Army and being promoted Major General, Ironsi had been through a number of high-profile courses and appointments. He had commanded a battalion, a brigade and a multi-national UN force on operations in the Congo (the last of these as an acting Major General), served as Equerry to Queen Elizabeth II during her visit to Nigeria in 1956, served as Defence Attaché at the Nigerian High Commission in London, and attended both the British Army Staff College at Camberley and the Imperial Defence College (now the Royal College of Defence Studies) in London. Notwithstanding all this, he appears to have been remarkably lacking in both organizational skill and political nous, if his performance at the head of the new federal military government was anything to go by.

Ironsi's appointment as GOC in the first place was an overtly political act. Major General Welby-Everard, the departing British GOC, clearly recommended Ogundipe, the third most senior of the four Brigadiers in contention (the others being, in order of seniority, Ironsi, Ademulegun, and Maimalari). In a top-secret memo to the Permanent Secretary of the Ministry of Defence, dated 14 September 1964, Welby-Everard set out the strengths and weaknesses, as he saw them, of the three viable candidates (see Appendix 1 on page 212). Maimalari, the only RMAS graduate amongst them, he discounted "as I consider him to be too young at present and not sufficiently mature." In his view, Ironsi's candidature was hampered by his having been away from Nigeria, and consequently out of direct contact with the army for the past three years, first as Military Adviser in London, then as a student at the Imperial Defence College and finally for the first six months of this year as the Commander of the United Nations Force in the Congo. Moreover, Ironsi had never commanded a brigade in Nigeria, and had held Battalion command for only 6 months in 1960-61. Finally, and most damningly (in this author's view), Welby-Everard stated:

> I have not been impressed by his military knowledge on the occasions when he has attended the GOC's conference and other meetings. It is also my duty to point out that there is a record against him of financial instability. My personal opinion is that I doubt whether he has either the professional military knowledge or the personal characteristics to make a good GOC.

Ademulegun was assessed as having,

> a wide and up-to-date knowledge of the army and its current problems, and his professional military knowledge is good. He is a forceful leader but somewhat intolerant in his opinions and hasty in his judgment. For this reason, he has a good many critics, not to say enemies, in the Army. There is no doubt in my opinion that he has the professional ability to make a good GOC and also has the necessary leadership qualities, but I fear he may not command the unswerving loyalty of all the officers.

Ogundipe, who was junior to both Ironsi and Ademulegun, was described as having,

> earned high praise for his military ability, fine character and powers of organisation. His professional military knowledge is good, and he possesses a sound and well-balanced judgment. He has an equitable temperament, and is universally respected by all ranks in the Army. He has the military ability, leadership qualities and the personal characteristics to make a good GOC.... After very careful consideration of all the military and personal factors involved, my opinion is that OGUNDIPE would make the best GOC, because I consider that he would be more likely to command the loyalty of the whole Army than either of the other two, and there would be less likelihood of opposing factions springing up within the Officer Corps. (Personal communication to the author, October 2016)

The appointment of the new GOC was to be made in the immediate aftermath of the imbroglio surrounding the federal elections in December 1964 and January 1965. Ademulegun was very strongly favoured by the Sardauna, and also by many members of the federal cabinet. Azikiwe, on the other hand, lobbied very strongly on behalf of Ironsi, mainly through the medium of Chief Okotie-Eboh, with other pressure coming from Mbadiwe, Mbu and influential outsiders like Pius Okigbo.... He (Muhammadu Ribadu, the Minister of Defence) concluded that "to support Aguiyi-Ironsi was logically tenable on grounds of his seniority...."[3] His (Ribadu's) politics had overcome his normally shrewd judgment of character, and he was able to convince a wavering Abubakar. This, however, was not the end of the matter. Although the Sardauna was "only" the Premier of the North, everyone knew that real political power in Nigeria rested with him, and he needed to be brought on side. Following what were described as "heated exchanges" between the Sardauna and the Prime Minister, the latter sent Maitama Sule to Kaduna to make the case for Ironsi face to face with the Sardauna. Another argument ensued, but eventually, albeit reluctantly, the Sardauna relented — but insisted, perhaps presciently, "the country will regret it.[4] It is very tempting to speculate whether Nigeria's history would have taken a different course if Ribadu and the Prime Minister had accepted Welby-Everard's recommendation, and Ogundipe, not Ironsi, had been appointed GOC.

In any event, as has been seen, in taking over power following the Majors' coup, Ironsi may have been reaping where he did not sow. He had no preexisting ideas of what he intended to achieve as the head of the government and therefore began his time in office without any or any clearly thought-out ideas about what policies he intended to pursue. When asked by a journalist two days after the coup whether he intended to remain in power after the situation in the country returned to normal, he replied, "I hope not."[5]

There were other forces at play, which Ironsi failed to grasp immediately. First, he made no clear or decisive move to bring the January mutineers to justice, thus stoking the latent resentment of Northern officers and other ranks (especially the senior NCOs). Second, and on the other hand, the conspirators were viewed by the Southern intelligentsia as heroes for having swept the corrupt politicians out of power. The fact that they were being detained at all (especially after Ironsi was supposed to have agreed not to do so in negotiations with Nzeogwu), was anathema enough to the supporters of the mutineers, never mind any suggestion that they might actually be punished. Unfortunately for Ironsi, it could not be denied that the actions of the January coup makers violated all sorts of norms and laws of military conduct, and his failure to deal decisively with these violations only encouraged speculation that he was privy to the coup in the first place, and that it was all a gigantic Igbo plot.

Third, and possibly as a consequence of assuming power when not prepared for it, the new government appeared bumbling and inept in its handling of *both* military and political matters, giving the impression of making things up as it went along. For example, the government never formally announced what had happened to the military victims of the January coup, for in the absence of facts, all sorts of rumours and myths sprang up and flourished, often to the regime's disadvantage. One story held that Maimalari had somehow escaped his assassins and fled to Ghana; lured back by Ironsi on the pretext of negotiations, he had then been shot and killed by the latter in a dastardly fashion.[6] Fourth, the regime seemingly failed fail to understand that the perceptions of its actions could be just as important as the actions themselves, and the best examples lay in the appointments made to senior positions in the army after the coup and in the promotions which followed four months afterwards.

Of the fifty-three officers of the rank at major and above at the time of the coup, eight were dead (Ademulegun, Maimalari, Kur Muhammed, Shodeinde, Largema, Pam, Unegbe, and Adegoke); five were in prison (Banjo, Nzeogwu, Anuforo, Okafor, and Ifeajuna); five were members of the military government (Ironsi, Ejoor, Fajuyi, Ojukwu, and Katsina); one had transferred to the air force (Kurubo); and one was out of the country on a course (Adebayo). There were therefore only thirty-three senior officers available to fill the army's senior posts — which needed to be filled after the events of January — and twenty-four of these were Igbo or Igbo-speaking. Whilst it was therefore inevitable that the bulk of the appointments would come from this group, the regime perhaps should also have foreseen that there was a real risk that these appointments could be perceived as further evidence of an Igbo plot to replace the Northerners as the dominant force in the federation. Following the coup, both brigades were now commanded by Easterners (Bassey at the First Brigade and Njoku at the Second Brigade), as were three of the five Battalions (David Ogunewe at the First Battalion; Henry Igboba at the Second; and Israel Okoro at the Third). In addition, the Abeokuta Garrison and the army depot were also commanded by Easterners (Gabriel Okonweze and Festus Akagha, respectively). Finally, the only Northern officer in a senior staff position at Army HQ was Yakubu Gowon, albeit as Chief of Staff, Army; the rest were all Southerners.

The army promotions announced in May did not help matters, although, like the appointments issue, the problem lay more in how the act was perceived rather than in the act itself. Eleven majors were promoted substantive Lieutenant-Colonel, whilst fourteen others were made acting Lieutenant-Colonels. Eighteen of the twenty-five officers so promoted were Igbo-speaking, along with five Northerners, one Westerner, and one Midwesterner. Since the Easterners formed by far the greatest proportion of the eligible majors, this was hardly surprising. In addition, the Northerners were not, in actual fact, treated unjustly; the one Northern major promoted substantive Lieutenant-Colonel, Katsina, was the most junior of the eleven so promoted, whereas three of the four Northerners promoted acting Lieutenant-Colonel (Murtala Muhammed, Shuwa, and Haruna) were still only substantive captains.[7] Indeed, if anyone was to feel aggrieved by these promotions, it was the substantive majors from the West who had been passed over for promotion, e.g., Adekunle,

Obasanjo, Sotomi, Rotimi, and Ayo-Ariyo. It is also often forgotten that there were also Igbo-speaking substantive majors, such as Chude-Sokei and John Obienu, who were also passed over. And there was some justification for some of the Eastern majors now being promoted to substantive Lieutenant-Colonel, among them, Patrick Anwunah, Mike Okwechime, and Alexander Madiebo, as they were only getting what was long overdue. Of the five Nigerian cadets who passed out of Sandhurst in December 1956 (which included Madiebo, Anwunah, and Okwechime) the only Northerner (Gowon) had been promoted more than two years earlier, in April 1964, and another, Unegbe, in July 1965. (This, of course, could have simply been a reflection of the assessments by their superiors of differentials in performance and potential.) Whatever the merits of the exercise in military terms, it was a disaster in terms of its perception by both the general public and Northern SNCOs — yet another example of an Igbo government promoting their kinsmen to all the senior posts.

These difficulties, noxious as they may seem, were but child's play compared with what was to come.

On 24 May 1966, following a two-day meeting of the Supreme Military Council, Ironsi made a nationwide broadcast in which he announced the promulgation of Decrees 33 and 34, which banned political parties, abolished the regions, vested all executive and legislative power in the hands of the new national (formerly federal) military government, and unified the nation's public services under a single Public Service Commission. This decision represented a monumental political miscalculation for several reasons. First, for many in the North who had grown increasingly uneasy at the perceived government bias in favor of the Igbos — this decision appeared to confirm their worst fears; that they would now be taken over by the better qualified Southerners, who would fill all the top and mid-level positions in the single nationwide public service division. This sense of foreboding had been fuelled by some remarkably tactless and provocative behavior on the part of some Igbo residents of the North — as several accounts reported them to be engaged in offensive behavior such as holding parties to celebrate the demise of the Sardauna, displaying photos of Nzeogwu in the markets, and continually playing a recording in which a speech by the late Prime Minister was drowned out by gunfire.[8]

Second, the decrees appeared to preempt the recommendations of the several study groups appointed by Ironsi himself to look into the question of Nigeria's economic and political future, although the study groups had not yet reported (and, in any event, there had already been grumblings from the North about the region's relative under-representation in the membership of the National Unity Study Group, the Constitutional Review Study Group, and the National Planning Advisory Group). To make matters worse, Ironsi had appointed another Igbo man, Francis Nwokedi, as Sole Commissioner on Administrative Unification. Third, coming on top of the unrest amongst Northerners in the army described above, these decrees may have initiated resentment that would be transformed into concrete plans for action amongst Northern soldiers.

More immediately, however, riots broke out in several cities in the North, with the violence directed mainly, but not exclusively, at the Igbos and their property. Although it seems that at least some of the violence was spontaneous, there is fairly strong evidence to suggest that it was preplanned and coordinated, not least the fact that the violence broke out in several different places at the same time. The rioting went on for several days, and took some time to bring under control, partly because of the limited number of policemen and the fact that the majority of troops available were mostly Northerners who could not be fully relied on in these circumstances. Hundreds of people were killed and many more injured in the mayhem. In an attempt to bring the situation under control, a number of measures were announced by the government: the military governors would be posted away from their regions of origin, and sections of the Nigeria Police Force antiriot squads would also rotate. The First Battalion of the army in Enugu would swap places with the Fourth Battalion in Ibadan, and there would be military prefects appointed at the local level to be responsible for ensuring that government policy was carried out (given how overstretched the army was by this point, it is difficult to see how this last point could have been a realistic proposition). Finally, Ironsi himself would seek to lead by example, undertaking a nationwide tour, first visiting Kano, Zaria, Kaduna, and Jos in the North, before meeting with traditional rulers from across Nigeria in Ibadan on 28 July. It turned out to be his final official engagement as Supreme Commander.

As alluded to earlier, the circumstances under which Ironsi's government came to power and its performance once in office, did little to endear it to junior officers and senior NCOs of Northern origin in the army. The SNCOs, who had served much longer than the junior officers, were particularly outraged by the violations of the military norms of authority and hierarchy that the coup represented; the apparent ethnic bias only made matters worse. The feelings of anguish, resentment, and anger amongst Northerners in the country soon reinforced by similar feelings from many outside the service. The principal source of these feelings, nevertheless, came from students at Ahmadu Bello University (who would have been contemporaries at school with a lot of the Northern subalterns); it is possible, but by no means definite, that former NPC politicians weighed in as well. The key relationship, however, was that between the SNCOs and the junior Officers; the latter were thus being pressured from within and without the army to act. Subsequent to the May riots, the tensions, suspicions, and mutual hostility within the previously close-knit fraternity of army officers (and especially between the Northerners and the Easterners) became more and more overt, with each side suspecting the other of murderous plans. On the one hand, the Northerners claimed to fear that the Easterners were going to complete the "unfinished" job of 15 January by eliminating all remaining non-Eastern officers; whilst the Easterners claimed that the Northerners intended to "reestablish the dominance" of the North over the rest of Nigeria. Wherever the real truth lay, it is indisputable that the situation in the country and within the army on the evening of 28 July 1966 was akin to a barrel of explosives with an unlit fuse — and no shortage of potential detonators.

The coup that ended the Ironsi regime appears to have involved many different groups of plotters. As stated above, Northern junior officers were coming under pressure to act in order to avenge what was seen as the Igbo January coup. Some officers who attended a platoon commanders course run at NMTC, such as Lieutenants Muhammadu Jega and Sani Abacha, were reported to have written to the Chief of Staff (army), Yakubu Gowon, demanding that more senior Northern officers act, failing which they would do so themselves, and declaring that the senior officers would be responsible for whatever happened thereafter. (Such brazenness, even in the fevered atmosphere of the time, seems quite extraordinary, even unlikely, to this author — but these were far from normal times.) Elsewhere, in Lagos, the aforesaid more senior Northern officers were also conspiring to stage a coup in order to remove Ironsi from office, this conspiracy being led by Lieutenant-Colonel Murtala Muhammed (Inspector of Signals), Major Theophilus Danjuma (Staff Officer II at SHQ), and Captain Martin Adamu (Second Battalion). Other officers named as being involved in the plot included Captain Joseph Garba of the Federal Guards, and Lieutenants, Muhammadu Buhari (Second Battalion), Jeremiah Useni (Fourth Battalion), Shehu Yar'Adua (First Battalion), as well as Ibrahim Babangida, Abdul Wya, and B.S. Dimka (various units in Kaduna). All of these names would become depressingly familiar to Nigerians over the next decade or so in relation to coups.

The fuse appears to have been lit at Abeokuta Garrison, where the Commanding Officer, Lieutenant-Colonel Gabriel Okonweze, having been alerted on the night of 28 July, possibly by Lieutenant-Colonel Anwunah or by Lieutenant-Colonel Njoku, called a meeting of his officers in the Officers' Mess, told them of the alert he had received, and informed them of his decision to wake up and arm *all* troops as a precautionary measure.[9] An Igbo NCO is then said to have gone around the barracks to wake up the troops. In so doing, he alerted a Northern SNCO who, convinced that this was the beginning of the Easterners' "unfinished business", alerted his fellow Northerner, who was the unit armourer, and secured the unit armoury, ensuring that weapons were distributed only to Northern troops. Once armed, and under the direction of a Northern subaltern, the Northern troops proceeded to the Officers' Mess, where Okonweze and other Eastern officers were shot dead. Troops of Eastern origin within the barracks were rounded up and shot. The mutiny subsequently spread, over the next day or two, to Lagos, Ibadan, Kaduna, and Enugu, by which time Ironsi, along with his host, Lieutenant-Colonel Fajuyi (Governor of the Western Region) and several other officers and soldiers (mostly, but not exclusively, from the East) were dead or missing. Attempts by the military chain of command — and involving, at various times Brigadier Ogundipe (Chief of Staff, Supreme Headquarters), Commodore Wey (Head of the Navy), Lieutenant-Colonel Gowon (Army Chief of Staff), and Major Mobolaji Johnson (Military Administrator of Lagos), who were all at Police HQ in Lagos — to put down the mutiny and restore order were unsuccessful, largely because none of them was able to exercise effective command or control over the troops. First Johnson and then Ogundipe were told, point-blank, by Northern NCOs that they would not accept orders from them unless their Northern Captain, an officer junior to both of them, validated those orders. Ogundipe then dispatched Gowon to negotiate with the mutineers now holed up at the Second Battalion in Ikeja, only for them to insist that, as the most senior Northern officer left alive, he, Gowon, should instead act as their spokesman. There was febrile talk of the North seceding immediately from the rest of Nigeria, a position most forcefully advocated by Lieutenant-Colonel Murtala Muhammed and Captain Martin Adamu. (Majors Theophilus Danjuma and Shittu Alao and Captain Joe Garba are known to have been present, but it is not clear to what extent they supported Muhammed's position.) On the other hand, civilians such as Chief Justice, Sir Adetokunbo Ademola; Mr. Justice Muhammed Bello; Public Service Commission Chairman, Alhaji Sule Katagum; as well as the British High Commissioner and the US Ambassador, strongly advised against pursuing such a course. With some difficulty, Gowon managed to persuade his fellow Northern officers against secession; they agreed to remain as part of Nigeria but only on condition that he, Gowon, take over the leadership of the country.[10]

The tense standoff and the negotiations continued throughout the weekend, during which Nigeria effectively was without a government. Ogundipe and the others at Police HQ were effectively redundant at this stage. During the course of the standoff, Gowon spoke by telephone to the surviving military governors (Ejoor, Ojukwu, and Katsina) to keep them informed of events. Ojukwu insisted that, in the absence of Ironsi, Ogundipe, as the next most senior officer should have taken over, an unrealistic proposition in the circumstances, given the latter's lack of effective control over the situation. Eventually, Gowon went on air on 1 August 1966 to announce that he had assumed power as Supreme Commander and Head of the Military Government. Ojukwu responded by declaring, also on air, his position as stated above; and that, as he had not been party to the agreement that Gowon assume power, he would neither recognise him as Supreme Commander nor his authority. The battle lines had been drawn that would ultimately lead to the fragmentation of both the army and the country — and to a bloody Civil War.

NOTES

1. Miners p. 171.

2. Luckham p. 166.

3. Clark, Trevor. *A Right Honourable Gentleman: Abubakar from the Black Rock*. Edward Arnold, 1991, p. 714.

4. Ibid.

5. Luckham p. 46.

6. Ibid p. 52.

7. Miners p. 210.

8. Miners pp. 200-201; Luckham p. 271.

9. Omoigui, Nowa. *Operation Aure — The Northern Military Counter-Rebellion of July 1966*. www.segun.bizland.com/omoigui13 (accessed 27/6/2017).

10. Luckham p. 67-68.

CHAPTER 5

The Second Military Government: Prelude to War

I need not tell you what horror, what devastation and what extreme human suffering will attend the use of force. When it is all over and the smoke and dust have lifted, and the dead are buried, we shall find, as other people have found, that it has all been futile, entirely futile, in solving the problems we set out to solve.

— **Adeyinka Adebayo, 1967**

There were a number of interesting parallels between Nigeria's first and second military governments. First, neither one was led by men whose own actions had brought about the governments they headed; neither Ironsi nor Gowon had been involved in planning the coups that brought them to power. Second, and partly as a consequence of the first situation, neither Ironsi nor Gowon came to office with a clear plan or programme for government. Third, both governments were viewed as being the result of an attempt by one region to lord it over the rest of the country, initially by the Igbos in January and then by the Northerners in July. Fourth, both governments failed to prosecute (or, in the case of the second government, even to arrest) those who carried out the coups that brought them to power, and this created resentments that later erupted in cataclysmic events, i.e., the July coup and the Civil War respectively. Fifth, and perhaps most importantly, both governments were afflicted by some of the very problems the army claimed as reasons for its intervention once in power: to put an end to tribalism and regionalism. This defect would have serious consequences for both; the July coup in the first case, and the Civil War in the second. There was, however, one key difference between the two governments; whereas the Ironsi government started out being popular and only later lost its popular appeal, the reverse seemed to have been the case with the Gowon government, which started out with many skeptical about its legitimacy and viability, but which, once the war had broken out, enjoyed widespread support across the country (apart, obviously, from the Eastern Region).

Even at this early stage of being in power, therefore, it will be seen that the Nigerian Army had been shaped by Nigerian politics — and had been radically altered by its overt entry on to the political stage. In return, the army had begun to fundamentally change the course of Nigeria's political history by sowing the seeds of the impending Civil War (and before that by beginning the process of creating states, a most political act which will be discussed later).

In the previous chapter, the circumstances in which Lieutenant-Colonel Yakubu Gowon assumed the leadership of his country at the tender age of thirty-one were described. It might be useful, at this juncture, to pause and explore a little more about the man who would remain in charge of the affairs of Nigeria over the next nine years. Born on 19 October 1934 in Tuwan in present-day Plateau State, Yakubu Cinwa Gowon was the fifth of eleven children born to his parents, Yohanna and Saraya. His father was a farmer and had also become an evangelist for the Church Missionary Society (CMS) following his conversion to Christianity. He moved his family from Tuwan to Wusasa near Zaria in Kaduna State in 1936, when Yakubu was aged two. Yakubu's mother was the disciplinarian, and by all accounts was a firm subscriber to the adage that sparing the rod spoiled the child.[1] The family was by no means well off or affluent, and all the children had to help out on the family farm. Gowon attended the local primary school in Wusasa, where he excelled academically and won several prizes. He also participated in extracurricular activities such as sports and music. In 1950, Yakubu Gowon was admitted to Government College Zaria, where he appears to have done better on the sports field than he did in the classroom, if his school reports are anything to go by.[2] As he came to the end of his school days in 1953-54, Gowon's first instinct was to become a teacher so that he could start earning money to help support his family; he also considered, but soon discarded, becoming a doctor or an engineer. His school principal and vice-principal, both British expatriates, actively encouraged him to consider a career in the army (by this time, several Old Boys from the school such as Zakariya Maimalari, Umar Lawan, Abogo Largema, and Yakubu Pam had been either commissioned or were training to become army officers).

There was a history of military service in the family, for Gowon's two older brothers, Ibrahim and Peter, had both served in Burma with the army during World War II, and Ibrahim had been killed in action — a fact which was probably responsible for Saraya, Gowon's mother's lack of enthusiasm about the prospect of her third son also joining the army. We do not know what her feelings were when two of Gowon's younger brothers, Moses and Isaiah, subsequently joined the military, the former in the air force and the latter, the army. Gowon was not sure himself about a military career, and, according to his biographer Elaigwu,

> He prayed and then wrote down a number of professions — teaching, engineering, medicine and army on pieces of paper which he slipped into his Bible and prayed again. With his eyes closed he picked from among the pieces of paper — and he picked on the army.[3]

His mind now made up, Gowon attended and passed an interview at the Depot in Zaria, and then sat and passed the army entrance exam. A further interview followed at the Brigade Headquarters in Kaduna (his interview panel included the then Captain Wellington Bassey). After another interview at Army HQ in Lagos in May 1954, Gowon proceeded to the Regular Officers Special Training School in Teshie, Ghana, together with Patrick Anwunah, Arthur Unegbe, Alexander Madiebo, and Mike Okwechime. On completing the course at Teshie, and passing the West Africa Command Selection Board, Gowon and the others proceeded to the UK, where they sat and passed the War Office Selection Board before going to Eaton Hall in Chester. On completing this, he attended and passed the Regular Commissions Board before being admitted to RMAS in September 1955. On successful completion of the course at RMAS, Gowon was commissioned, at aged twenty-two, as a Second Lieutenant at midnight on 21 December 1956 in the usual Sandhurst tradition. As has been noted above in chapter 1, the process by which Gowon and his colleagues achieved their commissions was much longer and significantly more onerous than that for their British colleagues who were commissioned alongside them.

After passing out of RMAS at the end of 1956, Gowon attended the Young Officers Course and the Platoon Commanders Course at Hythe and Warminster, respectively, before returning to Nigeria in July 1957, where he was posted to the Fourth Battalion of the

Queen's Own Nigerian Regiment (QONR) in Ibadan as a Platoon Commander. Whilst with QONR, he attended a number of courses, including the three-inch Mortar Course at Teshie between March and May 1958 and the Support Arms Course at Netheravon in the UK between May and August 1959. Upon his return from the latter, the now Lieutenant Gowon was appointed Adjutant of QONR. In January 1960, Gowon was deployed on operations to the Southern Cameroons as a Platoon Commander, and then between November 1960 and June 1961, to the Congo as part of the Nigerian contingent in the UN Force. Upon his return, and now a Captain, Gowon was posted to a staff job at Army HQ. The following year, and still a Captain with less than six years commissioned service, Gowon attended the Army Staff College in Camberley. Upon his return to Nigeria in early 1963, he was promoted Major and posted back to the Congo as Brigade Major of the Nigerian Brigade in Lualuabourg; the following year, in April 1964, he was promoted Lieutenant-Colonel and appointed Adjutant General; he was not yet thirty, and had been a commissioned officer for less than eight years at this point. In May 1965, he was sent to attend the Joint Services Staff College in the UK, and had just returned from this course to take command of the army's Second Battalion in Ikeja when the January 1966 coup took place, following which, as we have seen, he was made the Chief of Staff of the Army by Ironsi, and then took over the leadership of the country after the events of July 1966. He was not yet thirty-two years old, had less than ten years service as a commissioned officer, and had never commanded anything larger than a thirty-man platoon.

Given the prevailing situation in the army and in the country at the time Gowon took up the reins of leadership, even an older and much more experienced leader would have already had his work cut out. It would hardly have been surprising if Gowon initially seemed to be struggling and out of his depth. Large sections of the army were unruly and very clearly not under control. (Murtala Muhammed must shoulder a large degree of the blame in this regard, as his behavior was insubordinate, to put it mildly; which included urging Northern soldiers in the First Battalion in Enugu to try and seize control, demanding an immediate invasion of the East, and barging in uninvited to meetings of the Supreme Military Council.) Gowon's legitimacy as Supreme Commander was not accepted by one of the Military Governors (Ojukwu), and the future seemed bleak. In a shrewd move, Gowon announced the pardon and release of a number of people serving prison sentences, most notably Awolowo and Enahoro and, later, Dr. Okpara, which had the effect of buying the new leader, at least in the short-term, the support of the South, and the time to try and consolidate his grip on power.[4] Tense negotiations ensued, on 8 and 9 August 1966, between the central and regional governments, which resulted in provisional agreements (i) that troops would be withdrawn wherever possible and returned to their regions of origin (save for the security of Lagos, as the capital of the country being placed in the hands of the Supreme Commander), (ii) that legislation creating unitary government should be repealed, and (iii) that a conference be arranged for the political leaders of the regions to discuss the country's future.[5]

Gowon opened the so-called ad hoc Constitutional Conference in Lagos on 12 September 1966, with delegations from all four regions and Lagos in attendance. In his address to the conference, he set them two tasks: first, to produce a recommendation for the country's future constitutional arrangements from amongst four options: (i) federation with a strong centre, (ii) one with a weak centre, (iii) a confederation, or (iv) "an entirely new arrangement which will be peculiar to Nigeria and which has not yet found its way into any political dictionary"); and second, to come up with an interim arrangement to tide the country over until such time as the chosen constitutional arrangement could be effected.[6] On the first task, each of the delegations submitted memoranda with their proposals, ranging from "a union of four virtually independent Regions" (East) and "a similarly oriented proposal for autonomous states" (North) to "eight States and a strong Central Government" (West) and at the centre "twelve States with a relatively weak Government" (Midwest) and "a multi-state Federal structure" (Lagos). On the second task, only the West and Lagos initially submitted memoranda: the Midwest joined a month later.[7] After a five-day adjournment, the conference reconvened on 20 September 1966, at which time the Northern delegation appeared to have amended its position, coming out strongly in favour of a strong central government and the creation of individual states that would not have the right to secede from the nation. This course change may have been the result, according to Kirk-Greene, of

....some even stronger pressure....said to have been exercised by
Middle Belt elements, notably Tiv, in the army, physically outside
the conference hall or personally at a higher level, and to have at
least included the approval of Lt Col Gowon, himself a Northern
minority man.....there was little reason to expect the Middle Belt
minority leaders to let slip this chance to secure that recognition
of status denied to them during years of parliamentary opposition,
political persecution, nugatory alliances with southern parties and
open resistance that had been their lot over the previous decade.[8]

On 25 September, the conference steering committee, comprising the
leaders of the delegations, submitted an interim report to Gowon.
This report, which included a recommendation for the creation of
states endorsed by all the delegations, save that of the East, also
included the following agreements regarding the army, which, in the
light of what was to follow, is worth quoting at length:

1. There shall be a Nigerian Army, which shall be organized in
   Regional Units *composed entirely in each Region of personnel
   indigenous to that Region.* (author's emphasis)

2. The operational control of the units in each Region will be the
   responsibility of the Regional Commander.

3. Directions with respect to the maintaining and securing of public
   safety and public order within the Region or any part thereof may
   be given to the Regional Commander by the Security Committee
   in that Region, and the Regional Commander shall comply with
   those directions or cause them to be complied with.

4. The composition of the Security Committee shall be as follows:
   i. The Governor of the Region;
   ii. The Head of the Regional Government;
   iii The Regional Commander;
   iv The Commissioner of Police;
   v. The Minister in the Region responsible for Public Order.

5. *Training facilities, Ordnance Depots and other Army stores
   shall be organized on a Regional basis. Recruitment shall be the
   responsibility of the Regional Commander acting in accordance with the
   policy laid down by the Security Committee.* (author's emphasis)

6. At the national level there shall be a Defence Council which shall be responsible for—

   a. laying down military policy which should include the strength of military personnel in each Region, types and quantities of weapons, equipment, minimum standards of recruitment, promotion, discipline, etc.;

   b. overall operational control of the Regional units in the event of—

      i. external aggression;

      ii. inter-Regional conflict; and

      iii. the Regional Security Committee requesting the Council for military assistance to cope with any security situation within the Region beyond the capability of the Regional Unit.

   c. the control of Defence Industries

7. The Defence Council will consist of—

   i.   The Head of the State of Nigeria;

   ii. The Head of the Central Government;

   iii. The Heads of the Regional Governments;

   iv. The Chief of Staff;

   v. Regional Commanders;

   vi. The Minister of Defence.

8. The office of Chief of Staff shall be held in rotation by the Regional Commanders for fixed periods not exceeding twelve months.

9. The Defence Council shall be served by a Defence Secretariat under the Chief of Staff. The personnel of the Secretariat shall be drawn from the Regions in equal numbers.

Similar arrangements were proposed for the Navy and the Air Force (although the document was silent on how or why, for example, the Northern Region would have a Navy).[9]

It seems fairly obvious that, should these proposals become enshrined in any future constitution, the Nigerian Army (and indeed the Nigerian Navy and Air Force), as known up to that point, would effectively cease to exist, and would amount to little more than regional militias. As it turned out, the interim report was soon academic. After the conference adjourned for the annual Independence Day celebrations (it was scheduled to reconvene on

24 October), there was an outbreak of violence in the North, which dwarfed anything that had gone before. The catalyst for the violence varies, depending upon whom one spoke to: the Northern version was that the violence was triggered by reports on Radio Cotonou, rebroadcast by Radio Kaduna in both English and Hausa, of Northerners being killed in the East; whilst the Eastern version holds that the killings were all premeditated. What is beyond doubt is that thousands of Nigerians, mostly Igbos, were killed over the weekend spanning the end of September and the beginning of October 1966, and over the next few days and weeks that followed. The violence was not limited exclusively to the North. It was significant that the violence was not purely a civilian affair as Northern troops massacred several Easterners at Kano Airport on 30 September, and two days later, "a platoon of the Fifth Battalion mutinied, killed an officer and their Regimental Sergeant Major, forced the Battalion's Commanding Officer to flee for his life, and went on the rampage in the town".[10] The final death toll may never be known with certainty (it certainly ran into the thousands), but this orgy of bestial butchery spelled the end for the Constitutional Conference. The efflux of Easterners from the North, which had begun after the May riots, now turned into an exodus of biblical proportions. According to Luckham, "By mid-October there were practically no Ibos left in the North, and not many non-Ibo Easterners either"; and he estimated that more than a million Easterners fled back to the East.[11] In response, Ojukwu ordered all non-Easterners to leave the East, on the basis that, in the light of the killings in the North, he could no longer guarantee their safety. On 3 October, Gowon made a moving speech to the rump of the Constitutional Conference in which he expressed regret and sadness about the violence, and, interestingly in the light of their later dealings, appeared to support Ojukwu's expulsion of non-indigenes from the East:

> The Governor of the East has said that because of this renewed violence, he had no alternative but to ask non-Easterners in the East to go back to their own homes. "I think he is justified; I will tell you that"....If we are alive and if we are determined, we can get this country back to its proper shape. "I am determined to do that even if it means my life. I give you my word for it".[12] (author's emphasis)

The following day, Ojukwu summoned a meeting of the Eastern Consultative Assembly, which, having considered the report of the Eastern delegation to the Constitutional Conference, resolved that, until all the decisions taken at the meeting on 8-9 August were fully implemented, and "until immediate compensation is paid by the Federal Military Government for the lives and properties of Easterners lost in the disturbed areas of Nigeria, the Eastern Nigeria Delegation should no longer participate in future Constitutional Conference."[13]

They were never to return. Ojukwu made a broadcast on 22 October setting out the conditions under which the Eastern delegation would return to the Constitutional Conference, which included the removal of Northern troops from Lagos and the West, and the use of the police to maintain security in Lagos for the conference. Gowon, who insisted that the conference would reconvene as scheduled on 24 October, promptly rejected these conditions. The conference reconvened, sans the Eastern delegation, and adjourned again after a week for what proved to be the last time. On 17 November 1966, the federal government adjourned the conference indefinitely after it became clear that the Eastern delegation would not return unless its preconditions were met, which the federal government was not prepared to do. Over the next couple of months, the federal and Eastern Region governments (or more accurately, Gowon and Ojukwu) exchanged accusations as to where the blame lay for the impasse. Offers made by the federal government for meetings in Benin, in Akure, and on a naval ship at sea were rebuffed by Ojukwu; in turn, Ojukwu's invitation to Gowon and to his fellow military governors to a meeting in Calabar or Port Harcourt were declined. Something extraordinary was required to resolve the impasse.

That extraordinary something was provided by Lieutenant-General Joseph Ankrah, the head of Ghana's military government (President Nkrumah had been overthrown in February 1966 whilst out of the country on a state visit to China). Ankrah now offered the use of Peduase Lodge, Nkrumah's luxurious weekend retreat at Aburi, just outside Accra, as a venue for a meeting of the Supreme Military Council, in the hope that Ojukwu would agree to this, which he did. The two-day meeting began on Wednesday 4 January 1967. Present were Gowon, Adebayo, Ojukwu, Ejoor, Katsina, Wey, Johnson

(Administrator of Lagos), Kam Selem and Omo-Bare (Inspector-General and Deputy Inspector-General of Police, respectively). Also in attendance were senior civil servants from the federal and all the regional governments. The participants returned to Nigeria on the evening of the fourth, and returned to Ghana the following morning, Thursday, 5 January. After an opening address in which he urged his visitors to do their best to reach agreement on a lasting solution to Nigeria's problems, Ankrah withdrew and left the Nigerians to it.

There is widespread agreement amongst commentators on this period of Nigeria's history that of all the attendees, Ojukwu was by far the best prepared; the only one with a clear idea of what he wanted to achieve. This might therefore be an opportune point to take a closer look at the man who, together with Gowon, would have a major impact on the course of Nigerian history not just over the next few years but arguably over several years to come.

It would be difficult to find any two people whose antecedents and upbringing were more divergent than Ojukwu's and Gowon's. Chukwuemeka Odumegwu Ojukwu was born in Zungeru in Northern Nigeria on 4 November 1933, the son of a businessman, Louis Odumegwu Ojukwu. Ojukwu Sr. hailed from Nnewi in present-day Anambra State and made a fortune from his transport business. He subsequently diversified his business interests, and was later knighted as Sir Louis. His son, meanwhile, was brought up with the proverbial silver spoon in his mouth, a far cry from Gowon's more humble beginnings. Ojukwu first attended CMS Grammar School in Lagos, then transferred a year later to King's College, also in Lagos. As a teenager, his father sent him abroad at a public school (Epsom) in England from which he gained a place at Lincoln College at Oxford University, where he obtained a degree in History in 1955. He returned to Nigeria where he declined to take his place in his father's burgeoning business empire and instead took up a post as an Assistant District Officer in the colonial administration. In 1957, and again in defiance of his father's wishes, Ojukwu applied to join the army, and, after successfully completing the short-service course at Mons, was commissioned in March 1958, more than a year after Gowon. As a graduate, however, his seniority was backdated by several months, which was to be a source of friction in the future. It might be useful at this point to set out their respective seniority dates for promotion in each rank:[14]

GOWON		OJUKWU	
Rank	**Date**	**Rank**	**Date**
Second Lieutenant	19/10/55	Second Lieutenant	22/9/55
Lieutenant	9/9/57	Lieutenant	22/9/57
Captain	19/10/61	Captain	22/9/61
Major	09/03/63	Major	07/03/63
Lieutenant-Colonel	01/04/64	Lieutenant-Colonel	01/04/64

After commissioning, Ojukwu, like Gowon, attended courses at Warminster and Hythe in England and Teshie in Ghana before being posted to 5QONR, then based in Kaduna, as a Platoon Commander. Also like Gowon, he was trained at the Joint Services Staff College in the UK, and, again like Gowon, had held a senior staff position at Army HQ in Lagos (in his case as Quartermaster General). Unlike Gowon, however, he had also been a battalion CO, returning to command the Fifth Battalion, now based in Kano. He was serving in this latter position when Ironsi tapped him to become Military Governor of the Eastern Region after the January 1966 coup.

In addition to being by far the best-educated man around the conference table, Ojukwu was also the most able. He came armed with memoranda that set out his positions, and was adroit in his manipulation of the others, e.g., first, getting them to agree to renounce the use of force as a means of solving Nigeria's problems, for he was well aware that at this stage there was no way he could win in a direct military confrontation with the rest of the federation. (This was precisely the reason Murtala Muhammed had been urging an immediate invasion of the East — to bring Ojukwu to heel.) One gets the impression that many of his colleagues (with perhaps the possible exception of Wey and Katsina, who seemed more prepared to be blunt and robust in their dealings with Ojukwu) were so relieved that Ojukwu had finally deigned to join them that they seemed to approach proceedings with a degree of bonhomie that belied the seriousness of the issues at stake. As John de St. Jorre put it, they saw it more as:

> an informal, ice-breaking gathering in the style of an officers' mess committee meeting, the first, they hoped, of many to come.... little detailed preparation was done beforehand...there was an assumption....that the main priority was to get on talking terms with the East again, patch up the basic problems in a general way and leave the "small print" and the follow-up action to the civil servants and the "legal boys"....with such an improvement in personal relations, future meetings of the Supreme Military Council in Nigeria would present no difficulty and would, therefore, occur frequently, enabling residual problems to be ironed out.... [Ojukwu, on the other hand], came to Aburi to re-write the Nigerian constitution — and largely succeeded.[15]

That said, it should also be noted that the participants were grappling with several difficult and contentious subjects, such as the fate of Ironsi, the legitimacy (or otherwise) of Gowon's accession as Supreme Commander and Ojukwu's refusal to recognise him as such, as well as the future of the army and the country. Regarding the first two, Ojukwu pointedly said to Gowon and to the others that

> ...any break at this time from our normal line would write something into the Nigerian Army which is bigger than all of us and that thing is indiscipline....How can you ride above people's heads purely because you are at the head of a group who have their fingers poised on the trigger?...You announced yourself as Supreme Commander. Now, Supreme Commander by virtue of the fact that you head, or that you are acceptable to people who had mutinied against their commander, kidnapped him and taken him away?

In response to Ojukwu's expression of revulsion at the murder of Eastern officers and soldiers in July 1966, Katsina asked him why he had not expressed similar revulsion at the murders of senior Northern officers in January 1966. Ojukwu's response was to avoid taking any opportunity of putting his revulsion (if indeed he felt any) to the January killings on record; instead he pointed out that in January, soldiers from all four regions had participated in the murders of officers and politicians from all four regions, whereas in July, officers and soldiers from one region only (the North) had killed their colleagues from mainly one other region (the East). Whilst this may have been true, it was perhaps not particularly helpful in the circumstances and could reasonably be said to highlight Ojukwu's biggest character flaw: he did not seem to know how or when to back off momentarily in order to achieve broader long-term advantage. There always seemed to be a compulsion on his part to demonstrate to his colleagues how much more clever he was than them. De St. Jorre underscores this point again:

> Although a brilliant tactician, Ojukwu was a poor strategist. He constantly narrowed his future options and manoeuvrability for the sake of the short-term advantage.[16]

Philip Effiong, Ojukwu's wartime deputy concurred, describing him after the war thus:

> ...he had one weakness — he did not know when to apply the brakes. But it's purely because he was ambitious. He was a very able chap.[17]

As far as the future of the country and the army were concerned, Ojukwu managed to persuade his colleagues to agree to arrangements that, in essence, amounted to confederation in all but name. The recommendations by the ad hoc Constitutional Conference regarding splitting the army along regional lines were broadly followed. More fundamentally, the Aburi Conference participants agreed to a series of measures regarding the governance of the country, which stripped powers from the Supreme Commander (now to be called the Commander in Chief) and from the federal government in favour of the military governors and the regions. The executive and legislative authority that had previously been invested in the Supreme Commander was now to be invested in the Supreme Military Council

> to which *any* decision affecting the whole country shall be referred for determination provided that where it is not possible for a meeting to be held the matter requiring determination *must* be referred to Military Governors for their *comment and concurrence*.[18] (author's emphasis)

In effect, as the Federal Permanent Secretaries wasted no time in pointing out to Gowon on 20 January 1967,[19] the Commander in Chief would have no powers of control or dismissal over the military governors, who would in turn have veto power over Supreme Military Council decisions, a situation clearly incompatible with military rule. In addition, the Aburi Participants also pointed out that the Nigerian Army was in effect being dismembered and transformed into a number of regional armies; most tellingly, the Aburi agreement was such that "no authority is vested with the power for the use of the army, for external attacks on Nigeria" — a situation that fell very little short of complete lunacy. And there was more:

> Furthermore, it is observed that while Military Governors will have powers to appoint or approve appointments of Federal Government Servants, there is no corresponding power of the Supreme Military Council to even influence the appointments to senior posts in the Regional Public Services. This clearly makes the Federal Military Government subordinate to the Regional Governments.

Whilst there was clearly an element of senior federal civil servants protecting their individual turf and interests at play here, they nonetheless had a point. It is perhaps not surprising that, on his way back to the East, Ojukwu turned to his Chief Secretary (the Head of the Eastern Region's civil service) and asked, "Why were those people so jubilant?.... Do you think they have grasped the full implications of the decisions they have taken?"[20]

Gowon was made to realize, in fairly short order, that what had been agreed upon at Aburi could not be implemented to the letter if Nigeria was to continue as a federal government (if indeed there was to be a Nigeria at all). The task now before him was to find a way to backtrack from those elements of the Aburi decisions that in effect turned Nigeria into a confederation, and at the same time accommodate as many salient points as possible of the East's recommendations in order to maintain a united Nigeria. Unsurprisingly, Ojukwu insisted that the Aburi agreements be implemented to the letter, adopting the position that "On Aburi we stand: there will be no compromise".[21] A series of meetings were held in Benin, first, by the Solicitors-General of the federation and the regions on 14 January 1967; second, by the senior army officers (as well as representatives of the regions) on 24 January 1967; and then by the secretaries to the military governors on 17 February 1967, ostensibly to try and fashion a framework by which the agreements determined at Aburi could be implemented. At the same time, there was an increasingly acrimonious series of exchanges between the federal and Eastern regional governments and their respective information/mass media organs in which each side sought to blame the other for the rapid unravelling of the immediate post-Aburi feel-good atmosphere. The federal government's *Nigeria 1966 and the Eastern Region's January 15: Before and After*, were particularly illustrative examples of this series of publications that proved unhelpful in the prevailing atmosphere.

On 25 February 1967, Ojukwu upped the ante. In a dawn broadcast, he "threatened that unless the Aburi agreements were fully implemented by 31 March, he would feel free to give effect to them unilaterally."[22] Three days later, the Supreme Military Council met in Lagos without Ojukwu and reaffirmed that they continued to believe that Nigeria should continue to exist as a single undivided country. The government-controlled radio stations in Enugu and Kaduna persisted in hurling insults and accusations at each other. Lieutenant-Colonel Hassan Katsina, who as previously noted, was at Aburi and slightly more inclined than his colleagues to challenge Ojukwu, Katsina did not help matters by saying, on 9 March, that "if need be the East could be crushed in a matter of hours", which drew a retort from Ojukwu that "I feel we have crossed the line."[23] Given this febrile atmosphere, it was hardly surprising that Ojukwu again refused to attend a meeting of the Supreme Military Council held in Benin on 10 March to consider a draft decree arising out of the earlier series of meetings of officials and army officers in the same city. (Ojukwu alleged that he would not be safe attending a meeting of the SMC in Benin because of the presence of Northern troops in the West; but this apparently did not prevent him from paying a visit to Ejoor in the same city two days later.) The meeting resulted in the promulgation of Decree 8 of 1967, which conceded substantial ground to the East's point of view at Aburi; for example, executive and legislative power was vested in the Supreme Military Council (and not in the Supreme Commander, as had hitherto been the case), which in certain matters had to act with the explicit concurrence of all four military governors; and the army was reorganized into area commands along the agreed-upon lines at Aburi. There was, however, one key provision: "the concurrence of only three of the Governors, however, was required to declare a State of Emergency or to invalidate any Regional legislation that impeded the executive authority of the Federation, or endangered the continuance of federal government in Nigeria."[24] This provision was clearly designed to prevent Ojukwu and the East from holding the rest of the country to ransom.

Despite the fact that the decree was considered by several commentators (the Eastern minorities and the Lagos press, for example) to be "another major concession to the Military Governor of the East.... [and] "conferred more authority on the Regional Governments than the Civilian Premiers exercised at the peak of their powers," with the commentators adding that Gowon had "carried the principle of decentralization too far,"[25] the Eastern Region government rejected the Decree out of hand. On 31 March, Ojukwu issued a Revenue Collection Edict, which diverted all revenue raised in the Eastern Region from the federal government to Eastern Regional government coffers. A number of reasons were advanced for this, among them (i) claims that the federal government had failed to adhere to a pledge to pay salaries and other entitlements to workers of Eastern origin who had been forced to flee to the East for refuge from the killings; (ii) the effects of the associated influx of (according to the Eastern Regional government) almost two million refugees into the Region; and (iii) the alleged delay federal government's paying the East its "statutory share of centrally collected revenues."[26] There was probably some degree of truth in these claims. Gowon responded by suspending all Nigerian Airways flights to the East, describing Ojukwu's action in proclaiming this edict as "not really a revenue matter but a calculated attempt to subvert existing Federal institutions by unilateral action". This did not prevent Ojukwu from issuing a number of other edicts (the Legal Education Edict, the Statutory Body Edict, and the Court of Appeals Edict), all described as "survival edicts", and all of them in effect reducing or removing the authority of the federal government and its institutions in the East.

To this simmering cauldron was now added Awolowo's resignation from the ad-hoc Constitutional Committee (on the grounds that Northern troops stationed in the West constituted "an army of occupation" and that discussion of the military had been removed from the committee's terms of reference by the SMC), and his announcement at a meeting of the Western Leaders of Thought on 1 May [made in the presence of three attendees: The Governor (Colonel Adebayo), the Area Commander (Lieutenant-Colonel Olutoye) and the CO Third Battalion (Major Sotomi) that "If the Eastern Region is allowed by acts of commission or omission to secede from or opt out of Nigeria, then the Western Region and Lagos must also stay out of the federation."[27] Ejoor, in a broadcast on 19 May, stated his determination not to allow the Midwest "to be used as a battleground in a conflict born of revenge and aimed at the acquisition of naked power" and at the same time warning "against subversive elements within its borders working to make it an appendage of another Region" (this last being clearly aimed at the several Igbo-speaking officers of Midwestern origin, such as Nwawo, Nzefili, Okwechime, and Igboba, who had all fled to the Midwest after the upheavals of September-October 1966). The federal government responded to Ojukwu's "Survival Edicts" by ordering an economic blockade of the East, suspending postal and money order transactions between the East and the rest of the country, suspending foreign exchange transactions from that region, and revoking the passports of several prominent Easterners. On 4 May, a meeting was convened by the Chief Justice of the Federation, Sir Adetokunbo Ademola, of a National Conciliation Committee, which included Awolowo; the Chief Justice of the Eastern Region, Sir Louis Mbanefo; and the former Governor of the Eastern Region, Sir Francis Ibiam. This committee sent a delegation under the leadership of Awolowo to Enugu to confer with Ojukwu on 5 May in an attempt to avert secession. On 6 May, Ojukwu presented the delegation with a list of conditions under which the East would resume negotiations; these included a demand that "the economic strangulation of the East should be discontinued; the occupation of West and Lagos by Northern troops should end."[28] He said he would rescind his edicts if Gowon lifted the economic blockade of the East by 25 May. The Conciliation Committee's delegation met with Gowon in Lagos, and persuaded him to lift the blockade, which Gowon duly directed on 20 May should be lifted with effect from 23 May. The Inspector-General of Police made an announcement on 25 May that non-Western troops would be withdrawn from Ibadan and Abeokuta. Ojukwu responded, not by rescinding the edicts as he had promised, but by insisting that nothing had been said about the withdrawal of Northern troops from Lagos and Ikeja. He summoned a meeting of the Eastern Nigeria Consultative Assembly on 26 May, and subjected the members to a lengthy speech over several hours, in the course of which he boasted. "There is no power in this country, or in Black Africa, to subdue us by force." He asked the Assembly,

> as the representatives of the 14 million people of Eastern Nigeria to choose from (a) accepting the terms of the North and Gowon and thereby submit to domination by the North or (b) continuing the present stalemate and drift or (c) ensuring the survival of our people by asserting our autonomy.

Gowon, prior to this point, had been accused of indecisiveness and political ineptness. Not this time, however. In a swift political masterstroke, he addressed the nation in a 27 May 1967 broadcast and declared,

> a State of Emergency throughout Nigeria with immediate effect. I have assumed full powers as Commander in Chief of the Armed Forces and Head of the Federal Military Government for the short period necessary to carry through the measures which are now urgently required.

He announced the re-imposition of the economic blockade that had been lifted only a few days earlier. He also announced the abolition of the four Regions, which would be reconfigured into twelve states as follows: the former Northern Region would be carved into six states (including states for the Middle Belt minorities), whilst the former Eastern Region would be divided into three states, (including two states for the minorities). The Igbo heartland was now designated the East Central State and, interestingly, Ojukwu appointed as its Military Governor. Later the same day, the Eastern Consultative Assembly met and gave Ojukwu a mandate to "declare at the earliest date Eastern Nigeria as a free, sovereign and independent state by the name and title of the Republic of Biafra." In a broadcast on 30 May 1967, Ojukwu did just that.

The Rubicon had been crossed.

NOTES

1. Elaigwu, Isawa J. *Gowon: The Biography of a Soldier-Statesman*. West Books Publishers, 1985, p. 19.

2. Ibid p. 31.

3. Ibid p. 33.

4. Kirk-Greene, A.H.M. *Crisis and Conflict in Nigeria: A Documentary Sourcebook: 1966-1970*. Oxford University Press 1971, p. 55.

5. Luckham p. 304.

6. Kirk-Greene pp. 60, 219.

7. Ibid pp. 60-61.

8. Ibid p. 61.

9. Ibid pp. 234-235.

10. Luckham pp. 308-309; Siollun, Max. *Oil Politics and Violence: Nigeria's Military Coup Culture; 1966-1976*. Algora Publishing, 2009, pp. 134-135.

11. Luckham p. 309.

12. Kirk-Greene p. 255.

13. Ibid p. 258.

14. Miners p. 271.

15. De St. Jorre, John. *The Brothers War: Biafra and Nigeria*. Houghton Mifflin, 1972, pp. 92-93.

16. Ibid p. 120.

17. Effiong, Phillip. *Nigeria and Biafra: My Story*. African Tree Press, 2007, p. 160

18. Kirk-Greene p. 318.

19. Ibid pp. 340-344.

20. Akpan, Ntieyong. *The Struggle for Secession — 1966-1970: A Personal Account of the Nigerian Civil War*. Frank Cass, 1972, p. 53.

21. Kirk-Greene p. 82.

22. Ibid.

23. Ibid p. 84.

24. Luckham p. 320.

25. Kirk-Greene p. 86.

26.   Ibid p. 88.

27.   Ibid p. 415.

28.   Ibid p. 423.

CHAPTER 6

The Second Military Government: The Civil War Years

War is the continuation of politics by other means.
— Carl von Clausewitz, On War, 1832

T he army had at this stage done remarkably little soldiering in the eighteen months since intruding itself into the country's political scene. The consequences of this preoccupation with politics and the neglect of its primary role would soon be manifested in the less-than-stellar military performance of both sides in the Civil War that broke out on 6 July 1967, when the first shots were fired in anger near Garkem. It is well at this point to examine the military resources, in terms of men and materials, available to both sides with which to prosecute the war.

Prior to the upheavals of January, May, July, and September-October 1966, the Nigerian Army numbered some 10,500 officers and men; at the outbreak of war, that figure was down to about 7,000. In order to make up the shortfall, the federal government accelerated army recruitment, especially encouraging veterans to reenlist who had served at any time since 1939, and were under the age of fifty.[1] There was in particular a dearth of officers and soldiers in the technical arms, as these had mainly been Easterners who were now no longer available to the federal side. (Fewer than 200 of them stayed behind on the federal side, and these mainly comprised the Eastern minorities.) On further scrutiny of the officer situation, the federal side had an estimated strength of 220 combatant officers at the outbreak of war, if the first officers who passed out from the Nigerian Defence Academy (NDA) in 1967 are included; on the Biafran side, that figure was probably no more than seventy.[2] More generally, the Biafrans were much worse off. Prior to the war, the only army unit in the East was the First Battalion in Enugu, the rump of which, after the non-Easterners left in August 1966, numbered no more than 240 troops, the majority of them technicians and tradesmen.[3] To this number were added those officers and soldiers who managed to escape the carnage in the rest of the country and successfully make their way back to the East.

What both sides lacked were *experienced* combatant officers. There were in total some fifty-seven combatant officers commissioned before independence. Of these:

- Two were killed before 1966 (Ogbonnia in a car crash and Ezeugbana in the Congo)

- Thirteen were murdered in 1966 (Ironsi, Ademulegun, Maimalari, Kur Muhammed, Shodeinde, Largema, Fajuyi, Pam, Unegbe, Ekanem, Okonweze, D.O. Okafor, and Okoro)

- Two had joined the Cameroon Army when Southern Cameroon detached itself from Nigeria (Malonge and Kweti)

- Eight were engaged in nonmilitary roles as governors and ambassadors (Ogundipe, Adebayo, Bassey, Gowon, Ejoor, Katsina, Kyari, and Kurubo)

- Eight were in the Midwest Area Command and subsequently joined Biafra (Nwawo, Okwechime, Nzefili, Trimnell, Nwajei, Igboba, Ochei, and Keshi)

- Nineteen were on the Biafran side from the beginning (Imo, Njoku, Ojukwu, Effiong, Banjo, Anwunah, Madiebo, Akagha, Ogunewe, Eze, Amadi, Adigio, Brown, Ivenso, D.C. Okafor, Nzeogwu, Aniebo, Chude-Sokei, and Ude)

This meant that at the outbreak of war there were only five officers on the federal side commissioned before independence who were available for purely military duties (Ekpo, Olutoye, Obasanjo, Sotomi, and Akahan — the last of these killed in a helicopter crash shortly after the outbreak of the war). The Biafrans, on the other hand, had some nineteen officers (eighteen if Ojukwu is excluded) commissioned before independence, although Ojukwu then did his level best to cast away this advantage by falling out with several of his experienced officers (Njoku, for example, was imprisoned for a large chunk of the war) and executing one of them (Banjo). The situation seems even bleaker when one examines how many of these officers were staff trained. On the federal side, of the officers commissioned before independence, fifteen were staff-trained and one of the only two in a military role.... Akahan was killed early in the war, leaving Obasanjo as the sole staff-trained officer in a military role on the federal side. On the Biafran side, there were seven officers commissioned before independence who were staff-trained. Of these, Ojukwu was in a political post; Njoku was in jail (for a large chunk of the war; and Nzeogwu was killed early in the war — leaving only four officers available for primary military duties (Anwunah, Ivenso, Ude, and Amadi).[4]

The dearth of experienced leaders gave rise to a rate of promotions that far exceeded the rush to Nigerianisation a few years earlier. This was apparent at *all* levels of command. Of the seven men who served on the Nigerian side as Divisional Commanders during the war (Shuwa, Bisalla, Murtala Muhammed, Haruna, Jalo, Adekunle, and Obasanjo), only Obasanjo was commissioned before independence, and only Bisalla and Obasanjo were staff-trained. Officers who were not substantive Captains when war broke out became Brigade Commanders (including George Innih and Shehu Yar'Adua, who were commissioned as Second Lieutenants from RMAS in 1964). Senior NCOs and Warrant Officers often commanded platoons and companies. Several emergency and field commissions were granted (and several of them going to veterans who had responded to the call to return to the colours at the outbreak of war). One of the battalions that took part in the first assault on Onitsha across the Niger was commanded by an education officer, commissioned directly from university in 1964, who had never been trained as an infantry officer.[5] On the Biafran side, a few senior officers (commissioned before independence) such as Njoku, Akagha (briefly), and Ogunewe, had held unit commands prior to the outbreak of war. Others, such as Madiebo (commander of an artillery battery), Effiong (Director of Ordnance), Banjo (Director of Electrical and Mechanical Engineers), and Nzeogwu (Chief Instructor at NMTC) had also held leadership positions before the war, but their numbers were swiftly reduced, for example with Nzeogwu's death in action and Banjo's execution in the first few months of the war.

In the circumstances, therefore, the fairly unimpressive military performance of both sides is hardly surprising. Debacles such as the repeated bloody and unsuccessful frontal assaults across the Niger against Onitsha, the Abagana ambush, and the capture, encirclement, and recapture of Owerri provide first-hand examples of the inept handling of the war. To be fair, however, whilst there can be no doubt that the war was the direct result of the military's intervention in politics the previous year (and its consequent fragmentation along ethnic/regional lines), the subsequent inept way it was fought was not entirely due to incompetence. The inexperience of those on both sides who were responsible for fighting the war has been alluded to — but there is more to the story than this.

First, the war was initially viewed, at least on the federal side, as a "police action" that would be prosecuted and concluded in a matter of hours — therefore, as Major-General Abdullahi Shelleng pointed out, "Operational plans were tailored to the requirements of a police action, but they were soon found to be inadequate."[6] It was assumed that once the key towns of Enugu (the capital), Onitsha (the commercial hub), and Port Harcourt (the major port) were captured, the Biafrans would capitulate and the "police action" concluded. This turned out be a gravely erroneous assumption.

Second, there was a striking lack of coordination between and within the divisions. According to Major-General David Jemibewon, each of the divisions "operated more or less as a separate and independent army, and some of whose commanders behaved like tin gods."[7] The divisional HQs were a long way from Lagos, at the end of a tenuous communication link; and this simply reinforced their defacto autonomy. Stories abounded of each division having its own weapons procurement arrangements, and developing operational plans either without reference to the other divisions or the army HQ, or occasionally in flagrant contravention of directives from that body. There was therefore no coherent overall *strategic* approach to the prosecution of the war. As de St. Jorre put it:

> the rivalry between the three Divisions...covered every field from the honour and glory deriving from the capture of significant Biafran towns to the most cut-throat competition for arms, supplies and reinforcements from Lagos. Co-operation and co-ordination, hard enough to achieve in view of the huge mass of men, the vast tracts of difficult terrain and the poor communications, were rendered

virtually impossible by these rivalries which greatly harmed the Federal war effort....each (Division) had its own officers watching and waiting for the arms ships at Lagos docks....Recruits waiting at Ikeja airport for transport to take them to the 1st Division would suddenly find themselves on a plane heading for the 3rd, and vice versa....Yet more extraordinary was the fact that at least two of the Divisions had their own arms buyers operating in Europe independently of the Federal Government — though sending it their bills — at different stages of the war.[8]

Major-General Shelleng again:

It is rather unfortunate to note that most of the officials who were entrusted with the purchase of military hardware from abroad lacked national consciousness and were only interested in the kickbacks they could get from the deals. Glaring examples of these shortcomings could be seen when twelve 105mm artillery guns of Spanish origin were ordered in 1968. Of the twelve guns received, only one fired one round. Despite numerous complaints from the war front commanders against the poor performance of these guns, and against expert advice, 24 more of the same type were ordered and received later in the same year. These unpatriotic officials saddled the Nigerian Army with 36 Artillery guns that were only fit for a museum.[9]

Shelleng, interestingly, gives the impression that the "officials" concerned were civilians, and not his fellow army officers.

Third, given the above statement, it is obvious that there was no direct and effective "grip" on the army by its Commander-in-Chief. Gowon delegated the operational running of the war to Army HQ under its Chief of Staff, Katsina (who succeeded Akahan following that officer's death), and spent much of his energies dealing with the politics of the war; the endless rounds of peace talks, the efforts to limit international recognition of Biafra, the thorny issue of the international relief effort, etc. The trouble was that the Divisional Commanders appeared to have little respect for Katsina as an individual, or for Army HQ as an organization, and that they felt confident they could carry on as they wished without any adverse consequences from Gowon coming their way. In the view of many (including this writer), Gowon went a bit too far in giving his subordinate commanders the latitude to prosecute the war as they saw fit; empowering subordinates with the tactical discretion to conduct warfighting operations is all very well as long as that discretion is exercised *within* the boundaries of an overall operational strategic framework, which was clearly lacking here.

Four, and returning to the matter of inexperience at all levels of command, the *tactics* employed by both sides are also worth examining. With perhaps a hint of condescension, de St. Jorre described the war as being

> a nine-to-five affair, with recognisable breaks for meals and no night fighting". Another assessor concluded that "In military terms, it is a poor joke of a war....Sandhurst training is fine for officers who can count on a fair level of competence among their men, or alternatively who do not have wars to fight. It gives few clues to the handling of illiterate, inexperienced boys, fresh from the villages, understandably terrified at the sound of gunfire.[10]

A more credible critic — Major-General Alexander — delivered a no less damning assessment. Alexander, the first British member of an International Observer Team, and a former Chief of Staff of the Ghanaian Army who had led that country's contingent in the UN Congo operation earlier in the decade, observed:

> Federal forces advance astride the road towards the town, and when they get within three or four miles of it, they halt. They then start building up their ammunition. Before the assault they subject the outskirts of the town to artillery and armoured car fire. The Biafrans do not carry out a staunch defence of this objective. Once they have decided the Federals are about to attack, they pull out, taking everything movable with them, and the Federals move in firing every round of ammunition they have. After occupying the town, the Federal forces sit down and wait for their ammunition to be replenished, and the Biafrans counter-attack by fire. Ammunition control as we understand it is non-existent on the Federal side, and during an advance a Federal soldier fires every round in his possession, whether he is meeting resistance or not.[11]

This last is quoted at such length because it provides a synopsis of one possible explanation for why the war lasted as long as it did. But, there were two sides in this war, and the Biafrans share the blame for the incompetence with which it was prosecuted. As has been alluded to earlier, Ojukwu's relationship with his senior officers (at least two of whom, Imo and Njoku, were senior to him) was far from rosy. He appeared to distrust them, possibly because a fair few were opposed to secession, and this mistrust increased after Banjo, Ifeajuna, and two others were accused of attempting to overthrow him — tried and executed in September 1967 — in the early stages of the war. Njoku was fired from his position as Army Commander shortly thereafter and imprisoned for most of the war, and it seemed that the only way to escape sharing his fate as a senior Army officer in wartime Biafra was either to always agree with Ojukwu, or at least not to disagree with him overtly. The man who took over as Army Commander after Njoku was removed, Alexander Madiebo, has documented how Ojukwu kept his cards very close to his chest about the conduct of the war; not only did he frequently take decisions without reference to Army HQ, he was his own de facto quartermaster, issuing small arms for operations from the "State House" (wherever that happened to be at that time). Even before the war began, Ojukwu, according to Madiebo,

> leaned entirely on civilians for all military purchases including weapons. These weapons, when they arrived in Eastern Nigeria were hidden in villages around Nnewi, under arrangement outside military control. From there they were brought up to Enugu by night in trickles, and handed over to the Army. The Army, ignorant of what was available to it at any given time, could not plan in advance. In addition, this system proved to be a colossal waste of money because a good percentage of these weapons were unserviceable.[12]

It was hardly surprising, then, that from the very first battles of the war in July 1967, the Army Commander, Njoku, was complaining to Madiebo that

> with all the fighting going on the whole day, he had failed to convince Ojukwu to show or tell him where the available arms and ammunition were hidden. As a result, Njoku went on, it was impossible to plan and issue any sensible orders to the fighting troops, for he had very little ammunition left under his control.[13]

Given the fact that the Biafrans were greatly outnumbered and outgunned, and were fighting on their own territory, it should have been clear from the start that their best bet lay not in a head-on confrontation in conventional set-piece battles with the federal army, but in unconventional guerilla warfare that would help neutralize the federal side's strengths. The problem was that the Biafran commanders had been trained in exactly the same conventional manner as their federal counterparts and, like them, seemed to have some difficulty in thinking outside the box.

Having looked at the impact its involvement in the political sphere had on the army's *military* performance during the war, what was the army's pre, intra and postwar impact on the country's political scene?

First and foremost, the creation of the twelve states was clearly a momentous political step. Although partly motivated by a desire to undercut Ojukwu by separating the Eastern minorities from the Igbo heartland, and thereby depriving him of the economic benefits of oil, food-producing regions, and access to the sea via Port Harcourt and Calabar, the exercise had ramifications beyond the old Eastern Region. Once started, the clamour for the creation of states, irrespective of their economic viability, has persisted to this day. Minorities in other parts of the country, the Middle Belt being the prime example, were also satisfied. Although the West lost a sliver of territory on its southern border to the new Lagos State, it remained largely unchanged (although this did not halt the cries for more states to be carved out from it). And the minorities in the Midwest, created under the Balewa administration, retained their autonomy from the old Big Three: Northern, Western and Eastern regions. Second, at the federal level initially, and subsequently at the state level, civilians (including old politicians like Awolowo, Enahoro, Tarka and Aminu Kano) were brought into the military government. This was not only a departure from the first military government under Ironsi, it set a precedent that endured until the return to civilian rule in 1999.

Third, there was the politics of the war itself. From the beginning, Gowon made it clear that this was a struggle, not against Easterners as a whole, but against "Ojukwu and his rebel clique", and he issued a code of conduct to the federal army at the start of the war; this, together with his "No victor no vanquished" approach, his refusal to hold Nuremberg-style trials at the end of the war, and his refusal to strike campaign medals for the war all helped to reintegrate the Igbos into the federation at the end of the war under the "Three Rs" banner — Reconciliation, Reconstruction, and Rehabilitation. (It should be pointed out, though, that some Biafran officers, especially those originally detained for complicity in the January 1966 coup and released by Ojukwu, as well as those in the Midwest Area Command who subsequently went over to the Biafran side, remained in detention until 1974.)

Fourth, there are few serious commentators who do not accept that political considerations helped to prolong the war. Whilst the federal blockade of Biafra was a key part of the federal strategy for winning the war, the resultant mass starvation, especially of children, created diplomatic pressure on the federal government not to block the activities of bodies such as the International Committee of the Red Cross (ICRC) and the Protestant and Catholic churches and their relief agencies, even though it knew full well that the airfields and air routes by which humanitarian aid was flown into Biafra was also the route by which arms and ammunition were brought in. In addition, the relief agencies provided Biafra with access to much-needed foreign exchange after the federal masterstroke of changing the Nigerian currency overnight in 1968, thus rendering useless the stocks of the old Nigerian currency held by the Biafrans. The starvation issue was ruthlessly (some would say cynically) exploited by the Biafrans, who recognised the powerful effect of images of starving children on Western television screens and newspaper pages; the resultant pressure by the Western public upon their governments soon led to arms embargoes against the federal government, and the donations poured in to the coffers of the ICRC and the churches, and other relief agencies. Under the terms of the Geneva Convention, the federal government was well within its rights to insist on inspecting and supervising the transport of any relief material to its destination and offered to permit daylight relief flights into Biafra, provided the flights were inspected and followed agreed routes. Ojukwu refused, because he knew that this would obviate the need for night-time relief flights, which provided cover for the arms flights. As de St. Jorre put it,

> the relief operation as it stood, though far from satisfactory in terms of saving lives, was doing Biafra a power of good abroad, publicizing its case and filling its coffers. A relief pact with the Nigerians would have taken the steam out of the first and dried up the second.[14]

Finally, the war itself, at least for a short time, was a uniting factor for the rest of Nigeria.

As pointed out earlier, at the outbreak of the war, the Nigerian Army numbered little more than 7000 troops; by the time the war finished some thirty months later, that figure had risen to the region of 250,000, an expansion by more than 3000 per cent.[15] This expansion in numbers was accompanied by significant, nay, major discrepancies between the training, experience, ranks, and responsibilities of its leaders at all levels, starting from the top; Gowon, who had been promoted Major-General shortly after the war broke out, had reached two-star rank less than eleven years after being commissioned from RMAS (in saner times, he would most likely have been no more than a Major, perhaps Lieutenant-Colonel, at best). A culture of expectation in terms of rapid advancement had thus been created amongst some officers, especially those who had started to feel comfortable and very much at home in positions of political power. Whilst an army of this size may have been necessary in wartime, there was no doubt that Nigeria in peacetime did not need such a bloated army, especially when one considers that the proportion of Nigeria's annual budget allocated to defence stood at 40 percent for the fiscal year 1970-71,[16] which was clearly unsustainable. There was therefore an obvious need to demobilize, but this in turn raised concerns about how the newly demobilized troops would be employed. These were all issues with which the federal military government, and Yakubu Gowon as peacetime Head of State, would now have to deal. As one writer succinctly put it,

> The war of Nigerian unity also threw up the kind of leader the country needed so desperately. Gowon is not of Lincolnian stature but he is cast in a similar mould; his faith, humility and plain good sense played a considerable part in saving Nigeria. *Whether he can perform the same service in peace as he did in war remains to be seen.*[17] (The emphasis here is mine.)

NOTES

1. Miners p. 229.
2. Ibid p. 230.
3. Madiebo, Alexander. *The Nigerian Revolution and the Biafran War*. Fourth Dimension Publishing, 1980, p. 97.
4. Miners pp. 343-344.
5. Ibid p. 233.
6. Tamuno, Tekena N. (Ed). Proceedings of the National Conference on Nigeria Since Independence, Vol 3. Ibadan University Press, 1980, p. 65.
7. Ibid p. 86.
8. De St. Jorre p. 275.
9. Tamuno p. 68.
10. De St Jorre p. 279.
11. Ibid.
12. Madiebo pp. 90-91.
13. Ibid pp. 129-130.
14. De St Jorre p. 246.
15. Tamuno p. 91.
16. Ibid.
17. De St Jorre p. 414.

CHAPTER 7

The Second Military Government: The Post-War Years

With malice toward none, with charity for all, with firmness in the right as God gives us to see the right, let us strive on to finish the work we are in, to bind up the nation's wounds, to care for him who shall have borne the battle and for his widow and his orphan, to do all which may achieve and cherish a just and lasting peace among ourselves and with all nations.
— **Abraham Lincoln, April 1865**

No Victor, No Vanquished (Yakubu Gowon, January 1970)

In the early hours of Sunday, 11 January 1970, Ojukwu, accompanied by a number of his top aides (Madiebo, Okpara, Akpan, and Mojekwu amongst them) flew out of Ulli airstrip, and out of Biafra, for the last time. The previous day, he had recorded his final speech to the Biafran people (what remained of them), which was broadcast *after* his departure, in which he said that

> in accord with my own frequent affirmations that I would personally go anywhere to secure peace and security for my people, I am now travelling out of Biafra to explore with our friends all these proposals....Our detractors may see this move as a sign of collapse of our struggle, or an escape from my responsibilities....I know that your prayers go with me as I go in search of peace and that, God willing, I shall soon be back among you. In my short absence, I have arranged for the Chief of General Staff, Maj-Gen Phillip Effiong, to administer the Government.

At no point did he say that this whole speech was an exercise in obfuscation, for not only were there no realistic peace "proposals" that he was leaving to pursue, he had actually already left Biafra in the full knowledge that the war was over, and that he was not returning. His anointed successor, Effiong, in a broadcast on 12 January, made a pointed reference to "those elements of the old government regime who have made negotiations and reconciliation impossible and have voluntarily removed themselves from our midst....any question of a government in exile is repudiated by our people", a clear reference to his predecessor. Effiong ordered "an orderly disengagement of troops". Three days later, in front of Gowon at Dodan Barracks in Lagos, Effiong declared that

> we affirm that we are loyal Nigerian citizens and accept the authority of the Federal Military Government of Nigeria...the Republic of Biafra hereby ceases to exist.

In response, Gowon declared "we have arrived at the end of a tragic and painful conflict". He instructed his field commanders to

> put into immediate effect contingency arrangements for the mass surrender of secessionist forces...all field commanders will take all necessary measures to give full protection to surrendering troops... all Federal troops must continue to observe the letter and spirit of the code of conduct issued at the beginning of the military operations.

He went on to guarantee

> a general amnesty for those misled into rebellion. We guarantee the personal safety of everyone who submits to federal authority. We guarantee the security of life and property of all citizens in every part of Nigeria, and equality in political rights. We also guarantee the right of every Nigerian to reside and work wherever he chooses in the Federation as equal citizens of one united country....there is no question of second-class citizenship in Nigeria.[1]

By any measure, this approach by Gowon was magnanimity almost without precedence...and was not necessarily an approach that all on the federal side agreed with.

The immediate tasks after the cessation of hostilities were to feed the affected population and begin to clear away the debris of war and to reconstitute the infrastructure in the affected areas. There were lingering resentments against some of the wartime humanitarian and relief agencies (Gowon famously said they could "keep their blood money, we don't need their help, we can do it ourselves",[2] and the main burden of the relief effort was borne by the Nigerian Red

Cross, to which the federal and state governments made available significant funds. The federal government also set up a National Commission for Rehabilitation to work alongside the Red Cross. One writer has estimated that about 60 million pounds had been spent on the relief and rehabilitation effort in the first year following the end of the war.[3]

On the political and administrative fronts, a Federal Commissioner, Mr. J.O.J. Okezie, was appointed to represent East Central State in the Federal Executive Council, and the civilian Administrator of the same state, Ukpabi Asika, was made a member of the Supreme Military Council, achieving parity with the military governors of the other eleven states. Those Easterners who had previously been employed in public service and in government-owned statutory corporations were to be reabsorbed if they so wished. The fears of those who had been appointed to replace the Easterners when they left were allayed when it was made clear that they would remain in their posts and suitable alternative arrangements made for the returnees. More pertinent as far as the present volume is concerned, were the arrangements regarding military personnel who had served in the Nigerian Armed Forces prior to the outbreak of the war. A board of officers was constituted to consider these cases. Several officers and men were reabsorbed into the Armed Forces (albeit with loss of seniority — Ebitu Ukiwe in the navy and Chris Ugokwe in the army being two examples). Others were either retired or dismissed (Ojukwu had been dismissed from the army at the outbreak of the war; others, such as those who had been implicated in the January 1966 coup — Ademoyega, Gbulie, and Udeaja, for example — were detained until October 1974 and then dismissed from the army).

On the tenth anniversary of Nigeria's Independence on 1 October 1970, Gowon made a broadcast to the nation. In this momentous speech, he announced a nine-point programme as a prelude to returning the country to civilian rule by 1 October 1976. This programme included:

1. Reorganisation of the Armed Forces
2. Implementation of the National Development Plan and the repair of the damage and neglect of war
3. Eradication of corruption from national life
4. Settlement of the question of creating more states

5. Preparation and adoption of a new constitution
6. Introduction of a new revenue allocation formula
7. Conduction of a national population census
8. Organisation of genuinely national political parties
9. Organisation of elections and installation of popularly elected governments in the states and in the centre

Leaving aside for a moment the feasibility of achieving such an ambitiously extensive programme in six short years (how, for example, did he propose to *eradicate corruption*?), the speech received a mixed reception from Nigerians. On the one hand, there were those, mainly in the political class and their acolytes, who thought six years was too long a time to wait for the restoration of civilian rule; on the other hand, there was a school of thought that held that Gowon had made himself a hostage to fortune by setting a target date, against which he would be measured and which would simply escalate expectations. In any event, it would be useful to examine each of the points in this programme in turn.

First, the reorganisation of the Armed Forces. As mentioned earlier, the army, by the end of the war, had swollen dramatically from a prewar strength of 10,500 to 250,000. Not only were the majority of these, both officers and other ranks poorly trained, they were also poorly housed and equipped, and constituted an unsustainable drain on the nation's resources. The majority of the substantial defence budget was consumed by recurrent expenditure on personal emoluments, with little left over for capital expenditure on facilities, equipment, and training. Perhaps hamstrung by fears of the impact on society due to the large numbers of returning men familiar with the tools and the use of violence, and with little gainful employment to return them to, Gowon kicked the can down the road and did little or nothing about this matter. (To be fair, it must be remembered that there had been a wave of armed robberies after the war, which had necessitated setting up Armed Robbery Tribunals, and resulted in several public executions of armed robbers by firing squads.) The army's restiveness with poor living conditions was worsened by a perception that Gowon was increasingly preoccupied by nonmilitary affairs and becoming distant from his primary military constituency. (indeed, after Gowon's overthrow, his successor specifically cited this matter as one of the reasons for removing him from office.)

Second, the implementation of the Second National Development Plan. This plan, envisaged to run from 1970 to 1974, involved an attempt to define clear national objectives, which the implementation of the plan was designed to deliver. These included nebulous and difficult to measure concepts such as "a just and egalitarian society" and "a land of bright and full opportunities for all citizens". Gowon was fortunate that the period of the plan coincided with a huge boom in oil prices, partly assisted by the 1973 Yom Kippur War between Israel and several Arab countries in the Middle East, which meant that the government was not lacking in the funds with which to carry out this ambitious project. Whether it was similarly well endowed with the ability to successfully and competently execute the plan was another matter entirely. (The ports being clogged up for several months by an armada of ships carrying cement for the construction boom triggered by the plan, and the resultant financial loss to the nation, due to the huge sums paid to the carriers in demurrage fees is but one example.) That said, the Gowon government enacted a number of measures during this period that have had an enduring impact on the country. In 1972, Nigeria changed from driving on the left (a relic of the colonial era) to driving on the right. The following year, Nigeria ditched the colonial currency of pounds, shillings and pence and adopted the indigenous Naira and kobo; the old imperial measurements of length and weight were also done away with, and the metric system adopted. The Gowon government also instituted the National Youth Service Corps (NYSC) scheme, which was conceived as a vehicle whereby university and polytechnic graduates, who had been educated free at the state's expense, would give something back to the country by donating their newly acquired skills to the country for the first year after graduation; the fact that they would serve in states other than their states of origin would help the cause of national unity, and they would be paid an allowance for doing so. The Nigerian Enterprises Promotion Decree of 1972 was designed to increase the participation of the indigenous Nigerian population in the private economic sector, which had hitherto been dominated by expatriates. An Agricultural Development Bank was established to facilitate investment in the agricultural sector — this, and other initiatives mentioned above, achieved varying levels of success and effectiveness. Some, like the NYSC scheme, driving on the right, and decimalization of currency, weights, and measures have become permanent fixtures on the Nigerian scene.

The Gowon regime, feeling flush as a result of the resumption of full oil production after the end of the war, allied with sky-rocketing oil prices during the oil-boom years, set up, first, the Adebo Commission in 1971, and subsequently, the Udoji Commission in 1972, to review the public services in order to promote efficiency and effectiveness, and also to review the existing wage and salary structures therein. The Adebo Commission report led to the establishment of the Udoji commission, which, in its 1974 report, recommended a salary-scale structure that would be applicable to federal, state and local government services, as well as to the armed forces, police, judiciary, universities and other public services. The report also (and this part is often forgotten) made recommendations regarding an open reporting system to aid performance evaluation and to promote other modern management styles and techniques. Unfortunately, the focus was squarely on the recommended salaries and wages; dissatisfaction with these provoked a series of wildcat strikes, despite the existence of decrees outlawing them. In the meantime, because of the widely perceived notion that salaries had been increased several fold, inflationary pressures rapidly took hold, with some prices increasing up to threefold, thereby wiping out any expansion in purchasing power.

Third, the eradication of corruption from national life. This was probably the most unrealistic point in the programme, and, as it transpired, one which failed most miserably. To begin with, there seemed to have been little consideration given to the simple fact that, as long as human beings were involved, corruption was inevitable. Gowon and his government, by an imprudent choice of words, set itself up to fail — and fail it did. A large chunk of the blame must be laid at the feet of Gowon, who, although never demonstrably shown to be corrupt, nonetheless appeared unwilling or unable to deal swiftly or decisively with his many subordinates (both military and civilian) who undoubtedly were. In mid-1974, allegations of corruption were made against, first, Joseph Tarka, Federal Commissioner for Communications; and subsequently against Joseph Gomwalk, the Governor of Benue-Plateau State (which was Gowon's home state).

The press was up in arms, demanding that Tarka either resign or be sacked, and questions were asked as to why Gowon allowed Tarka to remain in his job when, earlier in the year, Brigadiers Adekunle and Sotomi, who had been implicated in the London trial of a Nigerian woman for drug trafficking, had been retired despite their protestations of innocence. In the end, Tarka bowed to the pressure and resigned from office a few weeks later. The Gomwalk case was similar, but with a different outcome. Gomwalk was accused in a sworn High Court affidavit in August 1974 by a businessman, Aper Aku (himself later to become a civilian Governor of Benue State) of "financial wrongdoings in the award of contracts and expenditure of public funds."[4] Gowon this time summoned Gomwalk to Lagos and asked him to respond to Aku's allegations against him. Gomwalk provided a lengthy, point-by-point rebuttal of the allegations, which was subsequently published in the newspapers. Gowon then publicly cleared Gomwalk of any wrongdoing, to the displeasure of several segments of Nigerian society, particularly the press and students. Gowon was unapologetic in standing his ground, and it is hard to escape the suspicion that, having had his fingers burned by the Tarka affair, he was determined not to be so easily rolled over in the Gomwalk case, and went as far as stating that the rash of affidavits and allegations against his subordinates were in fact aimed at tarnishing him personally.[5]

The most significant issue on the corruption front, however, concerned many of the state governors. Several of them had well-deserved reputations for graft, and for publicly flaunting the proceeds of their corruption. On more than one occasion, they had demonstrated a willingness to act as if unencumbered by any threat from the centre to their continuation in office. Indeed, as one of them, the aforementioned Gomwalk openly declared openly in a 1974 interview:

> The autonomy is complete. In fact, the Federal Government doesn't know what we are doing, in that they don't direct us with reference to what we should be doing....when making your own budgets, you don't have to submit it to the Federal Government...the Federal Government reads of Benue-Plateau State budgets in the newspapers as anybody else does. The states are completely autonomous.[6]

In these circumstances, it is hardly surprising that ten of the twelve governors under Gowon were subsequently found, after his overthrow, to have been significantly corrupt, and forced to forfeit several of the proceeds of said corruption to the federal government. Gowon was faced on several occasions with demands that the governors be called to order, or, better still, replaced. He had himself, in his Independence Day broadcast to the nation on 1 October 1974, set a deadline of 31 March 1975 to appoint new governors — this was not the only promise made in that broadcast that he would go on to break (see below). He nevertheless did not follow through (despite subsequently claiming that some of them had actually *requested* to be reassigned). According to Elaigwu, Gowon claimed that:

> they approached me and asked me to change them in the interest of the nation and also in order to allow some of their colleagues "to come and taste what they think we have been enjoying all the times. Let them come and have some of the headaches we have been living with all this time. Please change us". And I told them it was my decision, and that "I would change you as, and when, I deem it fit."[7]

He went on to advance a number of reasons for not replacing the governors by the promised deadline, some of which, if true, beggar belief. Amongst these were the desire to minimize disruptions to the schooling arrangements for the old and new governors by not making changes before the advent of the long summer holidays. (Had this not been thought about before setting the self-imposed deadline? Had the schooling arrangements of the governors' children been taken into account at the time of their appointment in May 1967?) Another reason was his wish for the incumbent governors to remain in the saddle at the time of the state visit from Queen Elizabeth II of England to Nigeria, scheduled for mid-October 1975. As if all this was not bad enough, he went on to suggest that he wanted the governors to remain in post until *after* the Festival of Arts and Culture (FESTAC), which was at that time scheduled to take place in November-December 1975 because

> the people who knew the problems involved, the people who had been with me, who had been along with me all the time in preparing this festival, should help me see it successfully carried out before they left.[8]

Fourth, settlement of the question of the creation of new states.
Between 1970 and 1974, the Gowon government was faced with a
multitude of demands for new states. These included demands for
a Port Harcourt State to be carved out of Rivers State; for a separate
Benue State and a Plateau State out of Benue-Plateau; Wawa (Enugu)
State out of the East Central State; and Osun, Oyo, Ogun, and
Ondo States out of the Western State. There were also demands for
a Cross River State out of the South Eastern State; Zaria State out
of the North Central State; and Borno and Bauchi states out of the
North Eastern State. The agitation for state creation was sometimes
accompanied by bitter sectarian accusations and counter-accusations
of "domination"; Asika, then Administrator of East Central State,
famously described some of the agitators as "nattering nabobs of
negativism" who would "rather rule in hell than serve in Paradise."[9]
Gowon was moved to complain about "the floods of petitions and
newspaper advertisements that have tended to aggravate or embitter
relations between people that have lived together for decades"[10]
but he only had himself to blame for raising expectations too high.
In any event, although several of these states were subsequently
created, the Gowon government did not create a single additional
state before it was overthrown. Having said that, it must be noted
that, unlike Gowon's twelve-state structure with equal numbers of
states in the North and in the South, all subsequent state-creation
exercises (which have *all* been carried out by military regimes) have
consistently resulted in more states in the North than in the South.

**Fifth, the issue of the preparation and adoption of a new
constitution.** Although the Gowon government did virtually
nothing in this regard, it did institute a number of measures that
have had a significant impact on later Nigerian constitutions. These
began with Decree 14 of 1967, under which the states were created.
This decree stipulated that the new states would have similar powers
to those of the regions from which they were created. Decree 27 of
the same year, however, stated that the "Legislative and Executive
powers of the twelve newly created states in Nigeria are limited
for the time being to residual matters"....for the exercise of matters
in the concurrent legislative list, "specific consent of the Federal
Government is required."

Hitherto, both regional and federal governments had the power to deal with matters on the concurrent list — the new decree therefore represented a limitation on the power of the states vis-à-vis those previously enjoyed by the regions. More was to follow. Decree 17 of 1967 gave the federal government the power to prohibit the circulation of newspapers in any part of Nigeria (hitherto a regional affair). In 1968, the federal government, desperate to accumulate foreign exchange to finance its war effort, took a dim view of a request by the Northern states to the Nigerian Produce Marketing Company (NPMC) to suspend overseas sales of their groundnuts and responded by passing a decree which compelled the NPMC to take directions only from the Federal Ministry of Trade. Decree 50 of 1968 prohibited state marketing boards from borrowing from commercial or private banks; only the Central Bank could now lend to the marketing boards. In 1975, through Decree 7, the federal government instituted a uniform system of personal income tax across the entire country, resulting in significant losses in tax revenue to some states. The assault on the powers of the states continued through the transfer of primary and secondary education from the residual to the concurrent list, and the transfer of university education from the concurrent to the exclusive list (which meant only the federal government could now establish and run universities). The cumulative effect of these and other measures, allied with the vast expansion in federal government revenues from the oil boom, was to greatly expand the powers of the federal government and reduce those of the states, a situation that persists to this day.

Sixth, and closely related to the previous point, the introduction of a new revenue allocation formula. This issue of revenue allocation had always been a contentious one in Nigeria and following the creation of twelve states from the previous four regions, it became more so. Immediately after the creation of the new states, Decree 15 of 1967 had been promulgated, which set out the basis for the distribution of each region's share of the Distributable Pool Account (DPA) amongst the states created from that region (which clearly applied most to the states created out of the old Northern and Eastern Regions, the West and Midwest Regions having remained largely unchanged). There was much wailing and gnashing of teeth about this by the states concerned, which claimed that the Decree 15 approach was too arbitrary. In 1968, the Dina Commission was set up to review this matter. The states rejected its report, and its recommendations (which included fixing the proportion of mining rents and royalties payable to the states at 10 percent) were shelved (but almost all quietly reintroduced later). Instead, the federal government, between 1969 and 1974, paid 45 percent of mining rents and royalties to the states. The DPA was shared on the basis of 50 percent being equally divided between the states, and the other 50 percent on the basis of the population of each state. As the income from oil boomed, the disparity between what was accrued to each state became quite glaring. By way of example, the two major oil-producing states (Rivers and Midwestern), which between them accounted for 7.3 percent of the country's population, received between them over 40 percent of the total allocation to the states; the other ten states, with more than 90 percent of the country's population between them, received just under 60 percent of the DPA.[11] There was a predictable outburst of howling, as the Western and Northern states, which had been firm proponents of the derivation principle in the good old days of cocoa and groundnut pyramids, now experienced a Damascene conversion, and were now apostles of the creed of need, not that of derivation. It was against this background that Gowon announced, in his Independence Day broadcast on 1 October 1974, that the revenue allocation formula was to be revised in two major ways: first, the question of revenue allocation would no longer be a constitutional but a legislative matter, and second, the federal government would now ensure that each state was to be able to fund at least two-thirds of its budget from a combination of its own tax income and federally collected revenues (i.e., the DPA). Beginning April 1975, 100 percent of offshore oil revenues would now be paid into the DPA, as well as 80 percent of onshore revenues. This formula remained extant until 1981, when reviewed by the civilian Shagari administration.

Seventh, and equally as contentious as the sixth, conducting a new national population census. Previous attempts at conducting a census in 1962 had created such political ructions that it had to be abandoned and repeated the following year, and the results from that census were not universally accepted. The issue, as always, was that political power and allocations of federal revenues were both dependent, to a large extent, on population; and the fact that the

North was consistently held to be more populous than the South was a running sore point. Another attempt was made in 1973 by the Gowon government, starting with the inauguration in July of that year of a National Census Board chaired by the former Chief Justice of the federation, Sir Adetokunbo Ademola. The exercise itself was conducted at the end of November and the beginning of December 1973; 130,000 enumerators, accompanied by an equal number of (unarmed) soldiers (presumably to keep the enumerators on the straight and narrow) were employed. Provisional results released in May 1974 put the country's population at just under 80 million, again with the majority (almost two-thirds) in the six Northern states (51.4 million as opposed to 28.4 million). Overall, the country's population, according to these figures, had increased by more than 40 percent over ten years, despite having been gripped by a civil war for a quarter of that time. The backlash was not long in coming, and a Census Data Review Committee was set up to examine the figures. Gowon had been scheduled to announce the results of this review in his October 1975 Independence Day broadcast — as events turned out, he never had the opportunity to do so. The successor regime of Murtala Muhammed cancelled the 1973 Census figures.

The last two points, the eighth and ninth in this programme, the organisation of "truly national political parties" and the organisation of the elections of new governments at state and federal levels. Neither of these would be achieved by the time Gowon was overthrown in July 1975. The principal reason for this was contained in the 1 October 1974 broadcast to the nation:

> Four years ago, when I gave 1976 as the target date for returning the country to normal constitutional government, both myself and the military hierarchy honestly believed that by that date, especially after a bloody Civil War....every Nigerian would have learnt a lesson, there would have developed an atmosphere of sufficient stability....Regrettably, from all the information at our disposal, from the general attitude, utterances and manoeuvres of some individuals and groups and from some publications during the past few months, it is clear that those who aspire to lead the nation on the return to civilian rule have not learnt any lessons from our past experiences... There is no doubt that it will not take them long to return to the old cut-throat politics that once led this nation into serious crisis.

We are convinced that this is not what the honest people of this country want....Our own assessment of the situation as of now is that it will be utterly irresponsible to leave the nation in the lurch by a precipitate withdrawal which will certainly throw the nation back into confusion. Therefore, the Supreme Military Council, after careful deliberation and full consultation with the hierarchy of the Armed Forces and the Police, have decided that the target date of 1976 is in the circumstances unrealistic...I want to make it abundantly clear, however, that we have not abandoned the idea of a return to civilian rule.[12]

Gowon went on to promise that new federal commissioners were to be appointed on 1 January 1975, and new governors for the states by 1 April 1975; he adhered to the former promise (in part, at least) and, as already seen failed to adhere to the latter. Taken in the round, it will be seen that of the nine points set out in his speech four years earlier, which were supposed to pave the way for a return to civil rule by 1976, he failed to achieve six of them, and managed to achieve only three (the census, the development plan, and the revenue allocation formula). This less than stellar performance helped to pave the way for the coup of July 1975 that removed him from office.

Other writers — historians and journalists — have described the atmosphere in and around the army towards the end of the Gowon regime. Not only were there a significant number of senior officers in political/administrative as opposed to military roles, there were also an increasing number of junior and middle-ranking officers who had never served under a civilian regime and for whom the concept of military subordination to civil authority was an alien one. For the remaining purely professional officers, there were concerns that many new entrants to the army's officer corps were signing up not with professional military aspirations but instead with political aspirations to office as governors or commissioners. Senior military brass went around accompanied by armed soldiers in large, siren-blaring convoys — woe betide the ordinary motorist or pedestrian who did not get out of the way quickly enough. One of the worst offenders in this regard was Gowon himself; his movements resulted in large stretches of roads being lined with armed soldiers and police and closed off for hours, bringing misery and inconvenience to motorists. There was also a significant disconnect between the military governors, several of whom had amassed great wealth illicitly (and were not shy about flaunting it), and their colleagues in purely military postings, many of whom yearned for a chance to partake of the perceived material spoils of political office.[13]

Whilst there were a number of officers in favour of Gowon's transmutation from a military head of state to a civilian president,[14] for others, the decision to renege on the pledge to hand over power in 1976 was the last straw. This issue had been discussed at a senior officers conference in September 1974. According to Elaigwu, there was a clear majority view supporting the extension of military rule, and very few officers (notably Brigadier James Oluleye) openly opposed the extension. Based on interviews with officers present at the meeting, Elaigwu asserts:

> All officers interviewed confirmed that Danjuma supported the extension and even stressed that the military, like politicians, had a right to rule. This contradicts the opinion expressed in Lindsay Barrett's book that General Danjuma opposed military rule after 1976 and said so at the meeting. So also was there no evidence that General (then Col) Garba opposed extended army rule. Thus the decision to extend army rule was not Gowon's but the army's. But as Commander-in-Chief, Gowon was ultimately responsible for the decision.[15]

Rumours started to circulate of coup plots, and soon came to the attention of the head of the Special Branch of the Nigerian Police, M.D. Yusuf, who in turn brought the matter to Gowon's attention. Both Yusuf and Gowon were surprised by some of the names mentioned as being linked to the plot; these included Colonel Joseph Garba, the Commander of the Brigade of Guards, which was responsible for Gowon's protection; Colonel Anthony Ochefu, the army's Provost Marshal and Colonel Abdullahi Mohammed, Director of Military Intelligence. It was noteworthy that amongst the leading plotters were a group of young colonels, who, as subalterns, had played a key role in the July 1966 coup that resulted in Gowon assuming the leadership of the country; Colonel Ibrahim Taiwo, Lieutenant-Colonels Shehu Yar'Adua, Ibrahim Babangida, Paul Tarfa, Muhammadu Buhari, and Sani Bello (Bello, who as Ironsi's ADC, had been captured along with his boss and had been present at the time of his murder, managing to facilitate the escape of his fellow ADC, Andrew Nwankwo of the air force, whilst Ironsi and Fajuyi were being assassinated by their captors.) Gowon expressed incredulity that these rumours could be true, and wondered whether they were provocations to tempt him into eliminating those he viewed as his close aides. Yusuf, on the other hand, was much more hard headed about the whole thing and encouraged Gowon to take the reports seriously and act on them, even offering to confront Garba directly if necessary. Gowon dissuaded him from doing so, and said he would speak to Garba himself. He eventually did so shortly before departing the country to attend an OAU summit in Uganda. Unsurprisingly, Garba denied any knowledge of or involvement in a coup plot. Gowon's response was to say that if, indeed, Garba was involved in a coup, it would "be on your own conscience and let it be without bloodshed".[16] He then departed for Uganda, which turned out to be his swan song as Nigeria's Head of State.

The coup that removed Gowon from office took place on the ninth anniversary of the coup that brought him to office; unlike that one, however, it was a bloodless affair (Nigeria's first), despite having been planned by pretty much the same set of people. The prime movers of the July 1966 affair — Murtala Muhammed, Theophilus Danjuma, and Martin Adamu, all by now Brigadiers — were fully informed of the plotters' plans, and although they were not direct participants on this occasion, they had all made it clear that they would not oppose Gowon's removal. (Notwithstanding this, one of them, Adamu, subsequently declined to make the radio broadcast announcement of Gowon's overthrow — that task fell instead to Garba.) That tacit approval, allied with Gowon's absence from the country and the fact that officers in key positions such as Garba, Abdullahi Mohammed, and Ochefu were amongst the conspirators probably contributed to the bloodless nature of the coup. There was mild panic amongst the plotters when Gowon's ADC, Lieutenant-Colonel William Walbe (who had, as a subaltern nine years previously, overseen the murder of Ironsi and Fajuyi in a bush outside Ibadan) returned unexpectedly from the OAU Summit, ostensibly to retrieve a file that Gowon had inadvertently left behind;[17] notwithstanding this, he was soon neutralized by the plotters, and the coup proceeded as planned. In the early hours of 29 July, Garba came on the radio to announce that

the Nigerian Armed Forces decided to effect a change in the leadership of the Federal Military Government. As from now, General Yakubu Gowon ceases to be the head of the Federal Military Government and commander in chief of the Armed Forces of Nigeria.

The wheel had turned full circle.

Yakubu Gowon had assumed the mantle of leadership of his country at a time of grave and bloody uncertainty. He was young and inexperienced, and within a year was leading a country divided in a bloody and bitter civil war. It is probably not unfair to him to say that the war was, in many respects, the making of him as a leader; and whilst his conduct of the war *militarily* was hardly stellar, his handling of it *politically*, both during and immediately afterwards, was critical in shaping the Nigeria of today. He had served his country well in war and just after; he was unable to do the same in peacetime. Nonetheless, his conduct in accepting his ouster from power was exemplary. He issued a statement making it clear that

> I on my part have also accepted the change and pledged my full loyalty to my nation, my country and the new Government. Therefore, in the overall interest of the nation and our beloved country, I appeal to all concerned to cooperate fully with the new Government and ensure the preservation of the peace, unity and stability of our dear motherland....and call upon all of you to give the new Government of our nation the same support and cooperation in the interest of our beloved country.[18]

Gowon left Uganda as a private citizen, and, after a brief stopover in Lome, the capital of Togo, proceeded to the UK to join his family, who had been there on summer holidays whilst he was in Uganda. He subsequently decided to enroll at Warwick University to study for a degree in Political Science, and eventually, as he hoped, quiet retirement into private life. Things were to turn out quite differently.

NOTES

1. Elaigwu pp. 136-137.

2. Ibid p. 142.

3. Ibid pp. 144-145.

4. Ibid p. 189.

5. Ibid p. 190.

6. Ibid p. 167.

7. Ibid p. 214.

8. Ibid p. 215.

9. Ibid p. 184.

10. Ibid.

11. Ibid p. 178.

12. Ibid pp. 198-199.

13. Siollun pp. 170-174.

14. Ibid p. 172.

15. Elaigwu p. 238.

16. Siollun pp. 175-177.

17. Ibid p. 178; Elaigwu p. 229.

18. Siollun p. 181, Elaigwu p. 244.

CHAPTER 8

The Third Military Government: Charting a New Course

In the endeavor to build a strong, united and virile nation, Nigerians have shed much blood. The thought of further bloodshed, for whatever reasons must, I am sure, be revolting to our people.
— **Murtala Muhammed, July 1975**

Having effected Gowon's removal from power, the plotters set about the task of constituting a government to replace the one he had led. First of all, the top echelon were cleared out of the armed forces and the police — officers of the rank of Major General and above (or equivalent rank in the navy and air force) were retired. These included Vice Admiral Wey and Major-General Hassan Katsina, respectively, Chief and Deputy Chief of Staff, Supreme Headquarters; Major-General Ejoor (Chief of Army Staff), Rear Admiral Nelson Soroh (Chief of Naval Staff); and Brigadier Emmanuel Ikwue (Chief of Air Staff). Major Generals Adeyinka Adebayo and Emmanuel Ekpo were also retired. Kam Selem and Theophilus Fagbola, respectively Inspector-General and Deputy Inspector-General of Police were retired, as were all the military governors and the administrator of the East-Central State.

Next, having decided that none of those involved in the coup would be beneficiaries of it in terms of being appointed to political and administrative roles, the plotters approached their superior officers, whose tacit approval of the coup attempt they had obtained, to take over the reins of power. Murtala Muhammed, Olusegun Obasanjo, and Theophilus Danjuma were told that the plotters wished them to assume the leadership as a sort of troika, with Muhammed as Head of State, Obasanjo as Chief of Staff Supreme Headquarters; and Danjuma as Chief of Army Staff. Represented by Joseph Garba,

Shehu Yar'Adua, and Abdullahi Mohammed, the plotters also set out their demands that decisions would be taken by a majority vote of the Supreme Military Council, and that any decision opposed by two-thirds of the council's membership could not be implemented. Murtala balked at this and, his legendary fiery temper coming to the fore, insisted that he would not be hamstrung in this way if he assumed the leadership. When the young colonels pointed out that if he maintained his refusal, they could always nominate someone else, and that they would make sure the reasons for his refusal were disclosed to his loyalists in the army, he exploded once again, saying that he would not be blackmailed. It reportedly took the intervention of Obasanjo and Danjuma to pour oil on troubled waters before Murtala finally accepted the position of Head of State.[1] [It should be pointed out that other writers suggest that Danjuma was the initial choice for Head of State, an offer he declined; but this may well be the result of confusing the aftermath of the July 1975 coup with that of the February 1976 coup. (See below.)]

In a broadcast on 30 July, Murtala Muhammed set out the reasons for Gowon's ouster. According to him:

Nigeria has been left to drift. This situation, if not arrested, would inevitably have resulted in chaos and even bloodshed....after the civil war, the affairs of state, hitherto a collective responsibility, became characterized by lack of consultation, indecision, indiscipline and even neglect....things got to a stage where the head of the administration became virtually inaccessible even to official advisers; and where advice was tendered it was often ignored. Responsible opinion, including advice by eminent Nigerians, traditional rulers, intellectuals, et cetera, was similarly discarded. The leadership, either by design or default, had become too insensitive to the true feelings and yearnings of the people.[2]

Murtala went on to announce the appointments of the new service chiefs (in addition to Danjuma for the army, Commodore Michael Adelanwa, Colonel John Yisa-Doko, and Mr. M.D. Yusuf were appointed to head the navy, air force, and police, respectively). He also announced the new military governors for the twelve states, in which, contrary to their stated original intentions, several of the plotters featured (Buhari, Sani Bello, Ibrahim Taiwo, Abdullahi Mohammed, and Anthony Ochefu). The structure of government was reorganized, with state governors no longer being members of the Supreme Military Council (to which another five conspirators were appointed — Garba, Yar'Adua, Babangida, Muktar Mohammed, and Alfred Aduloju); only one member of Gowon's Supreme Military Council was reappointed — Bisalla. The governors were made members of a new body, the National Council of States. The Federal Executive Council remained, and again, a number of those who had brought about the coup were appointed to it, although all civilian commissioners under Gowon were sacked. Murtala also announced a review of the political programme, the setting up of panels to advise on the creation of new states and a new federal capital, to cancel the 1973 Census, and to postpone the Second World, Black and African Festival of Arts and Culture (FESTAC).

This is perhaps an appropriate juncture to examine in closer detail the new Head of State and Commander in Chief of the Armed Forces. Who was Murtala Muhammed? He was of Hausa extraction, born Murtala Kurawa on 8 November 1938 in Kano's Kurawa quarter (from which he derived his initial surname, later changed to the one the world came to know him by). One of several children of Risqua Muhammed and Uwani Ramatu, he came from a line of Muslim clerics (his grandfather, Sulaiman, and his great grandfather, Salihu Dattuwa, were both *Alkalin Kano* and Chief Qhadi of Kano). He attended Gidan Makama primary school in Kano, and then, following in the footsteps of several other Northern army officers such as Maimalari, Kur Mohammed, Largema, Pam, and Gowon, enrolled at Government College Zaria in January 1952. Together with his classmate Muhammed Shuwa, he joined the army and followed the familiar path from the regular officers' Special Training School at Teshie in Ghana (where one of his instructors was Ojukwu) to RMA Sandhurst in England, from which he was commissioned in 1961 alongside Shuwa, Ibrahim Haruna, Emmanuel Ikwue, and Iliya Bisalla. Opting for the Signals Corps, he attended the Young Officers Course at the Royal School of Signals (RSS) in Catterick, North Yorkshire, before returning to Nigeria. Like many young officers of his generation, he served in the Congo as part of the Nigerian contingent in the UN Peacekeeping Force; upon his return to Nigeria, he was appointed the Aide de Camp to Dr. M.A. Majekodunmi, then the Administrator of the Western Region following the federal government's declaration of a state of emergency in that region. The following year, 1963, he was promoted Captain and appointed Officer Commanding of First Brigade Signals Troop in Kaduna; following an advanced course at the RSS in Catterick, he was promoted Temporary Major and given command of the Second Brigade Signal Squadron in Lagos in 1964. In May 1966, although technically still only a substantive Captain, he was promoted Acting Lieutenant-Colonel by Ironsi, who also made him Inspector of Signals. In passing over substantive Majors such as Obasanjo, Adekunle, Rotimi, Ayo-Ariyo, Obienu, and Chude-Sokei, Ironsi was hoping to placate Northern elements in the army who were restive as a result of his continued failure to bring the January coup plotters to trial. (Shuwa and Haruna were also promoted at the same time as Murtala.)

Ironsi's actions in promoting him did nothing to stop the twenty-seven year-old Murtala from spearheading the conspiracy (along with Danjuma and Adamu) that resulted in the bloody countercoup of July 1966 and Ironsi's demise. As outlined earlier (see chapter 4 above), Murtala was a fiery advocate of Northern secession after the July coup, and only agreed to Nigeria remaining one country on the condition that Gowon, as the most senior surviving Northern officer (although by no means the most senior officer in the armed forces hierarchy), took over the reins of leadership of the country. That he had insisted on Gowon's accession was no barrier to Murtala's consistent behaviour in a manner that undermined Gowon's authority, behavior that he would never himself have tolerated from a subordinate (see chapter 5). Following the Biafran invasion of the Midwest in August 1967, Murtala was appointed Commander of the hastily cobbled together Second Division, with which he succeeded in driving the Biafran Army out of the region. Murtala achieved this in part by his willingness to commandeer for his division's use of men and materials earmarked for other divisions, and in part by the even more ramshackle Biafran defensive performance.

Murtala and controversy were never far away from each other. Allegations were made that troops of the Second Division under Murtala's command looted the Benin branch of the Central Bank, and made off with several million pounds; counter allegations were made that in fact the retreating Biafrans had taken the money. Following the capture of Benin, Murtala went on the radio and stated:

On behalf of the Head of the Federal Military Government and Commander in Chief of the Armed Forces, I appoint Lieutenant Colonel Samuel Ogbemudia as the Temporary Administrator of the Midwestern State of Nigeria.[3]

The trouble was that, Murtala had not bothered to consult Gowon, or seek his authority to make this appointment; but, notwithstanding this, Ogbemudia remained in post until Gowon was removed from office eight years later. Much worse was to follow. On the arrival of Second Division troops in Asaba, just across the Niger from Onitsha, several hundred Midwestern Igbo civilians, mainly men and boys, were summarily executed, allegedly on Murtala's orders, for "collaborating with the enemy."[4] This disgraceful episode was never formally investigated nor was anyone ever held responsible for it, although Gowon, several years later, apologized for it.

Having secured the Midwest, Murtala now contemplated taking the battle to the Biafrans. Against instructions from Supreme HQ in Lagos, and in the face of strong disagreement from his old classmate and fellow Divisional Commander Muhammed Shuwa, and from Murtala's own subordinate Brigade Commanders, Murtala twice launched an ill-considered attempt at a direct opposed river crossing to take Onitsha. Prior to the first attempt, a meeting was held between the two Divisional Commanders and their respective staff to review the plan; underscoring the fiery nature of the disagreement between Murtala and Shuwa, it is reported that one of the staff officers had to physically interpose himself between the two men to stop them from coming to blows.[5] On both attempts, the attack was bloodily repulsed by the Biafrans at great cost in men and materials. Murtala reportedly persisted in his attempts to capture Onitsha via an opposed river crossing on the advice of religious soothsayers.[6] Only after being repulsed the second time did he finally agree to carry out the unopposed crossing further up the Niger at Idah and attack Onitsha overland from the North. Even this did not proceed entirely as planned, as the Biafrans launched the famous Abagana ambush in which they destroyed a long and unwieldy supply column. Following this debacle, Murtala reportedly took himself off to Kano and thence to the UK on vacation without the knowledge or consent of Army HQ, an astonishing display of indiscipline if true. Allied with the shockingly inept attempts to capture Onitsha by an opposed river crossing in direct contravention of Army HQ advice and the subsequent allegations of war crimes committed by troops under his command at Asaba, it is hard to think of anyone more deserving of facing court-martial than Murtala. Instead, he was merely replaced as Second Division Commander by his course mate, Ibrahim Haruna, then promoted Colonel and reappointed Inspector of Signals. He remained in this post until the end of the war and beyond. In October 1971, just before his thirty-third birthday, and after ten years service as a commissioned officer, he was promoted Brigadier and attended the Joint Services Staff College in the UK, after which, in 1974, Gowon appointed him Federal Commissioner for Communications, a post he held (along with his army job as Inspector of Signals) until his appointment as Head of State following Gowon's removal from office.

Murtala quickly established a reputation as a man of action who was also "a man of the people". He did not move into Dodan Barracks, the official residence of the Head of State, but continued to live in his private residence in Ikoyi. In stark contrast to his predecessor, Murtala shunned the elaborate security arrangements that had accompanied Gowon's movements. Gone were the road closures, the armed troops lining his route, and the extensive convoys — instead, Murtala was frequently observed stuck in Lagos' notoriously ensnarled traffic accompanied only by his driver, orderly, and ADC. On more than one occasion, he was spotted driving himself, alone, in his private car. All entreaties from others, including his military colleagues, about paying more heed to his personal security were swept aside in Murtala's typically brusque fashion. He was to pay a high price for this cavalier attitude.

The new government swept into action with a speed that was perhaps intended to draw a stark contrast with the perceived indecisiveness of the Gowon regime. The restructuring of the policy and decision-making apparatus at the top levels of the government (referred to earlier), with at least one of the new bodies created, the National Council of States was enshrined in subsequent civilian constitutions, albeit in a modified form (including the current one). The Murtala regime was the first to appoint governors to run states other than those from which they hailed (for example, appointing Anthony Ochefu and Zamani Lekwot to the East Central and Rivers states, respectively).

More controversially, the government embarked on a massive purge of the public service and government-owned statutory corporations across the country. Ostensibly aimed at removing the corrupt and the inefficient, and at instilling a sense of discipline, in reality it became an arbitrary exercise in score-settling, and spared no one, from the high and mighty (judges, including the nation's chief justice; university vice-chancellors, chief executives of teaching hospitals, military governors, among this last group; the recently-appointed Colonel Anthony Ochefu, who was one of the principal plotters in the coup that brought Murtala to power) to the low (cleaners, drivers, janitors). All were retired, terminated, or summarily dismissed. Diplomats, military officers, high- and low-ranking civil servants all felt the impact of the purge. Due process went out the window. Never before or since have public servants experienced the feelings of anxiety and impending doom as in those five months between August and December 1975, when they listened to the news on the radio and television to find out if they had lost their livelihoods; and many came to realise their fate this way. In several instances, those who fell victim to the purges were summarily ordered to surrender government property in their possession, and to move out of government quarters within two weeks, rendering many families homeless overnight. Arguably, the greatest consequence of this exercise was to shatter the professionalism and feelings of job security that hitherto existed in the civil service. For those fortunate enough to survive the purges, seeing their superiors, contemporaries, and subordinates become jobless and homeless overnight was a wake up call. Realising that the same thing could happen to them, many took the view that, unlike their colleagues, they would not be taken by surprise. What had hitherto been a reasonably (but by no means totally) professional and efficient civil service now became one where civil servants all had an eye out for the main chance. Many began to explore ways of using their positions to enrich themselves, so that they would not be left homeless and penniless if they became victims of future purges. Others, having seen colleagues they knew to be innocent purged, decided that if they themselves were to be so treated, they might as well be purged for true and valid reasons. Either way, the civil service in Nigeria has never been the same since.

On the political front, the regime was no less busy. In a broadcast to the nation on Independence Day, 1 October 1975, Murtala announced a four-year transition programme leading to handing over power to an elected civilian government on 1 October 1979. As part of this programme, a Constitution Drafting Committee (CDC) was set up, under the chairmanship of the distinguished lawyer and one-time politician, Chief F.R.A. Williams. This all-male body initially consisted of fifty members, but was reduced to forty-nine after Chief Obafemi Awolowo declined to serve on it. A Constituent Assembly (CA), consisting of a mix of elected and appointed members, would then examine and ratify the draft constitution that would follow, and the new constitution, under which the new civilian government would operate, would come into force after final approval by the Supreme Military Council. The end product, the 1979 Constitution, was by no means a perfect document, but it has had far-reaching consequences for the subsequent history of Nigeria. First, it marked a departure from the old Westminster-style form of government, in which executive power lay in the hands of a prime minister, and introduced the enduring concept of an executive, US-style president, into the Nigerian political scene. Second, it formed the foundation upon which the current 1999 Constitution was built. Third, the issue of religion reared its head in a *constitutional* sense for the first time — although eventually deleted from the Constitution, the issue of Sharia Law remains extant in today's Nigeria. Fourth, statutory bodies like the Code of Conduct Bureau and the Public Complaints Commission were for the first time given a constitutional basis, as was the principle of federal character in the cabinet, other senior government positions, the boards of parastatals (and, as subsequently amended by the Supreme Military Council, in the officer corps of the armed forces). All of these issues remain extant in today's Nigeria.

The other significant domestic political act of the Murtala regime was the creation of seven new states on 3 February 1976. Prior to this exercise, there had been twelve states in the country, split equally between the North and the South. Now, that equilibrium disappeared:

• Of the original twelve states, seven were unchanged apart from minor boundary adjustments, and with some name changes [Lagos, Kano, Kwara, Rivers, South-Eastern (now Cross River), North-Central (now Kaduna), Mid-West (now Bendel)].

- Of the other five states, the Western State was split into three new states (Ogun, Ondo, and Oyo); the East-Central into two (Anambra and Imo); the North-Eastern into three (Bauchi, Borno, and Gongola); Benue-Plateau into two (Benue and Plateau); and North-Western into two (Niger and Sokoto).

This meant that there were now ten states in the North as opposed to nine in the South, a lopsidedness that has persisted and grown until the present. Subsequent state-creation exercises, all by military governments, have maintained this imbalance:

- 11-10 – when there were twenty-one states;
- 16-14 when there were thirty states; and
- 19-17 with the current thirty-six state structure, all in favour of the North.

Given the fact that both the 1979 and the 1999 Constitutions provided for each state to have an equal number of senators, and for the number of members of the House of Representatives to be allocated on the basis of population; and since the 1963 Census figures continued to be used at the time the 1979 Constitution came into being, and that this showed the Northern states as having the majority of the population, it did not require the brains of an archbishop to work out that the new arrangement would enshrine a greater degree of *legislative* political power in the North — one of the very reasons that had indirectly led to the First Republic coming to such a bloody end at the hands of the majors of January 1966.

Murtala's relationship with his primary constituency, the army, was mixed. While he personally had a strong following in the army, it did not necessarily mean that all his regime decisions and actions were universally popular. In typically forthright and decisive fashion, the regime tackled head on the thorny question of post-Civil War demobilization that Gowon had shied away from. The army had grown from a strength of 10,000 in January 1966 to around 250,000 by the end of the Civil War four short years later. Defence as a proportion of government expenditure had grown from less than 10 percent in 1966 to 45 percent in 1976; 90 percent of this was consumed by salaries and other recurrent expenditures. Chief of Army Staff Danjuma, was quoted as saying that

Since the Civil War, the Nigerian Army has been run as a social service, maintaining and paying an exceedingly large body of men that we do not really need and whom we cannot properly equip.... We are about the only Army in the world where serving soldiers die of old age.[7]

The prospect of redundancy was not one which appealed to many of the officers and men in the army, particularly those who had gained emergency field commissions during the war and had become used to the prestige and the feeling of untouchability that came with being a military officer during the time of military governance.

It was against this backdrop that, on 8 January, a series of promotions were announced in the armed forces. Murtala was promoted from Brigadier to General, going from one to four stars in one fell swoop. He was just over thirty-seven years old and had been a commissioned officer for less than fifteen years. Given that his promotion was backdated to the day of the coup in July 1975, he technically had become a four star general at the age of thirty-six; assuming normal promotion progression, he would have been no higher than a Lieutenant-Colonel. Obasanjo, although senior to Murtala, was promoted to three-star rank as a Lieutenant-General, also with effect from July 1975. Danjuma also became a three-star Lieutenant-General, but with effect from 1 January 1976. Murtala's contemporaries Bisalla, Shuwa, and Haruna, all senior to Danjuma, were promoted to two-star rank as Majors-General. This particularly rankled Bisalla, who, as Federal Commissioner of Defence, was now junior in rank to Danjuma, one of his Service Chiefs (the other Service Chiefs, Adelanwa and Yisa-Doko, were also promoted to two and one-star rank, respectively; it is not unreasonable to suppose that the other officers superseded in this manner (Haruna and Shuwa) were not favourably impressed either, especially since neither of them, unlike Bisalla, had the consolation of a seat on the Supreme Military Council. Bisalla reportedly protested so strongly about Danjuma's elevation over him that Murtala and Obasanjo met with him in an attempt to calm the situation down, but they remained unmoved as far as revising any of the promotions. This decision may have been significant in what was to shortly transpire.[8] Other writers suggest that Obasanjo counseled Murtala against leaving an officer so palpably disgruntled as Bisalla in such a sensitive post as Defence Commissioner; Murtala's response was apparently to reassure Bisalla that Danjuma's promotion was political, and that, militarily, "Danjuma would still take his place behind the Defence Minister."[9] If so, this was patent nonsense. The other promoted officers, all from Brigadier to Major General, were the four GOCs (Alani Akinrinade, Martin Adamu, Emmanuel Abisoye, and John Obada), as well as Gibson Jalo (Commandant NDA), James Oluleye (Federal Commissioner for Establishments and member of the Supreme Military Council), Henry Adefope (Federal Commissioner for Labour), and Olufemi Olutoye (Federal Commissioner for Youth, Sports and Culture). The promotions were limited to the higher echelons of the military, and did not include any officers below flag rank.

The state-creation exercise turned out to be Murtala's last significant act as Head of State and Commander in Chief of the Armed Forces of the Federal Republic of Nigeria.

On 13 February 1976, Murtala's disregard for his personal safety became his undoing. As his soft-skinned Mercedes Benz stood stationary in a traffic jam near the Federal Secretariat in Ikoyi, Lagos, several army officers walked up to the vehicle and opened fire with automatic weapons. Murtala; his ADC, Lieutenant Akintunde Akinsehinwa; and his driver Sergeant Adamu Minchika, were killed. His orderly, SSgt Michael Otuwe, although seriously wounded, survived. The assassins, Lieutenant-Colonel Bukar Dimka, Major Ibrahim Rabo, Captain Malachy Parvwang, and Lieutenant William Seri, made good their escape — for a time. Dimka subsequently went on the air to broadcast:

> I bring you good tidings. Murtala Muhammed's hypocrisy has been detected. His government is now overthrown by the young revolutionaries....all senior military officers should remain calm in their respective spots. No divisional commander will issue orders ....any attempt to foil this plan from any quarter will be met with death. You are warned, it is all over the 19 States....everyone should be calm. Please stay by your radio for further announcements. All borders, airports and seaports are closed until further notice. Curfew is imposed from 6am to 6pm. Thank you. We are all together.

Dimka subsequently showed up at the British High Commission and demanded that the High Commissioner, Sir Martin Le Quesne, pass a message on to Gowon in London, requesting him to "come to Togo and wait". Unsurprisingly, Le Quesne declined to do any such thing, notwithstanding the fact that Dimka had clearly been drinking, and was accompanied by armed soldiers.

Whilst Dimka was engaged in his ultimately futile murderous and quasi-diplomatic tasks, his accomplices had not been idle. In a clear attempt to decapitate the regime, hit squads had been deployed to eliminate the other two leading members of the government: Obasanjo and Danjuma. For a variety of reasons, one being that Obasanjo was delayed leaving home by a visit from Colonel Olu Bajowa, who had come to ask for a name for his newborn son; and another, that the officer detailed to eliminate Danjuma failed to carry out his task because the Army Chief was in the company of the Chief of Naval Staff and two senior Army Staff Officers at the designated ambush point (the Marina Jetty), both officers — Obasanjo and Danjuma — escaped and were able to rally effective opposition to the coup, and eventually crush it. The bulk of this task was directed by Danjuma from a more secure location at Bonny Camp (enabled by the folly of the plotters in failing to sever communication links) and involved a number of officers whose names were either already familiar to the Nigerian public, or would soon become so, such as Domkat Bali and Ibrahim Babangida; other names less familiar to the public, such as Major Chris Ugokwe (who had been reabsorbed into the army at the end of the Civil War, albeit with loss of seniority) were no less involved in crushing the coup. Several army formations broadcast declarations of loyalty to the Murtala regime. A few short hours later, the coup had been quashed, and, once the smoke had cleared, it transpired that among the casualties was the Governor of Kwara State, Colonel Ibrahim Taiwo, who had played such a key role in the plot to oust Gowon seven short months earlier. Others who had been penciled in for elimination, such as Colonel David Jemibewon, Military Governor of Oyo State, and the aforementioned Babangida, escaped.

Once it became clear that the coup had been successfully thwarted, it was necessary to appoint a new head of state; and also necessary to round up and bring to justice those involved in plotting and executing the coup. First, though, the slain Murtala needed to be laid to rest. A military aircraft flew his body to his hometown of Kano, where he was buried according to Muslim rites. Amongst those accompanying the body at the airport in Lagos were Obasanjo, Danjuma, and Obada.

M.D. Yusuf, and Hassan Katsina, the former Deputy Chief of Staff, Supreme Headquarters, were among those present at the funeral. A seven-day period of national mourning was declared. The Supreme Military Council (SMC) met to appoint a successor to Murtala. The obvious choice was Obasanjo. As Murtala's second in command, his appointment would be entirely consistent with military norms. The fact that it was not so straightforward in practice was proof positive of the corrosive effect on the army's involvement in politics. Several members of the SMC advocated the appointment of Danjuma, especially since he had played such an active role in suppressing the revolt; still shaken by the shattering events, Obasanjo himself was reported to have supported Danjuma's elevation, and offered to retire in order to smooth Danjuma's path.[10] Perhaps mindful of the fate of Ironsi ten years earlier, after assuming power following an unsuccessful coup planned by officers of a similar ethnic background to himself, Danjuma declined the offer and insisted that the normal rules of seniority and succession be followed, and that Obasanjo be appointed. (The coup had been executed by mainly Christian officers from Northern minority ethnic groups, the region of Danjuma's birth, although he was not one of the plotters, and had resulted in the removal from office by assassination of a Muslim Hausa-Fulani head of state.) Other officers (Babangida, Mukhtar Muhammed, and Ibrahim Alfa) reportedly approached Joseph Garba to consider taking over, but he rebuffed them.[11] Obasanjo continued to resist the pressure from his colleagues to succeed Murtala, and reportedly only gave in after Abisoye intervened to say that if he, Obasanjo, continued to refuse to take over, the SMC might as well send for Dimka to do so.[12] Once Obasanjo was appointed, his previous post, as Chief of Staff, Supreme Headquarters, was now vacant. In making an appointment to this post, the members of the SMC would have been mindful of a number of factors, e.g., the need to appoint a Muslim (Obasanjo and Danjuma were both Christians), and a Hausa-Fulani one to boot, in order to maintain the religious and ethnic balance at the top tier of government. Moreover, for the group that had engineered Gowon's removal, it was necessary that the person appointed to this role be an insider. Taking all this into account, the choices narrowed down to Lieutenant Colonels Yar'Adua and Buhari. Yar'Adua eventually got the nod, as Buhari was deemed too inflexible to be a success in a political post (somewhat ironic, given that he would subsequently become both a military head of state *and* an elected civilian president, the latter by defeating a sitting president in 2015, which had never before happened in Nigeria). Upon his appointment, Yar'Adua was promoted Brigadier. In his maiden speech as Head of State, Obasanjo vowed to continue with his predecessor's policies.

Housekeeping done, the regime now turned its focus squarely on bringing those responsible for planning and carrying out the coup to account. The January 1966 plotters, although arrested, were never tried, whilst the July 1966 and July 1975 plotters were not even arrested; indeed, several of them even became members of the government. Ironically, since no one in Nigeria had ever before been tried for coup plotting, there was no existing law that adequately dealt with the present situation, and it was deemed necessary to rectify this. The very first decree signed into law by Obasanjo as the Head of State, therefore, was the Treason and Other Offences (Special Military Tribunal) Decree No 8 of 1976. This provided for the establishment of a Special Military Tribunal (SMT) to try military personnel and civilians for offences such as treason or murder, irrespective of whether or not the offences had been committed before the decree came into force. The fact that the tribunal was empowered to pass death sentences made the retrospective nature of this decree even more troubling. That civilians would also fall under the ambit of military law in this case only added to the concerns, but such was the level of emotion surrounding the failed coup that very few (if any) voices were raised in protest. A military Board of Inquiry (BOI) was set up to investigate the coup under the chairmanship of Major-General Emmanuel Abisoye, GOC 3rd Division. Its members included Deputy Inspector General of Police Adamu Suleiman, Captain Olufemi Olumide of the Nigerian Navy, and Lieutenant-Colonels Mukhtar Muhammed, Joshua Dogonyaro, and Mamman Vatsa (Dogonyaro and Vatsa themselves were subsequently involved in the planning of coups). Some 220 military personnel and civilians were arrested and interrogated in relation to the coup, of which number the BOI sent some 130 to the SMT for trial. These, however, did not initially include the most visible participant in the coup, Dimka, who had somehow managed to escape from the radio station and had gone on the run; he was not captured until almost three weeks later. The SMT, chaired by another of the GOCs (Major-General John Obada of the Lagos Garrison Organisation), acquitted fifty-six persons, found thirty-one military personnel and one civilian guilty, and sentenced all thirty-two plotters to death by firing squad. Among them were the Federal Commissioner for Defence, Major-General Bisalla, who had been so vociferous in his opposition to Danjuma's promotion over his head, and a civilian, Mr. Abdulkarim Zakari of the Nigerian Broadcasting Corporation, who was Mrs. Gowon's older brother and had allegedly been responsible for providing the martial music played on the day of the coup as well as for admitting Dimka into the radio station and showing him where to go on the day of the coup. The death sentences were confirmed by the SMC, whose members included the Chairman and two members of the BOI (Abisoye, Olumide, and Mukhtar Mohammed) and the President of the SMT, Obada — thus creating a clear *prima facie* case of conflict of interest. Notwithstanding this, on 11 March 1976, these thirty-two individuals were publicly executed by firing squad in Lagos, at the Bar Beach and at Kirikiri Prison. The executions were televised and photographs of bullet-riddled bodies were widely published in newspapers. The fairness of the trial would be a matter of much concern in later years. Leaving aside the *ex post facto* nature of Decree 8 of 1976, some of those acquitted by the first SMT were retried by a second SMT, chaired by Brigadier Pius Eromobor. (Gowon's younger brother, Captain Isaiah Gowon, being one example, received a fifteen-year sentence at his retrial for an offence for which he had initially been acquitted). For others, the story was much grimmer. The former Governor of Benue-Plateau State under Gowon, Joseph Gomwalk, had been convicted of concealment of treason by the Obada SMT and sentenced to life imprisonment. When the sentence was passed to the SMC for confirmation, that body ordered a retrial by the Eromobor SMT; Gomwalk was again convicted, but this time sentenced to death.[13] Dimka and six others, including Gomwalk, were executed at Kirikiri on 15 May 1976.

By far the greatest drama surrounding all this was the allegation that Gowon had prior knowledge of and was implicated in the coup attempt. It will be recalled that Dimka had gone to the British High Commission to request that the High Commissioner, Sir Martin Le Quesne, pass a message on to Gowon in the UK, asking him to "come to Togo and wait", which Le Quesne had quite properly declined to do. In a statement released a week after the failed coup, the federal government claimed:

For all practical purposes, the intent of Lt Col Dimka was to restore General Gowon and his associates to power. As a matter of fact, the Federal Government has ample evidence to show that General Yakubu Gowon knew [of], and by implication approved, the coup plot. It is known that Lt Col Dimka had been in touch with General Gowon both directly and through some other participants in the abortive coup plot. One of the participants had confessed under interrogation that he personally went to the United Kingdom several times to brief General Gowon about the plan.[14]

On the basis of this statement, and even before Dimka had been arrested and interrogated, Gowon was tried and convicted in the court of public opinion, with calls for him to be brought back to the country, dismissed from the army, and all his entitlements stopped; and with newspaper editorials describing him as "A plotter for all seasons", "General Gowon has betrayed Nigeria", and "Gowon's blood-stained hands".[15] Gowon, whilst acknowledging that Dimka had accompanied some others to visit him at his London home, very strongly and robustly denied the allegation that any discussion about a coup had taken place, pointing out that at least two other people had been present the one and only time he met Dimka, and that Dimka had been somewhat intoxicated.

Under interrogation after his arrest, Dimka further implicated Gowon, claiming that he had visited Gowon in the UK to discuss the plot, and that Gowon had instructed him, on his return to Nigeria, to contact Bisalla for further instructions regarding the plot (thereby further implicating Bisalla, who was already under suspicion after claims by one of those arrested, Lieutenant-Colonel T.K. Adamu, that he had reported the plot to Bisalla. Bisalla denied that Adamu had done any such thing, and was released. He was reportedly on the verge of being completely exonerated when Dimka was arrested).[16]

On 6 March, a day after Dimka's arrest, Yar'Adua, the new Chief of Staff, Supreme Headquarters, wrote to Gowon inviting him to appear before the Board of Inquiry to respond to the allegations made against him. Four days later, on 10 March, and before he had replied to Yar'Adua's letter, Gowon received a letter from the Acting High Commissioner at the Nigerian High Commission in London, informing him of the decision of the Supreme Military Council to suspend the privileges previously extended to Gowon, such as the payment of his retirement benefits in the UK, the payment of his rent, and the payment of the salary of a valet/batman. On 12 March, Gowon replied to Yar'Adua's letter of 6 March. In this letter, he indicated his willingness to cooperate with the Board of Inquiry; he was, however, concerned that the 20 February statement by the federal government had led to such a hostile reaction from the public that he was not satisfied that he would be safe if he were to return to Nigeria, and he offered to meet with the BOI either in the UK or in any other neutral country upon which he and the federal government could mutually agree. Yar'Adua replied on 22 March, saying that as the matter was an internal Nigerian affair, it would be "improper for the Board to hold sessions outside the country", and offered a guarantee for Gowon's safety if he returned to Nigeria as requested. In an attempt to persuade Gowon of the federal government's *bona fides*, Yar'Adua stated in his letter that Gowon's younger brother, Air Force Major Moses Gowon, who had been detained as part of the investigations into the coup attempt, had been released after being cleared by the BOI, and had returned to normal duties. On receipt of this letter on 27 March, Gowon took the precaution of telephoning Nigeria to confirm the veracity of Yar'Adua's claim that Moses Gowon had indeed been released and had returned to his normal duties, only to be told that the younger Gowon was still in detention. (He was not released until July 1976, and was subsequently discharged from the Air Force.) This persuaded Gowon that he could not rely on the federal government's assurances about his safety, and, perhaps wisely in the circumstances, he declined to return to Nigeria. The federal government thereupon formally requested his extradition to Nigeria by the British government, which refused the request. The federal government responded by dismissing Gowon from the army and declaring him a wanted man. He remained a wanted man until 1 October 1981, when the civilian President Shehu Shagari rescinded that order. This was not a pardon, as Gowon had made clear through his legal representatives; he would not accept a pardon, as he had never been convicted of any crime. Gowon's rank and benefits were not restored to him until 1986, by the then (military) President, Major-General Ibrahim Babangida, about whom there will be more later.

Murtala Muhammed had been in power for less than seven months. The swashbuckling, devil-may-care attitude that had characterized his early career in the army remained very much in evidence during his period as Head of State, and it may be argued that it directly led to the circumstances in which his tenure in office (and his life) came to such a violent and predictable end. His brash, in-your-face style and his disregard for his personal safety were displayed in July 1966 when he informed Lieutenant-Colonel Patrick Anwunah and again in 1975 when he told M.D. Yusuf that he was planning a coup, and that they could do whatever they liked with the information — or in 1967 when he insisted on a frontal assault on Onitsha and in 1975/76, when he dismissed his colleagues' admonitions to take more care about his personal security as Head of State.

Any objective assessment of Murtala Muhammed's legacy, both military and political, must result in a mixed scorecard. In political terms, whilst it is true that on the one hand he set the nation on the path to a return to civil rule, and that several of the constitutional provisions set in place as a result remain extant in today's Nigeria, it also true on the other hand that responsibility for the decimation of the civil service and the structural imbalance in Nigeria as the result of the 1976 state-creation exercise must be laid at his door as the leader of the government that visited both of these events on Nigeria — the effects of both actions lingering to this day. On the military front, he must be given credit for halting the Biafran advance into the Midwest in August 1967 with a hastily cobbled together division. Nevertheless, but he must also be held responsible for the undoubted war crimes committed by troops under his command. (Even if those crimes were not committed at his direction or with his knowledge, he had a responsibility to bring the guilty parties to account, which he failed to do.) He must also be held responsible for the inept and bloody way in which he stubbornly insisted on a frontal assault on Onitsha, which resulted in needlessly high casualties amongst his troops, especially when he was acting in defiance of guidance from Army Headquarters. If the highest priorities of a commander in a time of war are the accomplishment of his mission and the welfare of his troops, Murtala can scarcely be adjudged a stellar success at his primary calling, the profession of arms.

It now remained to be seen how his successor would fare.

NOTES

1. Siollun p. 82.

2. Ibid p. 232.

3. Omoigui, op cit.

4. Siollun p. 163.

5. Ibid p. 164.

6. Ibid p. 165.

7. Ibid p. 190.

8. Ibid p. 192.

9. Onukaba, Adinoyi. *Olusegun Obasanjo: In the Eyes of Time*. Spectrum Books 2007, p. 7.

10. Siollun p. 198.

11. Onukaba p. 30.

12. Ibid p. 32.

13. Siollun pp. 210-211.

14. Elaigwu p. 256.

15. Ibid pp. 258, 275-276.

16. Siollun p. 210.

Nigeria's first crop of commissioned military officers. **From left to right sitting**: Capt Adeyinka Adebayo, Captain Philip Effiong, Captain Imo, Major Samuel Adesoji Ademulegun,Major Wellington Bassey, General Forster, Major JTU Ironsi, Major Ral Shodeinde,Captain Zakaria Maimalari, Captain Conrad Nwawo, Captain David Ejo **Middle Row standing**: Lt Igboba, Lt George Kurubo, (non Nigerian standing nex¹ to Kurubo), Lt J. Akaga, Lt Patrick Anwunah, Lt Louis Ogbonna, Lt Chukwuemek Odumegwu Ojukwu, Lt Eyo Ekpo, Lt Arthur Unegbe, Lt Abogo Largema. **Back Row**: Lt Hilary Njoku, 2nd Lt Nzefili, 2nd Lt Ogunenwe, 2nd Lt Shadrak, L¹ Madiebo, 2nd Lt Anthony Eze, Lt Yakubu Gowon, 2nd Lt Sylvanus Nwanjei, Lt Yakʋ Pam, 2nd Lt Hassan Katsina. Those not in the picture are Captain Kur Mohammed, Lt Victor Banjo and Lt Micha Okwechime.

Sir Abubakar Tafawa Balewa, Federal Prime Minister and Head of the Nigerian Government under the Northern Peoples Congress (NPC), 1960-66: assassinated in the January 1966 coup.

Dr. Nnamdi Azikiwe, "ceremonial" President of the Nigerian Federation in a coalition government of his party the National Council of Nigeria and the Cameroons (NCNC) with the Northern Peoples Congress (NPC), 1960-66

Chief Obafemi
Awolowo, leader
of the Federal
opposition party, the
Action Group (AG)
imprisoned for treason
in 1962, incarcerated
at the time of the
January 1966 coup, and
released by the Gowon
regime following the
July 1966 countercoup.

Sir Ahmadu Bello,
Sardauna of Sokoto,
the powerful Premier
of the Northern
Region, assassinated in
the January 1966 coup.

Chief Samuel Ladoke Akintola, Premier of the Western Region, assassinated in the January 1966 coup.

Dr. Michael Okpara, Premier of the Eastern Region who escaped assassination in the January 1966 coup.

Major Patrick Chukwuma "Kaduna" Nzeogwu, most widely known of the ringleaders of the January 1966 coup who led the assault operations in Kaduna, during which the Sardauna was assassinated.

Nigeria's first military head of state, Major General J.T.U. Aguiyi-Ironsi (Jan 15 1966-July 29 1966).

Head of State Major General J.T.U. Aguiyi-Ironsi (center) surrounded by his military governors (L to R) Major Hassan Katsina (Northern Region), Lt. Colonel Adekunle Fajuyi (Western Region), Lt. Colonel Emeka Odumegwu Ojukwu (Eastern Region) and Lt. Colonel David Ejoor (Mid Western Region)

The Commander in Chief during the Civil War.

General Yakubu Gowon with HM Queen Elizabeth II
during his state visit to the UK in 1973.

Ojukwu's swearing in as Head of State of Biafra, following the
declaration of secession in 1967.

Ojukwu inspecting a parade of Biafran soldiers during the civil war.

*** Lt. Murtala Mohammed (in uniform) at a church service as a young officer and Aide De Camp to the former Administrator of Old Western Region Dr. M.A. Majekodunmi (1962).

*** General Murtala Mohammed addressing the Inaugural Meeting of the Constitution Drafting Committee, flanked by Chief Rotimi Williams and Lt. General Obasanjo, October 18, 1975.

*** Lt Gen Obasanjo with Andrew Young, US Ambassador to the UN in 1977.

***Lt Gen Obasanjo and his Service Chiefs at the Independence Day parade, October 1st 1978.

President Sheu Shagari won the 1979 Presidential Election on the platform of the National Party of Nigeria (NPN) and was removed from office in the December 1983 coup.

Major General Muhammadu Buhari, Nigeria's fifth military Head of State from December 1983 - August 1985.

*** Nigerian Head of State Major General Muhammad Buhari with Liberian leader Samuel Doe in November 1984. On the far right is Major General Tunde Idiagbon; Rear Admiral Aikhomu and Major General Babangida can be seen between Buhari and Doe.

*** Babangida's official
portrait as President and
Commander in Chief of
the Armed Forces

*** Flanking Babangida from L-R are Vice Adm. Aikhomu (CGS), Lt Gen
Domkat Bali (Chairman, Joint Chiefs) and Lt Gen Abacha (Chief of Army
Staff).

*** General Sani Abacha, Nigeria's "maximum ruler" from
1993-1998.

*** General Abdulsalami Abubakar, Head of State
(1998-99) appointed to lead the nation following the
sudden demise of Abacha in June 1998.

Completing a full circle, the Abubakar military
regime hands over power to a civilian administration
headed by a former military ruler now turned
civilian President, General Olusegun Obasanjo (rtd.),
on 29th May 1999.

CHAPTER 9

The Third Military Government: Return to Civil Rule

The Ballot is Stronger than the Bullet
— **Abraham Lincoln, May 1856**

The violent and bloody circumstances in which Murtala Muhammed's tenure as Head of State came to an end and Olusegun Obasanjo's began, had a marked impact on how the latter went about his business. For a start, the regime had been badly shaken by the ease with which Dimka and his associates had killed Murtala and had come perilously close to decapitating the government. Out went Murtala's low-profile, man-of-the-people approach; the leaders significantly beefed up the security around themselves, and Obasanjo himself moved into Dodan Barracks. The coup had taken seasoned coup makers like Murtala and Danjuma by surprise, and steps were now taken to ensure that that would not happen again. M.D. Yusuf offered his resignation as Inspector-General of Police, but it was refused; he did however lose jurisdiction over the police's Special Branch, which was subsumed into a new body, the National Security Organisation (NSO), headed by Colonel Abdullahi Mohammed, the erstwhile Director of Military Intelligence. Meanwhile, Murtala was honoured when the international airport in Lagos was named after him, and when his portrait adorned the 20-Naira currency note, then the highest denomination note in circulation.

Having examined the circumstances in which Olusegun Obasanjo came to power, it is worth taking a look at what is known of the man himself. Matthew Olusegun Fajinmi Aremu Obasanjo was born in Ibogun, near Abeokuta, the eldest child of Amos Adigun Obasanjo Bankole and Bernice Ashabi Akinale. His date of birth is not known with exactitude, as his birth was not registered; in subsequent years, it was calculated that he was born around 5 March 1937, using the establishment of the Baptist Church in Ibogun in 1935 as the reference point. Of several subsequent full and half-siblings, only one, his immediate younger sister, survived into adulthood. Although a relatively prosperous farmer, Obasanjo Bankole was determined that his only son would not follow him into the drudgery of farming, and enrolled him at the elementary school in a nearby hamlet in 1948, registering him as Matthew Olusegun Obasanjo, the surname he would be known by from then on. A bright pupil, he excelled academically, and, on at least one occasion, earned a double promotion. In January 1951, the young Obasanjo moved to Owu in Abeokuta to continue his education at the Baptist Day School. As he prepared for the entrance examination into secondary school, the family's fortunes took a turn for the worse, with his father's farms failing, with the result that Obasanjo Bankole upped sticks and moved away to seek a fresh start elsewhere. His wife, Obasanjo's mother, was now left with the task of bringing up her two children on her own. Obasanjo did more than his fair share, working several jobs in order to sustain himself and help the family, which included gathering and selling firewood, hauling sand for construction contractors, and working as a farm labourer. In December 1951, he sat and passed the entrance examination to the Baptist Boys High School, Abeokuta, where, despite having to work at the same time as study in order to pay his way through school, Obasanjo was able to maintain his record of academic brilliance.[1] Such was Obasanjo's academic achievement that he enrolled for and sat the London General Certificate of Education a year early, and passed all the subjects he entered for, including Mathematics and Additional Mathematics. He left school and took up a clerical job in Ibadan with the United African Company (UAC), followed by a brief teaching stint at a Modern School also in Ibadan. In 1957, he sat and passed the entrance examination to the University of Ibadan, but his straitened personal and family circumstances meant that he was unable to afford the fees. Whilst considering his options (which included seeking some form of scholarship), he happened across an advertisement in the *Daily Times* for the cadetship entrance examination for the Nigerian Army. More out of curiosity than real interest, he enrolled for the examination, passed it and a subsequent interview, and was accepted into the army which offered an escape from what has been described as "the stinging inadequacy that had been his life of 20 years."[2]

In March 1958, Obasanjo entered the Regular Officers Special Training School at Teshie in Ghana; his fellow cadets included several names that Nigerians (and readers of this text) would become familiar with such as Benjamin Adekunle, Folusho Sotomi, Humphrey Chukwuka, Henry Igboba, and Jacob Esuene. After successfully completing the six-month course at Teshie, Obasanjo was sent to the UK, where he attended Mons Officer Training School in Aldershot for a further six months; whilst at Mons, he received word from Nigeria that his mother had passed away. Upon successfully completing the course at Mons, Obasanjo received a Short Service Commission into the Nigerian Army in 1959, and was posted to the Nigerian Army's Fifth Battalion, then stationed in Kaduna. In October 1960, Obasanjo deployed with the rest of the battalion to the Congo as part of the UN Force under the command of Ironsi. One of his fellow subalterns was Chukwuma Nzeogwu. Upon the unit's return to Nigeria in May 1961, Obasanjo, at his own request, was posted out of the infantry into the fledgling army engineers as its second Nigerian Officer (after Captain Mike Okwechime). The following year, he was promoted Troop Captain, and attended a course at the Royal College of Military Engineering in Chatham, Kent, in the UK. On his return to Nigeria in July 1963, Obasanjo was posted to the Army Field Engineering Squadron in Kaduna as a Troop Commander; he subsequently became the Officer Commanding the squadron. Excelling in the Captain-to-Major promotion exam in September 1964, he was promoted Major before, in March 1965, attending the Indian Army School of Engineering in Poona and the Indian Defence Services Staff College in Wellington. He returned to Kaduna, via London and Kano, in early January 1966. Two days after his return, Nigeria experienced its first military coup, in which both Obasanjo's close friend, Nzeogwu, as well as Gbulie, his second-in-command in the Field Squadron, were both significant players. Following the countercoup in July 1966, and the subsequent breakdown in discipline in the army and the wider Nigerian society, Obasanjo left Kaduna for Lagos in February 1967 to take over as Head of the Army Engineers from Lieutenant-Colonel Mike Okwechime, who had, with other officers of Igbo origin, joined the exodus from the Northern and Western Regions and Lagos to the Eastern and Midwestern Regions. Following the outbreak of the Civil War in July 1967, and the Biafran incursion into the Midwest the following month, Obasanjo was appointed Commander of the Second Area Command in Ibadan. He remained in this post until he was appointed GOC of the Third Marine Commando Division of the Army in May 1969, in succession to Adekunle. He was by now a Colonel, after only ten years as a Commissioned Officer, and his appointment (and indeed those of the other GOCs appointed at the same time) could legitimately be seen as yet another example of the influence upon the army of its involvement in politics; one Yoruba officer had to be replaced by another. Under Obasanjo's command, the Third Marine Commando Division (3 MCD) recaptured Owerri (the earlier loss of which had triggered the reshuffling of the GOCs). Shortly thereafter, Ojukwu escaped into exile, Biafra surrendered, and the war was won. It fell to Obasanjo to accept the Biafran surrender, and a few days later, to escort the defeated Biafran leadership to Lagos for a more formal surrender to Gowon as Commander-in-Chief.

Following the war, Obasanjo returned in 1971 to his former post in Lagos as Commander of the Army Engineers, and was promoted Brigadier at age thirty-four, and with only twelve years commissioned service under his belt. In 1974, along with Bisalla, Obasanjo attended the Royal College of Defence Studies (RCDS) in the UK, and, following his return to Nigeria from RCDS, was in January 1975, appointed Federal Commissioner for Works and Housing by Gowon. He was in this post at the time of the coup that removed Gowon from office in July 1975, and which led to Obasanjo's appointment as Chief of Staff, Supreme Headquarters.

Unexpectedly, and against his wishes, Obasanjo now found himself the Head of State and Commander-in-Chief of the Armed Forces. In his maiden speech to the nation, he made it clear that there would be no change in the policies of the federal military government, and also that all those found guilty of involvement in the abortive coup that resulted in Murtala's death would "be summarily dealt with in a military way". As has been noted in the previous chapter, this was not an idle boast, and a total of thirty-nine persons were executed by firing squad in March and May 1976 for their participation in the coup; several more were sentenced to terms of imprisonment ranging from two years to life.

Once the second and final round of executions dealt with the matters arising from the coup, the government settled back down to work. In May 1976, Obasanjo launched Operation Feed the Nation (OFN) in an attempt to "make this nation self-sufficient in basic food needs". The government promised to make several thousand tons of fertilisers available to farmers at heavily subsidized prices. The following month, the government announced an extension of the indigenisation decrees enacted by Gowon in 1974; now all foreign-owned banks would need to have 60 percent (hitherto 40 percent) of their equity in Nigerian hands. Furthermore, those companies affected by the 1974 decree, which had not thus far complied with the provisions of the earlier decree, were to have their assets frozen and taken over by the government with immediate effect. A new commodity marketing system was created with the establishment of a price-fixing authority and seven commodity boards. The federal government intervened in the private rental market, determining (ultimately an exercise in futility) what rents should be in Lagos and directing the state governments to take similar measures. Restraints were placed on wage increases in an attempt to rein in inflation. On the foreign policy front, the government reaffirmed its determination to make Africa the centerpiece of its foreign policy, and restated its commitment to the liberation struggles in South Africa, Angola, and Mozambique. To underline the point, Nigeria led the way in announcing, in July 1976, a boycott of the Montreal Olympics in protest of the participation of New Zealand, whose Rugby team, the All Blacks, were touring South Africa — several countries in Africa followed Nigeria's example. In September, the government launched the Universal Primary Education (UPE) scheme.

The journey back to civilian rule began with the submission of a draft constitution to the government by the Constitution Drafting Committee on 14 September 1976 (two members of the committee submitted a minority report as a result of what were described as differences "on fundamental points of conception and principle from the majority"). In October, the new draft constitution was released to the public for discussion and comment, and a Constituent Assembly (CA) set up to receive and collate submissions on the Constitution from the public. The CA was to consist of 203 elected members; every state would have five members for the sake of equality, and the remainder would be elected by local governments in each state on the basis of each state's population, with the number of elected representatives from each state ranging from seven from Niger State to sixteen from Kano State. As has already been mentioned (see chapter 5), the new draft constitution represented a significant departure from all of Nigeria's previous constitutions in many ways. In November 1976, Obasanjo inaugurated a 24-member Federal Electoral Commission (FEDECO) under the chairmanship of Mr. Michael Ani, and which included four female federal government representatives. In September 1977, the government appointed Mr. Justice Udo Udoma of the Supreme Court to chair the Constituent Assembly, with Mr. Justice Buba Ardo, Chief Judge of Bauchi, Borno, and Gongola states, as his deputy; twenty other members were appointed at the same time to serve on the CA, including women and representatives of industry, labour, students, and traditional authorities. The CA had its inaugural sitting in Lagos on 6 October 1977.

On 29 March 1978, the federal government promulgated the Land Use Decree, which vested all the land within the territory of a state (less land vested in the federal government for the use of its agencies) in the hands of the state government, which would hold the land in trust for the people of the state. In July 1978, Obasanjo announced that, as part of the transition to civilian rule, the nineteen state military governors were to be reassigned to military duties, and that nineteen military administrators were to be appointed to replace them. Furthermore, several military federal commissioners were to be redeployed to purely military duties, amongst them Brigadier Joseph Garba (External Affairs) and Colonels Mohammed Magoro (Transport), Muhammadu Buhari (Petroleum) and Ahmadu Alli (Education). Other military federal commissioners who retained their political appointments, such as Major-Generals Henry Adefope (Labour), James Oluleye (Finance), and Muhammad Shuwa (Trade), would retire from the army upon the transition to civilian rule — so too would Obasanjo and his deputy, Yar'Adua. The following month, August 1978, the CA submitted the new Constitution to the Supreme Military Council (SMC) for ratification; the CA was subsequently formally dissolved on 20 September 1978. On 21 September 1978, Obasanjo made a broadcast to the nation in which he announced that Decree No 25 of 1978, which promulgated the new Constitution into law with effect on 1 October 1979, had been signed, and that, as a consequence, the ban on politics had been lifted. He also announced that the SMC had made a number of amendments to the Constitution, notable amongst them provisions enshrining therein the National Youth Service Corps, the Land Use Decree, the Public Complaints Commission, and the National Security Organisation. The SMC amendments also made it unconstitutional for a public official holding an executive position (including members of all legislative bodies) to operate foreign accounts. The regime had, by both word and deed, demonstrated that it was truly serious about delivering on its promise to return Nigeria to civilian rule, in stark contrast to its predecessor.

Within twenty-four hours of the ban on politics being lifted, the formation of several political parties was announced. Eventually, the Federal Electoral Commission approved the registration of five of these parties — the Unity Party of Nigeria (UPN), National Party of Nigeria (NPN), Nigerian Peoples Party (NPP), Great Nigerian Peoples Party (GNPP), and the Peoples Redemption Party (PRP). Electioneering started in earnest and elections for the Senate were held on 7 July 1979, followed by elections into the House of Representatives a week later, on 14 July. On 21 July, elections for the State Houses of Assembly were held, followed a week later by elections for the state governors. Finally, on 11 August, the presidential election was held, with five candidates in the contest; on 17 August, FEDECO declared Alhaji Shehu Shagari of the NPN the winner. Predictably, the other candidates and their parties kicked up a fuss, and rejected the declared result as "a fraud". Legal challenges were mounted and eventually, on 26 September 1979, the Supreme Court ruled against Awolowo of the UPN and in favour of Shagari of the NPN.

At a parade on 1 October 1979, Shehu Usman Aliyu Shagari took the oath of office, and became the President of the Federal Republic of Nigeria and Commander in Chief of the Armed Forces. General Obasanjo and Major General Yar'Adua (both had been promoted earlier in 1979) saluted smartly and stepped back. Military rule was over — for now.

There can be no doubt that Obasanjo deserves credit for seeing through the transition programme as set out by his predecessor. The question arises, however, as to the extent to which he was an author of the policy as opposed to simply following the laid-down blueprint.

Even if this latter situation was the case (though there is evidence to suggest that it was not), carrying it through was no mean feat. Similarly, questions quite legitimately arise as to the extent of the contribution he made to ending the Civil War after taking command of the Third MCDO Division in May 1969: was he the innovator who came up with the masterstroke strategy to swiftly end the war, or did he just happen to have had the good fortune to be put in command at a time when the die was cast and Biafra was on its last legs? Again, even if the latter was true, it still required some military nous in order to bring the war to a successful conclusion. Was it simply a coincidence that his style of leadership in both situations, plodding when compared to his predecessors (Adekunle at the Third MCDO Division and Murtala as Head of State), delivered the goods on both occasions? Or was it that, in both cases, a steady hand on the tiller was what was required after the preceding fireworks? Any objective assessment of the impact of Obasanjo's time at the helm of affairs must include giving him credit for being the first military leader in Nigeria's history to voluntarily hand over power to a civilian regime. It must also be acknowledged that several measures put into place during his time as Head of State have had an enduring impact (for good or for ill) on Nigeria's political and economic history; the Land Use Decree and the Indigenisation Decree. Conversely, other measures such as the attempt to manipulate rents, the ban on public officials operating foreign accounts, and the OFN and the UPE schemes proving less successful or enduring.

And what of Obasanjo the man? How did Obasanjo the man impact the style of Obasanjo the leader? And to what extent did the upbringing of Obasanjo the boy impact on Obasanjo the man and Obasanjo the leader? Much has been made by other commentators of Obasanjo's vindictiveness, his capacity to bear grudges over a long period of time against those whom he believed had slighted him, his ruthlessness in casting aside those for whom he felt he no longer had any use.

Perhaps his biographer, Adinoyi Onukaba, best sums him up:

...Obasanjo is a study in ambivalence and ambiguity...he is often too quick to judge others who are less fortunate while overlooking the unfair advantage the military gave to people like him. Although he has worked very hard for everything that has come his way, it is also true that he owes a lot to providence — a fact he likes to play down....He is earthy and humble, but acutely sensitive about being slighted. He does not forgive easily and he can be quite vindictive... .a common criticism of him is that he thinks he knows it all....He has also been criticized by those who have worked with him, or for him, of using and dumping them when they are no longer of any relevance to him. It has been said that the only person that matters to Olusegun Obasanjo is Olusegun Obasanjo....He has been known to humiliate friends and sacrifice them if that will make him look good in the eyes of the world...[3]

It was perhaps not apparent at the time of Obasanjo's departure from the army, and from the public stage in 1979, but several of the traits described above would become more overt upon his return to power as a civilian-elected President some two decades later.

NOTES

1. Onukaba pp. 45-54.

2. Ibid p. 75.

3. Onukaba p. 36.

CHAPTER 10

The Brief Civilian Interregnum

Democracy substitutes election by the incompetent many for appointment by the corrupt few.

— George Bernard Shaw

hen leaving office, the Obasanjo regime bequeathed two of the existing Service Chiefs (Adelanwa of the navy and Yisa-Doko of the air force) and a new one (Akinrinade of the army was appointed to succeed the retiring Danjuma) to the new Shagari regime. In addition, there remained several senior officers still in service across all three services who had been part of the preceding military regimes: Bali, Babangida, and Jalo (army); Akintunde Aduwo, Ndubuisi Kanu, and Ukiwe (navy) and Yisa-Doko, Ibrahim Alfa, and Ita David Ikpeme (air force).

The new civilian government moved fairly swiftly to put its own men in place. In April 1980, the appointment of new Service Chiefs was announced, as Adelanwa and Yisa-Doko were retired, and Akinrinade moved into the largely ceremonial post of Chief of Defence Staff. In their places came Jalo as the new Chief of Army Staff, Aduwo as Chief of Naval Staff, and Abdullahi Dominic Bello as Chief of Air Staff. (Jalo was subsequently also kicked upstairs to replace Akinrinade as CDS when the latter voluntarily retired; Muhammed Inuwa Wushishi was appointed to replace Jalo as Chief of Army Staff.) Joseph Garba, who had played such a central role in removing Gowon from power, was also retired. The influence of politics in these appointments on the most senior posts in the armed forces was (perhaps unsurprisingly in a civilian government run largely by Northern politicians) pretty overt: at the time the Shagari administration was overthrown in December 1983, three of the four Service Chiefs were Northerners (Jalo, Wushishi, and Bello) as were all four army GOCs (Anthony Hannaniya, Muhammadu Jega, Muhammadu Buhari, and Zamani Lekwot), the Commander of the Brigade of Guards (Muhammed Bello Kaliel), the Inspector-General of Police (Adewusi), and the Director-General of the National Security Organisation (Umaru Shinkafi). Shagari might therefore be excused for feeling confident that he had all the bases covered to fend off any threat of a military coup against him. If he did, that confidence was greatly misplaced.

The truth was that the civilian regime had, right from the beginning, not covered itself with glory, and that by the time it was overthrown at the end of 1983, had lost credibility on several fronts. First, there was lingering resentment in many parts of the country about what many saw as the legal sleight-of-hand by the Supreme Court that had upheld Shagari's election as legitimate. Second, the new regimes, at both federal and state levels, and which involved politicians across all parties, soon developed a well-deserved reputation for graft and corruption that rivalled that of the politicians of the First Republic (many of them, including Shagari himself, appearing in leadership roles in the Second Republic). The ostentatious displays of ill-gotten wealth grated on a populace that now had to bear the brunt of "austerity" measures that had to be put in place after a major fall in oil prices which resulted in a significant reduction in government revenues. The Shagari regime also shot itself in the foot in its handling of one of its strongest financial backers, the businessman Moshood Abiola. Abiola nurtured strong presidential ambitions, and hoped that the payback for his financial largess to the NPN, as well as for his support for the government under the aegis of his Concord Group newspapers, would give him the party's nomination to run for president in 1983. He was to be disappointed with Umaru Dikko, Shagari's powerful Transport Minister, declaring that "The Presidency is not for sale to the highest bidder". Abiola, thoroughly disillusioned, now switched his press empire from a pro- to a very strongly anti-government posture. The final straw was the 1983 elections, which were blatantly rigged, at all levels, on an industrial scale. The time was right for the emergence of the several career coup planners who had been biding their time for the last few years. As Babangida subsequently put it:

We could have toppled that Government in 1982, before the [1983] elections. But we said no...we knew damn well that they were not going to conduct that election freely and fairly, and, therefore, we waited for the right time. You see, to stage a coup, there is one basic element that everybody looks for; there must be frustration in the society.... We found the coup easier when there was frustration in the land.[1]

Babangida also confirmed the enabling role played by elements in the media (including Abiola's Concord Group) in shaping the atmosphere in the country to make it more conducive to military intervention, and in funding the coup:

There was the media frenzy about how bad the election was, massively rigged, corruption, the economy gone completely bad, threat of secession by people who felt aggrieved. There was frustration within society and it was not unusual to hear statements like, "the worst military dictatorship is better than this democratic government".... We couldn't have done it without collaborators in the civil society — collaborators in the media, collaborators among people who have the means. Because the means were not easily available, but we received some from people who were convinced it was the right thing to do... The elite who participate want recognition, maybe patronage as time goes by.[2]

The stage was now set for the plot that would remove Shagari from office. This, however, was not the first such plot. Whilst there had been much speculation about plots to remove the Shagari government from power, the only overt plot was instigated by a civilian, Alhaji Bukar Mandara, a disaffected contractor whose contract to supply food to the army's Brigade of Guards had been revoked following the return to civilian rule, and who had been trying to recruit soldiers from within the Brigade to participate in overthrowing the government. Mandara was arrested, tried, and convicted of treason, although his conviction was later overturned on appeal. (It is difficult to imagine such a plot, or an appeal, taking place under a military regime.) In any event, a much more seasoned group of coup plotters was coming together, and they would not be quite the amateur as Mandara had been. Men like Babangida, Buhari, Abacha, Ibrahim Bako, and Aliyu Mohammed had an impressive record of successful coup plotting under their belts, dating back almost two decades to July 1966; to their ranks were added younger and (as it turned out), no less-talented coup plotters such as Lieutenant-Colonels Haliru Akilu, David Mark, Tunde Ogbeha; and Majors Abdulmumuni Aminu, Sambo Dasuki, Lawan Gwadabe, and Abubakar Umar. Given the widespread level of support for the coup across the senior echelons of the army, as well as the fact that both the now retired Obasanjo and Danjuma were notified in advance and supported the removal from office of the man to whom they had handed power over four years earlier, the coup, which took place on the night of 30-31 December 1983, passed off largely uneventfully, with the exception of the death in Abuja of Brigadier Ibrahim Bako, who had been detailed to effect the arrest of President Shagari. (This appears to have resulted from the surprising failure of such a seasoned group of coup plotters to achieve the effective suborning of the Brigade of Guards, who were responsible for Shagari's protection; it was in the course of the resistance put up by the Company of the Guards Brigade on duty at the State House on the night of the coup that Bako was killed.)

On the morning of New Year's Eve 1983, Nigerians woke up to the by now familiar strains of martial music on the radio, with an unfamiliar voice announcing that he and his colleagues in the armed forces had, in their self-appointed role

> as promoters and protectors of our national interest, decided to effect a change in the leadership of the government of the Federal Republic of Nigeria and form a Federal Military Government....accordingly, Alhaji Shehu Usman Shagari ceases forthwith to be the President and Commander-in-Chief of the Armed Forces of Nigeria.[3]

The voice on the radio was that of the Commander of the Army's Ninth Mechanised Brigade, Brigadier Sani Abacha. It was a voice with which Nigerians were to become only too painfully familiar.

NOTES

1. Siollun, Max. *Soldiers of Fortune: Nigerian Politics Under Buhari and Babangida (1983-1993)*. Cassava Republic Press, 2013, p. 9 (Siollun SOF)

2. Ibid, p. 11

3. Ibid, p. 18

CHAPTER 11

The Fourth Military Government: War Against Indiscipline

This generation of Nigerians, and indeed future generations, have no country other than Nigeria. We shall remain here and salvage it together.
— **Muhammadu Buhari, December 1983**

The new regime moved swiftly to stamp its authority on the armed forces and the rest of the country. The appointments of Major-General Muhammadu Buhari as the new Head of State and of Brigadier Tunde Idiagbon as the new Chief of Staff, Supreme Headquarters, were announced, as were those of the new Service Chiefs (Major-General Babangida for the army, Rear Admiral Augustus Aikhomu for the navy, and Air Vice Marshal Ibrahim Alfa for the air force). Major-General Domkat Bali was appointed Defence Minister. All previous Service Chiefs (Jalo, Wushishi, Aduwo, and Bello) were immediately retired, and held in detention in Bonny Camp in Lagos for a few days until the dust had settled and the new regime was in complete control. Several other officers, senior to or the contemporaries of the key players in the new regime were either retired or posted out of the country as Ambassadors. Declaring itself an offshoot of the Murtala/Obasanjo regime, the new government swiftly adopted the same structure of government the aforesaid regime had used, with a Supreme Military Council, (Initially, the SMC was an entirely military body from which state governors were excluded; subsequently, the Inspector-General of Police, the Director-General of the NSO, and the Attorney General of the Federation, none of them military personnel, were appointed to it.) a Federal Executive Council (with both military and civilian Federal Commissioners), and a National Council of States (which the state governors were members of). Some of the newly appointed officers (Buhari, Idiagbon, Bali, Vatsa, and the Service Chiefs, to name but a few) sat on more than one, and in some cases, all of these bodies. Northerners heavily dominated the newly devised SMC. Three of the four GOCs, for example, were Northerners — Abacha, Salihu Ibrahim, and Yohanna Kure — and, until the Inspector-General of Police and the Attorney-General were added, there were only five Southerners on the sixteen-member council; the addition of Etim Inyang and Chike Ofodile (Inspector-General and Attorney-General, respectively), brought the number of Southerners to seven out of a total of nineteen members (the third addition to the SMC, NSO Director-General Rafindadi, was also a Northerner). Military governors were also appointed and were largely posted to their states of origin, another departure from the Murtala/Obasanjo model.

The two men at the helm of the new government, Buhari and Idiagbon, were stern and uncompromising disciplinarians, and, in addition to the long-standing cankerworm of corruption, saw it as part of their job to tackle corruption's twin — indiscipline. It will be recalled that, following Murtala's death in the February 1976 coup and Obasanjo's ascent to the top job, Buhari had been considered for the number two position as Chief of Staff, Supreme Headquarters, and had lost out to Yar'Adua on that occasion as he was considered "too inflexible" to serve in a political position. Buhari was now in the most political position of all, Head of State, and this is perhaps an opportune time to take a closer look at Nigeria's fifth military leader.

Muhammadu Buhari was born in Daura in present-day Katsina State on 17 December 1942. He was the youngest child of both his parents. His father, Hardo Adamu, the Fulani headman of Dumurkol village near Daura died when young Muhammadu was only four years old, and he was brought up by his mother, Hajia Zulaihatu Musa, a Hausa lady who had been previously widowed. He attended primary school in Daura before going to the Katsina Model School in 1953. He attended Katsina Provincial Secondary School (later known as Government College, Katsina) between 1956 and 1961, where one of his classmates was Shehu Yar'Adua. They both enrolled in the Nigerian Military Training College (NMTC) in 1962, from where Buhari proceeded to Mons Officer Cadet School in Aldershot, from which he received a short service commission into the Nigerian Army as Second Lieutenant in January 1963 (his friend Yar'Adua went on to RMA Sandhurst, England, and was not commissioned till the following year). Buhari returned to Nigeria and was posted to the Second Battalion, then stationed in Abeokuta as a Platoon Commander. He attended the Platoon Commanders course at NMTC from November 1963 to January 1964; later that year, he attended a Transport Officers course at the British Army Mechanical Transport School in Borden, England. He returned to the Second Battalion, by this time stationed in Lagos, and, as a Lieutenant, played a key role there in the July 1966 coup that resulted in Ironsi's death and Gowon's accession to power. (Buhari subsequently played a leading role in the coups of July 1975 that deposed Gowon and the one of December 1983 that deposed Shagari.) Buhari saw active service in the Civil War, performing in both regimental and staff roles as Adjutant, Brigade Major, Battalion CO, and Brigade Commander. Like many of his contemporaries, promotion rates during the war were rapid, but with a significant disparity between ranks and responsibilities. Promoted Captain in January 1968 and Major two years later, he was Assistant Adjutant General at HQ First Division from 1971 to 1972, and attended the Defence Services Staff College in Wellington, India, in 1973. On his return to Nigeria in 1974, he was appointed acting Director of Supply and Transport at Army HQ as a Lieutenant-Colonel. As previously mentioned, he played a key role in the coup that removed Gowon from power, and was appointed Military Governor of the then North Eastern State, remaining there as Governor of Borno State after the state-creation exercise in February 1976. Shortly thereafter, Buhari was appointed Federal Commissioner for Petroleum and Natural Resources by Obasanjo, and, following the creation of the Nigerian National Petroleum Corporation in 1977, became that body's first Chairman. As part of the transition to civilian rule, Buhari returned to purely military duties as Military Secretary at Army Headquarters in 1978, and became a member of the Supreme Military Council the same year. Following the handover of power to the civilian Shagari administration, Buhari, now a Colonel, attended the US Army War College in Pennsylvania in 1980. Upon his return to Nigeria, he held no fewer than three divisional GOC appointments, commanding successively the Fourth Infantry (now defunct), the Second Mechanised and the Third Armoured Divisions; it was in the last of these that he distinguished himself, leading the offensive against an incursion by Chadian troops into

Nigerian territory. Deploying his divisional headquarters forward from Jos to Maiduguri, he not only rapidly repulsed the incursion but also pressed forward onto Chadian territory, which earned him the displeasure of his political masters in Lagos. He was serving as GOC of the Third Armoured Division at the time of his appointment as Head of State.[1]

The new regime immediately swung into action to address the twin evils of indiscipline and corruption. On 20 March 1984, Idiagbon, the Chief of Staff at Supreme Headquarters, launched the government's War Against Indiscipline (WAI). Henceforth, perpetrators of "typical" Nigerian behaviour such as lateness, failure to queue, strewing litter in public and private, and breaking traffic laws with impunity would result in swift and sure retribution to the offender (including corporal punishment). The last Saturday of the month was declared Environmental Sanitation Day, and no vehicular traffic was permitted until late morning so that the populace could clean their surroundings at home. (This statute endures more than thirty years later.) The Shagari-era politicians were rounded up in the hundreds. The government set up military tribunals to try the erring politicians and officials, and although each of the tribunals had one judicial member, the majority of them were military officers. Furthermore, the decisions of these tribunals were not subject to the country's appellate courts — the only appeal possible was to the SMC. And, as if all that wasn't bad enough, the presumption of innocence until proven guilty was turned on its head, and it was now up to the suspects to prove their innocence of the charges leveled against them. In protest, the Nigerian Bar Association (NBA) forbade its members from appearing before the tribunals. Not surprisingly, several politicians (and at least one army officer, Colonel Peter Obasa, erstwhile director of the NYSC) were found guilty and sentenced to long periods of imprisonment, many in excess of twenty years. Whilst the government very firmly dealt with all those individuals it managed to lay its hands on, there were also several politicians who had either not been in the country at the time of the coup, or who had managed to slip away before they could be arrested. Prominent among these were the former Transport Minister Umaru Dikko; the former Attorney General, Richard Akinjide; the National Chairman of the NPN, Adisa Akinloye; and the former Senate President, Joseph Wayas. Many of them kept their heads down and tried not to draw too much attention to themselves; the exception to this rule was Dikko, who took every opportunity to lambast the new regime in Nigeria, granting several interviews to the media in Britain and beyond from his place of exile in London. That he was the Minister in the previous regime whose name was most closely associated with corruption only made things worse from the government's point of view. Dikko's attacks could not have endeared him to the new regime, and must have increased its yearning to silence him permanently. This was almost certainly the origin of the infamous Dikko affair (see below).

The regime's robust, take-no-prisoners approach extended to all those it saw as standing in the way of its redemptive mission. The infamous Decree No. 2 of 1984 gave the Chief of Staff, Supreme Headquarters the authority to detain persons he regarded as security risks for up to three months, renewable at his discretion, without charge or trial. The increasingly vocal opposition to the regime within civil society, by figures such as Beko Ransome-Kuti, Tai Solarin, and Haroun Adamu, resulted in their detention under this Decree.[2] Next in the firing line was the press. Decree No. 4 of 1984 made it a criminal offence to publish any article, irrespective of its veracity, that was designed to, or could, subject the federal or state governments or any public officer into ridicule or disrepute. (It is often forgotten that the same decree empowered the head of state to ban newspapers or magazines and to withdraw the licence of any electronic medium if he was satisfied that their behaviour was inimical to the public interest.)[3] Two journalists, Tunde Thompson and Nduka Irabor of *The Guardian* newspaper, were convicted and sentenced to one year's imprisonment for publishing an article (which, as it turned out, was almost entirely true) about posting senior military officers into diplomatic posts abroad. The regime thus managed, in one fell swoop, to alienate the country's press. When the medical profession's representative bodies — the Nigerian Medical Association and the Nigerian Association of Resident Doctors — had the temerity to enter into a dispute with the government, it responded by proscribing them and appointing military commandants for teaching hospitals. A similar fate befell the National Association of Nigerian Students (NANS).

Probably the most controversial step that the regime took on the law-and-order front related to illicit drugs. Decree No. 20 of 1984 imposed the death penalty on convicted drug traffickers. The decree was also made retroactive, so that those who fell afoul of it could be sentenced to death for offences committed *before* the decree became law. On 14 April 1985, three people were publicly executed by firing squad for drug trafficking, and at least one of them had committed the offence before the decree was promulgated. By refusing to set out intentions, never mind a timetable, as far as a return to civilian rule was concerned, the regime scored its own goal; whilst there was some merit in Buhari's rhetorical question as to whether it was "not more profitable to devote our time now to the task of restoring sanity to our society and making life more tolerable for our people than to the academic exercise of drawing up a timetable for the return to power to those who have only recently brought us to this economic and social precipice?"[4] It nonetheless represented an astonishing degree of myopia as far as the public mood was concerned, especially given the continued economic difficulties of inflation and unemployment. In an attempt to outflank politicians and others who had stashed huge amounts of raw cash, the regime changed Nigerian currency notes overnight, and imposed strict foreign exchange controls; one of those who fell afoul of this was the popular musician Fela Anikulapo-Kuti, arrested at the airport in September 1984 on his way out of the country to a concert tour overseas. He was subsequently sentenced to five years in prison for illegally taking foreign currency out of the country.

In foreign relations, the regime's most significant exploit was the Dikko affair referred to earlier. Umaru Dikko had proved himself to be a thorn in the side of the military elite even before Shagari's overthrow. In particular, there had been bad blood between him and Buhari stemming from Buhari's vigorous repulsion of the incursion by Chadian troops in 1983, whilst he was GOC of the Third Armoured Division. Earlier writers have described Dikko as having had Buhari put under surveillance. When Buhari complained directly to Shagari, who in turn questioned Dikko, the latter did not deny the charge, but instead advised Shagari to retire Buhari, as he could not be trusted.[5] Dikko had then made a bad case worse with his unrelenting criticism of the Buhari regime during his exile in London. In an audacious, if somewhat clumsily executed plot, elements of the Nigerian intelligence and security agencies, in collaboration with Israeli nationals who were more likely than not to have had links to that country's intelligence services, contrived to kidnap Dikko in broad daylight on the West London street in front of his house. Unfortunately for the kidnappers, his secretary had witnessed the assault and alerted the police, who in turn alerted all air and seaport terminals. The plan to ship Dikko to Nigeria aboard a Nigerian Airways cargo plane from Stansted Airport in a crate labelled as the diplomatic baggage of the Nigerian High Commission was foiled when airport customs officers — alerted by the police to be on the lookout — became suspicious of the two crates stamped "Diplomatic Baggage", which they then opened, finding a gagged and unconscious Dikko (as well as an Israeli anaesthetist) in one crate and two other Israelis in the other. The British authorities arrested several people for complicity in kidnapping Dikko, and impounded the plane. The Nigerian government retaliated by impounding a British passenger plane at Lagos airport. A tense standoff ensued until the British government released the Nigerian Airways plane, following which the British passenger plane was in turn released by the Nigerian government. Unsurprisingly, the whole incident severely strained diplomatic relations between the two countries, and the Nigerian High Commissioner was recalled to Lagos, while two High Commission officials suspected of involvement in the plot were declared persona non grata and expelled. (Full diplomatic relations between the UK and Nigeria were not restored for another two years). Four people (three Israelis and one Nigerian) were subsequently tried and convicted of involvement in the kidnap attempt and received long prison sentences.

By the middle of 1985, the government was deeply unpopular throughout the country. There were also profound divisions emerging within the regime itself. On the one side were the hardliners, Buhari and Idiagbon foremost amongst them, who were convinced that the regime was on the right track, and that the strong medicine being given to the sick patient (Nigeria), though bitter and unpalatable, was in the best long-term interests of the country's recovery. On the other side were those like Babangida and Bali, who were opposed to Decree No. 4, believing that the sentences handed out to corrupt politicians were too severe, and that the NSO had gone too far in putting even members of the SMC under surveillance. (Babangida even complained that his phones were being tapped.) In a classic demonstration of the ascetic rigidity for which he was famed,

Buhari conspicuously failed to "reward" any of the midranking and junior officers who had played roles in carrying out the coup that brought him to power with plum political appointments — and such officers, cultivated for years by Babangida, found in him a friendly ear to their complaints. Buhari may have unwittingly set the stage for the coup against him when he began an investigation into financial irregularities at the Ministry of Defence, a probe that directly threatened Babangida, who had, prior to becoming Chief of Army Staff, been the Director of Army Staff Duties and Plans. The investigation reportedly uncovered suspect financial transactions relating to the issuance of import licences under the preceding Shagari regime, involving a close ally of Babangida's, Colonel Aliyu Mohammed. That officer's explanations that these transactions had helped to raise funds to finance the coup that brought Buhari to power cut no ice with the Head of State, who retired Mohammed. As Babangida subsequently stated:

> There was a lot going in our favour.... We don't intervene when we know the climate is not good for it or the public will not welcome it. We wait until there is a (sic) frustration in the society. In all the coups, you find that there has always been one frustration or the other. Any time there is frustration we step in. And then there is demonstration welcoming the redeemers.[6]

There was now a perfect alignment of a restive public, widespread economic hardship, an alienated press, as well as a disgruntled military at both middle- and senior-rank levels, the last involving seasoned coup plotters like Babangida, Abacha, et al. The stage was set for a classic palace coup.

The plot to remove Buhari was hatched at the beginning of 1985. Although it was later described by one of the plotters as being "a collective decision of the military", this was clearly nonsense, as, by definition, a coup plot is kept within a close cabal for obvious reasons, and there is no doubt that Babangida was the moving force behind it. One of the army's most senior officers, Domkat Bali, is on record as saying that

> Hannaniya, Suleiman and I concluded among ourselves that Babangida was merely going to use the post [as Chief of Army Staff] as a launching pad to the presidency. So if we knew that early, Buhari too must have known. Yet he watched passively.

Bali goes on to claim that he warned Buhari about the plot, having been told about it by Joshua Dogonyaro and Colonel John Shagaya, only for Buhari to respond that he "had confidence in his guards' ability to do their job". Similarly, Idiagbon was reported to have been warned, in early 1985, by Colonel Chris Alli about rumours of a coup plot; Idiagbon's response, reportedly, was "Let them try".[7] On the night of 26-27 August 1985, whilst he was out of the country on pilgrimage to Saudi Arabia, they took him at his word.

Perhaps unsurprisingly for a coup whose planner-in-chief was the Chief of Army Staff, supported by key players such as Abacha, and greatly assisted by Idiagbon's absence from the country, the overthrow of Buhari was fairly swift and easily accomplished. Majors Abubakar Umar, Abdulmumuni Aminu, Lawan Gwadabe, and Sambo Dasuki, all strong Babangida loyalists, arrested Buhari in Dodan Barracks on the evening of 26 August. Brigadier Joshua Dogonyaro made an initial radio announcement at dawn on 27 August announcing the dissolution of the three main organs of government: the SMC, the Federal Executive Council, and the National Council of States. He lamented what he described as:

an absence of cohesion in the hierarchy of Government...[and]....a lack of unanimity of purpose among the ruling body. Subsequently,... the ruling body, the Supreme Military Council, has, therefore, progressively been made redundant by the actions of a select few members charged with the day-to-day implementation of the SMC's policies and plans.

This was followed up later in the day by another broadcast by Abacha that formally announced Buhari's overthrow and Babangida's appointment as the new President (a first for a military regime in Nigeria). Later that evening, the new President made his maiden broadcast to the nation, in which he laid bare the extent of the schism within Buhari's SMC that had led to his ouster, and which is worth quoting from at some length:

Let me at this point attempt to make you understand the premise upon which it became necessary to change the leadership. The principles of discussions, consultation and co-operation which should have guided the decision-making process of the Supreme Military Council and the Federal Executive Council were disregarded soon after the government settled down in 1984...it turned out that Major General Muhammadu Buhari was too rigid and uncompromising in his attitudes to issues of national significance. Efforts to make him understand that a diverse polity like Nigeria required recognition and appreciation of differences in both cultural and individual perceptions, only served to aggravate those attitudes...Major General Tunde Idiagbon was similarly inclined in that respect. As Chief of Staff, Supreme Headquarters, he failed to exhibit the appropriate disposition demanded by his position. He arrogated to himself absolute knowledge of problems and solutions, and acted in accordance with what was convenient to him, using the machinery of government as his tool. A combination of these characteristics in the two most important persons holding the nation's vital offices became impossible to contend with".[8]

Babangida went on to announce the immediate retirement of Buhari and Idiagbon from the army, as well as that of Lawal Rafindadi, the NSO's Director-General. The NSO was to be "overhauled and reorganized". He also announced the immediate repeal of Decree No. 4 and the release of those convicted and imprisoned under this decree. The issue of political detainees would be looked into "with despatch". The new regime would also review economic issues such as countertrade, negotiations with the International Monetary Fund (IMF), and the structural adjustment of the Nigerian economy. He promised that "fundamental rights and civil liberties will be respected", but also warned that "their exercise must not degenerate into irrational expression nor border on subversion". He, however, omitted telling the nation that one of his first acts upon coming to power was to reverse his friend Aliyu Mohammed's retirement order, and to reinstate him in the army at his former rank. (Mohammed subsequently went on to become, briefly, Chief of Army Staff.)

Muhammadu Buhari was in office as Nigeria's Head of State for some twenty months. He took over from a thoroughly discredited civilian regime that had done its best to run Nigeria's economy aground by a combination of rampant corruption and profound mismanagement. The farce that passed for the massively and blatantly rigged 1983 elections raised the spectre of the First Republic: there were simply no legitimate means available to the Nigerian electorate to eject a discredited government from office. The Buhari regime came into power, therefore, on a massive tide of goodwill of tsunami proportions and yet managed to squander this within those twenty short months (or perhaps even less), such that it was so easily ousted from office. There are a number of reasons for this.

First, Babangida had a point in his characterization of the personalities of Buhari and Idiagbon in his maiden speech. Ascetic, rigid, and uncompromising, they failed to grasp the simple fact that in order to *effectively* exercise power you have to *both* remain in office *and* carry people along, starting, in a military regime, with your colleagues in the armed forces. Second, Buhari and Idiagbon were no doubt motivated by a strong desire to expunge, as they saw it, the numerous ills afflicting the Nigerian society, but in their zeal, they almost killed the patient with the treatment. The manner in which they pursued the undoubtedly venal politicians was neither the most effective nor the most legitimate path they could have pursued, and had the effect of making the politicians look like the victims rather than the offenders (a pattern which appears to be repeating itself, three decades later, with a civilian President Buhari). Third, sweeping hordes of people into detention did not endear the regime to the masses, and the failure to effectively come to grips with the deteriorating economy did not help. Fourth, gratuitously alienating professional groups such as the medical and legal professions, not to mention the press, was both unnecessary and counterproductive. Fifth, and perhaps most importantly, alienating the very people who had brought them to power (the middle-ranking officers who had in fact physically executed the December 1983 coup) was unwise, and they compounded that initial folly by ignoring the rumours and warnings about an impending coup. The tensions within the SMC itself arose from a combination of individual and institutional factors. Bali perhaps put it best when he said that

> ...it was more like a power struggle between IBB and Buhari.... Idiagbon is also a man of integrity but the mistake he made was that he took his job far too seriously. At a point, he almost became like a bully...he became disrespectful to people who were senior to him. In fact, he was responsible for some of the problems that were later used as excuse for the overthrow of the Buhari regime.[9]

Finally, whilst the Dikko affair was a bold and imaginative attempt to get hold of one of the worst offenders (as they saw it) as far as corruption in the Shagari administration was concerned, the ham-fisted way it was executed meant that the regime's credibility on the international scene was greatly diminished — which worsened its negotiating position in its attempts to set the economy back on a sound footing.

Buhari the leader was history — for now. It remained to be seen how his successor would perform in the top job.

NOTES

1. www.Buhari2015.wordpress.com. Accessed 21/7/2016.
2. Siollun SOF p. 48.
3. Agbese, Dan. *Ibrahim Babangida: The Military, Politics and Power in Nigeria*. Adonis and Abbey Publishers, 2012, p. 183.
4. Siollun SOF p. 49.
5. Ibid p. 33.
6. Ibid pp. 51-52.
7. Ibid pp. 52-53.
8. Ibid pp. 57-58.
9. Ibid pp. 58-59.

CHAPTER 12

The Fifth Military Government: Enter Maradona

My colleagues and I are determined to change the course of history. This government is determined to unite this country. We shall not allow anything to obstruct us. We recognise that a government, be it civilian or military, needs the consent of the people to govern if it is to reach its objective. We do not intend to rule by force.

— **Ibrahim Babangida, August 1985**

Born in Minna on 17 August 1941, and known at various times in his earlier life as Ibrahim Maigari, Ibrahim Maigari Wushishi, Ibrahim Muhammadu, and Ibrahim Badamasi, Ibrahim Badamasi Babangida (as he has been known since he was commissioned into the army in 1963) was the elder of the two surviving children of Muhammadu Badamasi and Aishatu. His father's family was originally from Sokoto, and his grandfather Ibrahim eventually settled in Wushishi after leading an itinerant life that took him to various places, including Kano and Kontagora. He settled down when he married Halima; and their second child, and eldest son, Muhammadu Badamasi, became the messenger to the District Officer in Minna. Babangida's parents divorced when he was a young child, and they both died within a couple of years of each other, when Babangida and his younger sister Hannatu were still young children. Their paternal grandmother Halima, who had by this time also moved from Wushishi to Minna, brought them both up. Young Ibrahim attended the Gwari Native Authority School in Minna between 1950 and 1956 and the Provincial Secondary School in Bida between 1957 and 1962 (where he became Head Boy). His classmates at school included those who would become his fellow army officers: Abdulsalami Abubakar, Garba Duba, Gado Nasko, Mohammed Magoro, Sani Sami, Mamman Vatsa, and Sani Bello; all with the exception of Bello, would became generals, and several of them would cross paths with Babangida in the coup-plotting business. The government of the Northern Region, led by the Premier, Sir Ahmadu Bello, made strong and consistent efforts to persuade Northern schoolboys to sign up for a military career, and visited the Bida Provincial Secondary School twice in 1962 alone. Old Boys of the school who were already in the army included the likes of Muhammed Inuwa Wushishi, Ibrahim Taiwo, and Garba Dada. Among the politicians visiting the school to encourage the boys to enlist was the Minister of State for Defence, Ibrahim Tako Galadima (accompanied on one occasion by a handsome, smartly dressed young Captain named Yakubu Gowon).[1]

Babangida and his friends sat and passed the entrance exam to the Nigerian Military Training College (NMTC) in July 1962. (Note that the NPC-led federal government had by this time instituted a quota such that 50 percent of all entrants to the NMTC, as well as those on the final pass list, were to be from the North.) Together with Sami, Duba, Magoro, Bello, Vatsa, and Nasko, and after overcoming his family's objections to his choice of a military career, Babangida reported at NMTC on 10 December 1962 to enroll in Course Six. On completing basic training at NMTC (where he first came across a young cadet called Sani Abacha), Babangida was sent to the Indian Military Academy in Uttar Pradesh, India, where, on 26 September 1963, he was commissioned as a Second Lieutenant in the Royal Nigerian Army, as it was then known. Upon his return to Nigeria in January 1964, Babangida was posted to the First Recce Squadron in Kaduna. Having been rated by the directing staff in Uttar Pradesh with a C-minus (a low average), Babangida was interviewed on his arrival by the Brigade Commander, Brigadier Ademulegun, and informed that he was to be placed on probation for a year, with quarterly reports to assess his progress; the consequences of unsatisfactory progress did not need to be spelled out.[2] Fortunately for the young subaltern, the officer commanding the Recce Squadron, Captain Isong, took Babangida under his wing, and under his tutelage, Babangida blossomed to the extent that he was deemed to have made such satisfactory progress after six months that his probationary period was terminated on Ademulegun's recommendation. (For his pains, Isong would be murdered by men from his own unit in the July 1966 coup, in which Babangida was involved.)

Babangida's Recce Squadron, now under the command of Major Hassan Katsina, was involved in the pacification of the Tiv area in late 1964 following riots in the lead up to the federal parliamentary elections of December 1964; and Babangida, as a Troop Commander, received a commendation for his role in this Internal Security (IS) operation. The following year, in late 1965, Babangida's Recce Squadron was again deployed on another IS operation, this time to the Western Region, after widespread rioting broke out there in the wake of the massively rigged regional elections. The unit returned to its base in Kaduna on 12 January 1966. By now a Lieutenant, Babangida had not long returned from a night on the town in Kaduna in the early hours of Saturday, 15 January 1966, when his fellow subaltern in the Squadron, Lieutenant Chris Ugokwe, woke him up with news of Nigeria's first coup.[3] The new federal military government was only a few days old when Babangida left Nigeria for the UK to attend the Armoured Corps' Young Officers Course. By the time he returned to the country some four months later, there was a palpable air of tension within the army and throughout the country, arising largely from the increasingly widely held belief in Northern circles that the January coup was part and parcel of a broader plot by the Igbos to dominate Nigeria. Babangida was very much part of the conspiracy of Northern soldiers that led to the countercoup of 29 July 1966 that in turn led to Ironsi's overthrow and demise and ultimately to Gowon's accession to power (see chapter 4). It proved to be the first of several coup plots that he became involved in, either as conspirator or as intended victim.

When the Civil War broke out in July 1967, Babangida was back in the UK, this time the Armoured Vehicle Instructor Course. Along with many officers who were abroad on courses, he was hastily recalled and posted to the Twenty-first Battalion in the First Division area of operations. He subsequently took over command of the Forty-fourth Battalion and was promoted Captain in 1968. By this time, Babangida's reputation as an officer deeply concerned about the welfare of troops under his command was well entrenched, and the circumstances of the war made this concern stand out even more. Agbese recounts an incident where Babangida stood up for a soldier, a mess steward, whom he, Babangida, felt was being unfairly and harshly treated by a more senior officer, to the point that a shouting match ensued, and a physical altercation appeared imminent.[4] In April 1969, and by now a Major, Babangida was wounded in action near Uzuakoli, sustaining a gunshot wound to his chest. He was evacuated to the Lagos University Teaching Hospital, where he underwent treatment. This unwanted reminder of his mortality appears to have awakened Babangida's mind to the need to marry and start a family, and in September 1969, the twenty-eight year-old Major Ibrahim Babangida married Miss Maria Okogwu in Kaduna (she subsequently converted to Islam and changed her first name to Maryam). Babangida returned to the front after his wedding, and resumed battalion command until the end of the war.

In August 1970, Babangida was posted to the Nigerian Defence Academy in Kaduna as a Company Commander. He attended the Company Commanders Course at British Army School of Infantry later the same year, and returned to NDA, where he remained until 1972. Promoted Lieutenant-Colonel, he attended an Advanced Armoured Officers Course in the US, and on his return to Nigeria in 1973, assumed command of the Fourth Recce Squadron, then based in Badagry. He was in this role when Lieutenant-Colonel Shehu Yar'Adua recruited him into the plot to depose Gowon (see chapter 7). Once this was accomplished, Babangida was appointed a member of Murtala Muhammed's Supreme Military Council. He was, at barely thirty-four years old, its youngest member, and he was to remain a member of the SMC until power was handed over to the civilian Shagari government four years later. This early and prolonged exposure to the inner workings of the highest level of government offered an unparalleled opportunity to look, listen, and learn; and Babangida proved that he was not a dull pupil. He learned the art of building coalitions in order to get things done, best exemplified by his careful preparatory lobbying of his fellow SMC members (Yar'Adua prominent among them) to ensure that, in its consideration in February 1976 of the report of the Irikefe Panel on State Creation, the SMC designated Babangida's adopted hometown of Minna (and not Bida, as recommended by the panel) as the capital of the soon-to-be-created Niger State. In return, he supported Yar'Adua's opposition to carving out Katsina State from the then North Central State.[5]

On the morning of Friday, 13 February 1976, Babangida arrived at his office at the Ministry of Defence with a strategy in mind for the planned demobilization of the army, which was to be discussed at a meeting of the army's top brass. All his notions were very quickly dispelled. Informed of the coup against the Muhammed regime,

Babangida was ordered by the Chief of Army Staff, Danjuma, to "flush out" Dimka from the radio station where he was broadcasting news of the regime's overthrow. Realising that armour would be the key factor in the success or failure of the coup, Babangida headed to the Ikeja Cantonment to both deny it to the plotters and to use the armoured vehicles there to accomplish the task of dislodging Dimka from the radio station, for Danjuma had made it clear that the station was to be levelled, if necessary. Now at the head of an armoured column, Babangida made his way to the radio station, where he tried to persuade Dimka — an old friend whom he has described as being under the influence of alcohol at the time — to surrender. He was unsuccessful in this, and he went to Bonny Camp (whence Danjuma had by now removed himself) to report; Danjuma sent him back with a flea in his ear, repeating that his orders were that Dimka be flushed out, and not negotiated with. Suitably chastened, Babangida gave orders for the plotters to be dislodged from the station, a task that, by many accounts, was actually led not by Babangida himself but by Lieutenant-Colonel Chris Ugokwe (who had awakened Babangida in Kaduna ten years earlier with news of the Nzeogwu coup) and Majors Shagaya and Jimmy Ojokojo.[6] Either way, the coup was foiled, but Babangida's reputation for calmness and bravery under pressure was greatly enhanced. Babangida was much taken aback by the fact that several of those implicated in the coup (Majors Dabang, Gagara, and Kasai) were protégés of his; worse still was the fact that they had apparently been the most vocal in pressing upon their fellow conspirators the need to eliminate Babangida if the coup was to succeed.

Between January and July 1977, Babangida attended the Second Senior Officers Course at the then Army (later Armed Forces) Command and Staff College, Jaji. Promoted Colonel in 1977, Temporary Brigadier in August 1978 and Substantive Brigadier the following March, Babangida was one of the pioneer students at the Nigerian Institute for Policy and Strategic Studies in July 1979. The following year, he attended the US Navy Postgraduate School for a Defence Management Course. In 1981, Babangida was appointed to the position of Director of Army Staff Duties and Plans, one of the Principal Staff Officers at Army HQ. Promoted Major General in March 1983, less than twenty years after first being commissioned, he was appointed Chief of Army Staff following the coup that toppled the Shagari regime at the end of 1983. Now, just over two years later, he was in the top job.

Babangida has been described by one writer as

the first Nigerian ruler to come to power by design rather than by chance. He was at that time the only Nigerian military leader that actively sought political power prior to coming into office, prepared for it and waited patiently for it to come his way.[7]

The first order of business was to demonstrate that, whilst he might have been a senior member of the Buhari regime, he was definitely *not* Buhari Mark II. His first steps suggested that this was, indeed, the case. He took on the title of President, which no military leader had done before; as subsequent events were to demonstrate, this was no accident of nomenclature. The former Supreme Military Council was now to be known as the Armed Forces Ruling Council (AFRC). Supreme Headquarters became General Headquarters, and its Chief of Staff, the regime's number two man, was now to be known as the Chief of General Staff (CGS). Babangida, in a shrewd political move, appointed an Igbo naval officer, Commodore Ebitu Ukiwe, to this post. Major-General Bali now became, in addition to being Defence Minister, the Chairman of the Joint Chiefs of Staff. Abacha was rewarded for his support for the coup by being made Chief of Army Staff in succession to Babangida, while Rear Admiral Augustus Aikhomu and Air Vice Marshal Ibrahim Alfa were reappointed to head the navy and the air force respectively. Clearly determined to avoid making the same mistake that Buhari had made in not rewarding those who had executed the coup that brought him to power, the AFRC — whilst retaining all but three members of Buhari's SMC (Buhari himself, Idiagbon, and Mohammed Magoro) — was expanded in size to make room for Ibrahim Badamasi Babangida (IBB) loyalists such as Colonels Haliru Akilu and Raji Rasaki as well as Lieutenant-Colonel John Shagaya. Space was found for others as ministers (Lieutenant-Colonels Tanko Ayuba and Anthony Ukpo) or state governors (Lieutenant-Colonels David Mark and Chris Garuba, Majors Abdulmumuni Aminu and Abubakar Umar).

Babangida actively courted the press in his early days. Apart from repealing Decree No. 4 and releasing Irabor and Thompson, he made himself available to journalists on an informal basis, and created the impression of having an open-door consultative approach to governance. This was perhaps best demonstrated by the way he actively welcomed public opinion and comment on the question of whether Nigeria should seek a bailout from the International Monetary Fund (IMF). Correctly calculating that the Nigerian public's pride would be affronted by what they perceived as the international financial community's sticking its nose into Nigeria's business, the groundswell of opinion was against seeking the IMF loan, so Babangida announced that the loan had been rejected; instead, Nigeria would implement a home-grown Structural Adjustment Programme (SAP), which almost certainly caused greater hardship to Nigerians than the IMF loan would have done. This, from Babangida's point of view, didn't matter much; what mattered was that he had established his credentials as "the listening President". Other populist measures included suspending the executions of drug dealers under Decree No. 20, reviewing the convictions and sentences of the politicians jailed under the Buhari regime (then releasing them), releasing the jailed musician Fela Anikulapo-Kuti (the health minister's brother), and quickly setting a date (1990) for a return to civilian rule (this last would come back to haunt him). He also followed through on his promise to "overhaul and reorganise" the feared NSO, throwing open to the public its cells and detention centres, and splitting it into three separate organisations: the State Security Service for domestic intelligence and security matters, the National Intelligence Agency for external intelligence and security, and the Defence Intelligence Agency for the same functions within the armed forces. Trade unions such as the NMA and the NLC and bodies such as the NANS were brought in from the cold. Traditional rulers were flattered and celebrated.

There was a decidedly populist and political influence in his cabinet choices. Serving and retired military officers were strongly represented (Akinrinade, Bali, Vatsa, Patrick Koshoni, Nasko, Useni), as were civilian technocrats and intellectuals such as Professors Bolaji Akinyemi, Tam David-West, Jubril Aminu, Olikoye Ransome-Kuti, and Emmanuel Emovon, as well as Prince Bola Ajibola, erstwhile President of the NBA who had clashed with the Buhari regime on the tribunals issue. All, it seemed, was rosy — but Babangida, seasoned coup plotter that he was by now, knew better. He is quoted as having said:

> When I became the President, there were about 23 of us who were the coup plotters at that time and immediately the coup was successful, I sat the 23 of us together and said: congratulations, we made it but remember one thing, just like we took up guns and toppled a government, we also have to watch because somebody would one day want to topple us....[8]

Possibly not even he realized how prophetic those words would be.

In December 1985, barely four months after the coup that brought Babangida to power, the Defence Minister and Chairman of the Joint Chiefs, Major-General Domkat Bali, announced that the government had uncovered a coup plot involving officers from all three services; a week later, the Information Minister, Lieutenant-Colonel Anthony Ukpo, named those arrested — to the shock of many, among them Babangida's childhood friend, classmate, course mate, AFRC member, and Minister of the Federal Capital Territory, Major-General Mamman Vatsa. This reported plot was the first time officers from the navy and air force had been arrested for involvement in a coup in Nigeria (air force officers Shittu Alao and Mukhtar Mohammed had been involved in the conspiracies to overthrow Ironsi in July 1966 and Gowon in July 1975, but as those coups were successful, the officers were not arrested). A special investigation panel was set up, headed by another of Babangida and Vatsa's schoolmates, Major-General Sani Sami, which generated a list of suspects sent for trial by a Special Military Tribunal (SMT), headed by Major-General Charles Ndiomu. Defendants were convicted on evidence ranging from confessions by some, through fellow defendants' implications of others, to, at best, equivocal and circumstantial evidence against others — Vatsa among them. Thirteen defendants, including Vatsa, were sentenced to death. The AFRC, the sole reviewing authority under the decree that set up the SMT, met to consider the fate of the defendants. There was widespread clamour in civil society for mercy, and prominent writers such as Chinua Achebe, Wole Soyinka, and JP Clark, met with Babangida to urge him to spare their fellow poet, Vatsa. It was all to no avail. In a nationwide broadcast in the evening of 5 March 1986, Bali announced that Vatsa and nine others had been executed (by firing squad at Kirikiri Prison) "about an hour ago"; three others, Majors Moses Effiong, Tobias Akwashiki, and Edwin-West had their death sentences commuted to life imprisonment. The entire episode proved to have long-term ramifications for the armed forces and for the country. For the first time, service personnel had been tried and shot for *planning*, as opposed to actually carrying out a coup. The involvement of air force officers led to the air force being starved of funds by the regime, dramatically adversely impacting on its operational effectiveness. The case against Vatsa in particular continued to generate controversy, especially after Bali, some twenty years after the fact, publicly voiced his doubts about Vatsa's guilt and whether he ought to have been executed. (Some might ask questions about whether this represented a failure of moral courage on Bali's part for not speaking up at the material time.) In any case, if Babangida thought the Vatsa case would put an end of the controversies trailing his regime, he was very much mistaken.

Whilst the Vatsa coup issue was still ongoing, the Babangida regime became embroiled in another stormy issue, this time one that was entirely of Babangida's own making. Nigeria's history with the Organisation of the Islamic Conference (OIC) — now known as the Organisation of Islamic Cooperation — goes back to the summit held in Rabat, Morocco, in 1969, where the OIC was founded. A group of senior Nigerian clerics attended the conference; Gowon, preoccupied by the Civil War, but fully aware of the contentious nature of religious issues in Nigeria, had no appetite for stirring up any form of religious controversy and wrote to the corresponding Head of State and the conference's host, King Hassan of Morocco, to make it clear that the delegation was not an official Nigerian government delegation. The Nigerian clerics, led by Alhaji Abubakar Gumi, the then Grand Khadi of Northern Nigeria, were not admitted to the conference as delegates, but were allowed in as observers; subsequent Nigerian governments have resisted any change from this observer status to full membership.

Nigeria was invited to the OIC meeting scheduled to take place (again in Morocco, this time in Fez) in January 1986. Ordinarily, the procedure would be an instruction from the Ministry of External Affairs to the Nigerian Ambassador to attend the meeting as an observer. On this occasion, however, the Permanent Secretary in the Ministry took the invitation directly to Babangida, bypassing the Minister, Professor Bolaji Akinyemi. Babangida authorized the attendance of a Nigerian delegation at the conference, with full diplomatic cover, a decision about which Akinyemi was once again kept in the dark. The delegation, headed by the Minister of Mines and Power, Rilwanu Lukman, and which included Gumi, Alhaji Alhaji (a federal Permanent Secretary), Abdulkadir Ahmed (the Central Bank Governor), and Ibrahim Dasuki (the future Sultan of Sokoto), promptly applied for Nigeria's admission as a full member of the OIC, which was immediately granted (waiving the usual one-year waiting period stipulated in the OIC's own constitution). The matter was never formally tabled or discussed at the AFRC and so, when the story broke, senior members of the government — such as the Chief of General Staff (CGS), Commodore Ukiwe, and the Information Minister, Anthony Ukpo — denied it. The news created a huge furor, with Christians demanding that Nigeria's membership be withdrawn and Muslims in turn insisting that Nigeria must remain a member. In what would soon become familiar as a classic Babangida manoeuvre, he sought to defuse the tension (and kick the matter into the long grass) by appointing a panel, headed by one of his loyalists Lieutenant-Colonel John Shagaya, a Christian army officer from Plateau State, to report on Nigeria's membership in the OIC. Unsurprisingly, the report never saw the light of day.[9] The episode, however, sowed the seeds of future turbulence within the regime, which would soon come to a head.

The Chief of General Staff, Commodore Ukiwe, had been vociferous in his criticism of the OIC affair. Although the number two man in the regime, as a Commodore he was outranked by all the Service Chiefs (Abacha, Alfa, and Aikhomu); and his relationship with Abacha in particular was less than harmonious. The situation was further complicated by the fact that Ukiwe was, in terms of length of service, actually senior to all of them (and indeed also to Babangida), but had lost seniority upon his readmission to the navy after fighting on the Biafran side in the Civil War. The OIC affair had created bad blood, and events surrounding the twenty-sixth Independence Anniversary Parade on 1 October 1986 made matters worse. In protocol terms, as the number two man, Ukiwe should have arrived at the parade immediately before Babangida; the official programme for the event, however, had him arriving before Abacha. Ukiwe insisted that normal protocol be followed, and made it clear that if the proposed programme was not changed, he would refuse to attend the event. It was not, and he stuck to his guns and did not attend. This gave his enemies within the regime, led principally by Abacha, the opportunity they had been waiting for to engineer his removal from the position as Chief of General Staff. Ukiwe was retired and replaced by Aikhomu as CGS, with Rear Admiral Patrick Koshoni succeeding Aikhomu as Chief of Naval Staff. (Babangida made other changes to the AFRC at the same time, including replacing the Inspector-General of Police, dropping some members, appointing some new faces — including one of his protégés David Mark and his old school classmate Garba Duba — and expanding the AFRC membership overall by two.)

The dust had barely settled on these ructions at the highest levels of the government when the country was rocked by an event the likes of which had never been seen before in Nigeria. On 19 October 1986, Dele Giwa, one of Nigeria's leading journalists and the Editor-in-Chief of *Newswatch*, was blown up and killed by a letter bomb as he opened a parcel that ostensibly came from Babangida's office. Giwa and his colleagues, like many journalists, had initially enjoyed an amicable relationship with the regime, but, in recent months, that relationship had soured, with Giwa being questioned by various security agencies about several allegations (e.g., that he had obtained and was intending to publish the judgment of the military tribunal that condemned Vatsa and his colleagues to death, that he had planned to import arms into the country and foment a socialist revolution or that he planned to publish a story about Ukiwe's removal from office). The day prior to Giwa's death, his wife had taken a phone call from Colonel Haliru Akilu, the Director of Military Intelligence, who had asked for the exact address of Giwa's residence and for a physical description of the house because "Babangida's ADC would come by later to drop off an item for Giwa". The envelope delivered to the house was described as "heavy and bore a white sticker with Dele Giwa's name and address written on it. The sticker also bore the Nigerian coat of arms and an inscription 'From the office of the C-IN-C'. It was also marked 'secret and confidential' and warned that it should only be opened by the addressee"[10] Giwa's teenage son, who was described as "having received a similar parcel in the past for his father from the President", received the parcel and took the parcel to his father, (in his study with the magazine's London correspondent), with fatal results. The government promised to leave no stone unturned in order to get to the truth of the matter; almost three decades later, the case remains unsolved, and nobody has been brought to justice for Giwa's death. There remains a lingering suspicion, however, that the regime was responsible for his death.

As mentioned earlier, Babangida set the date of 1 October 1990 for a return to civilian rule. In apparent furtherance of this aim, he set up a political bureau, under the leadership of Dr. Samuel J. Cookey, to conduct a review of Nigeria's political history in order (i) to identify the problems which had impaired the country's political development and recommend ways of solving them, (ii) to identify a basic philosophy to guide future government activities, and (iii) to gather, collate, and evaluate contributions from the Nigerian public in order to a debate the way forward politically. He warned the seventeen-member bureau that he was not interested in "a regurgitation of the political models of the so-called advanced countries of the world". Over the nine months following the inauguration of the bureau on 13 January 1986, it met 149 times, and visited all 301 local government areas then in existence in the country, receiving almost 15,000 memoranda and 2,000 oral submissions.[11] Fourteen months later, the bureau submitted its report to the government (but not before the same government had announced, five months into the bureau's task, a ten-year blanket ban on *all* former public office holders since independence, with the exception of civilians who had served in military regimes). Notwithstanding Babangida's warning about not "regurgitating" political models from the "so-called advanced countries", the bureau recommended the same US-style executive presidential system that the country had run between 1979 and 1983. It recommended a transition programme towards achieving this end, designed to be "a training process that would eradicate the ills of Nigeria's political system". The majority of the bureau concurred with Babangida's stated exit date of 1 October 1990, but a minority disagreed, suggesting 1 October 1992 instead, on the basis that they did not believe the 1990 date allowed enough time for the transition programme to be successfully completed. The bureau also made recommendations that included having a two-party state (with the parties largely funded by government), a single five-year term for the president, a unicameral legislature; also creating more states, rejecting the zoning principle, allocating 10 percent of the seats in the legislature for women and labour leaders, and creating an agency for mass social mobilization. Babangida set up an AFRC committee under Major-General Paul Omu to consider the bureau's report and to make recommendations to the AFRC thereon. This committee recommended an end date of 1 October 1995 for the transition programme; however, the AFRC decided on the 1992 date. It also accepted the recommendations for a presidential-style government and for a mass mobilization agency, but rejected the recommendation for a single five-year term for the presidency.

On 7 September 1987, Babangida inaugurated a Constitution Review Committee (CRC) to examine any problematic details in the 1979 Constitution, headed by Mr. Justice Buba Ardo. When the CRC reported back to the government in March 1988, it concluded that "From the memoranda received from the public, the political bureau's findings and input from Government, it seems reasonable to conclude that there was nothing fundamentally wrong with the 1979 Constitution".[12] On 11 May 1988, Babangida inaugurated a partly elected, partly appointed Constituent Assembly under the chairmanship of retired Supreme Court judge, Mr. Justice Anthony Aniagolu. Babangida warned them that certain aspects of the draft Constitution, such as "federalism, presidentialism, the non-adoption of any state religion...the two-party system, the ban or disqualification placed on certain persons from participating in politics..." were off-limits, and that the Assembly should not waste time trying to change them.

In the meantime, on 23 September 1987, Babangida created two new states, Akwa Ibom out of Cross River, and Katsina out of Kaduna, thus bringing the total number of states to twenty-one. At the same time, he extended the ban on participation in politics to include all former public officials (whether civil servants, police, and military personnel) and businessmen who had been found guilty of corruption or abuse of office; they were all banned from politics for life. All politicians who had held elective, appointed, or party offices in the First and Second Republics, as well as Babangida himself (and all those who served in his administration) were banned from participation in politics until the end of the transition programme on 1 October 1992. A National Election Committee (NEC) was set up under the chairmanship of Professor Eme Awa. This body's first test was the conduct of local government elections on a nonparty basis on 12 December 1987. It was not an auspicious beginning. So egregious were the irregularities attending these elections that they had to be partly cancelled in ten states and in the Federal Capital Territory; in Lagos State, the entire election was cancelled.

A week before the submission of the draft constitution on 5 April 1989, Babangida extended the ban on participation in politics to include the members of bodies, at both federal and state levels, such as the NEC, the Code of Conduct Bureau, Mass Mobilisation for Self Reliance, Social Justice and Economic Recovery (MAMSER), the National Population Commission, and the Directorate of Food, Roads and Rural Infrastructure (DFRRI). This particular ban would last until the end of the transition programme in order "to create an environment for free and fair elections during the transition period and in order to ensure total impartiality on the part of the key institutions charged with central elements in the political transition programme".[13]   On 3 May 1989, the AFRC met to consider the draft constitution. That same evening, in a nationwide broadcast, Babangida announced the lifting of the ban on politics (save for those groups of people previously excluded) and also announced the new Constitution. The draft constitution submitted by the Constituent Assembly a month earlier had been significantly modified by the AFRC. Gone were the provisions for financial autonomy for the judiciary, the restoration of the position of head of the civil service, the single six-year term for the president, and the criminalisation of any take-over of the government via extraconstitutional means.

The resumption of political activity was being overseen by a new NEC Chairman, Professor Humphrey Nwosu, Awa having been fired on 28 February 1989; Awa had apparently come off second best in a power struggle with the AFRC as to which body the NEC or the AFRC was vested with the authority to approve and register the two political parties provided by the constitution. The NEC set stringent conditions for the registration of political parties. By the expiry of the 19 July 1989 deadline for the submission of applications, thirteen organisations had submitted applications; of these, the NEC forwarded a shortlist of six of these to the AFRC for consideration, however, adding the rider that it did not believe any one of them fulfilled all the required criteria for registration. It came as no surprise that the AFRC, on 7 October 1989, declined to approve any of the six parties put forward by the NEC; the real surprise was Babangida's announcement, in a nationwide broadcast the same evening, that the AFRC was going to create the two parties itself.

The National Republican Convention (NRC) was described as being "a little to the right", whilst the Social Democratic Party (SDP) was "a little to the left". The parties were going to be funded entirely by the government, leading to accusations that they would be nothing more than yet another pair of government parastatals. The NEC was directed to write the constitutions and manifestoes of both parties, which were duly submitted to the government on 3 November 1989, and the government released them a month later.

Notwithstanding all of this political activity, there were still several members of the armed forces, mainly members of Babangida's kitchen cabinet (the so-called IBB Boys), who were not persuaded that the politicians could be entrusted with running the country on their own, and they began to advocate an arrangement whereby the country would be run by a succession of military men transformed into civilian leaders, along the lines of the Egyptian experience. These officers, the IBB Boys, prominent amongst them the likes of Mark, Akilu, Gwadabe, Shagaya, Umar, Ogbeha, Rasaki, Dasuki, and Aminu, had undoubtedly been beneficiaries of Babangida's accession to the top job, and it is tempting to conclude that their wariness of a return to civil rule was underpinned by their unwillingness to give up the perks of their close association with power. Tempting, but perhaps not entirely justified, given the inescapable evidence (at the material time and subsequently) that the political class had not learned any lessons from the catastrophic decisions of the First and Second Republics. Whichever school of thought one belonged to, what was not in doubt was that Babangida empowered these officers with a degree of influence that far outstripped their ranks or nominal positions, and sowed the seeds of what a future Chief of Army Staff, Salihu Ibrahim, was to one day describe as "an Army of anything goes", where middle-ranking officers made "decisions about the posting, career progression and retirement of their own superiors."[14]

Both country and army would pay a heavy price for this lack of sophisticated behaviour in the future.

Babangida was a keen student of the art of coup plotting, and he was determined not to repeat the mistakes of some of his predecessors (Gowon and Buhari in particular) of failing to keep his finger of the pulse of his primary constituency, the army. He had rewarded those who had carried out the coup that brought him to power with choice appointments, but he also wished to ensure that the wider armed forces felt included in the government and also felt the material benefits therefrom. In what was a first in the history of Nigeria, Babangida created, on 5 June 1989, the Armed Forces Consultative Assembly (AFCA), comprising formation and unit-level commanders, selected staff officers, and senior NCOs, with the stated objectives, amongst others:

> to constitute an information management system for the Armed Forces as a channel of communication, whereby essential information about governmental matters, directions and thinking flows down the ranks, and reactions to these filter back right up to the apex... provision of critical advice to the Presidency and the Armed Forces Ruling Council over general policies, programmes and decisions of government...provision of a sense of belonging and participation of officers and men of the Armed Forces in government....[15]

What was perhaps not stated explicitly was that the Assembly offered a means of extending the largesse of government patronage further down the chain of command (thereby reducing the resentment by those not included in the inner caucus or not holding political posts of those of their brothers in arms who received political appointments); it also offered an opportunity to keep a close eye on those who were in positions powerful enough to incite the overthrow of his regime.

The creation of the AFCA was not Babangida's first (or only) tactic to consolidate his position and his grip on power. His choice of the title of President, although claimed by some to be a spur-of-the-moment decision after the August 1985 coup that brought him to power,[16] quickly became "an instrument to concentrate ever increasing power in his hands."[17] He reserved for himself (as opposed to the AFRC or the SMC in previous governments) the right to appoint the CGS, the service chiefs and the inspector-general of police; indeed, he appointed and fired the AFRC at his pleasure, and summoned meetings of that body when it suited him to do so. In addition to being, since December 1989, Minister of Defence, the heads of all the security and intelligence agencies reported directly to him, as did the governor of the Central Bank. All the organs of the transition programme, such as the Constitution Review Committee, the Constituent Assembly, and MAMSER were brought under the presidency. During his eight years in power, Babangida sacked and reconstituted the entirety of the AFRC three times; by the time he left office, only five of the original AFRC members remained in post (Abacha, Aikhomu, Nyako, and Dogonyaro, in addition to Babangida himself). Little wonder, therefore, that Bali described the regime as "a de facto one man dictatorship."[18]

Babangida frequently shuffled his officers around from post to post, not giving anyone of them the time and opportunity to create a rival power base, and continuously retiring some in order to create room to reward and promote others to take their place. It is hard to see how the perennial game of musical chairs in command positions could have enhanced the military's operational effectiveness in carrying out its primary task of defending the sovereignty and territorial integrity of the nation.

In December 1989, Babangida conducted a reshuffle of his government that resuscitated the religious controversy from the OIC affair four years earlier. He retired the service chiefs of the navy and the air force, Koshoni and Alfa respectively, and replaced them with Nyako and Nureini Yusuf. This meant that now Babangida and all his service chiefs, as well as the inspector-general of police, the national security adviser, and the director-general of the SSS were all Muslims. Whilst this would not necessarily be an issue in and of itself elsewhere, it certainly *was* an issue in a Nigeria, where such matters were viewed through partisan lenses, and particularly more so after the OIC furor. The matter was made worse by Babangida's simultaneous removal of Bali (a Christian) from his position as Minister of Defence and Chairman of the Joint Chiefs of Staff, to be replaced as Chairman by Abacha and as Defence Minister by Babangida himself. Declining the offer of becoming Minister of the Interior, Bali chose to retire. (As a sweetener, Babangida promoted him to General in retirement.) Bali's treatment, and Ukiwe's before him, as well as the perceived bias of the Babangida regime as being in favour of Muslims, were to play a role in the genesis of an event that would rock the Babangida regime to its core and mark a turning point in the history of Nigeria and of its army.

NOTES

1. Agbese pp. 10-11, 19-20, 34-35, 38.

2. Ibid pp. 49-50.

3. Ibid p. 71.

4. Ibid p. 101.

5. Ibid p. 123.

6. Ibid p. 133.

7. Siollun SOF p. 68.

8. Ibid pp. 75-76.

9. Siollun SOF pp. 107-109; Agbese pp. 352-354.

10. Siollun SOF pp. 102-103.

11. Agbese pp. 264-265.

12. Ibid p. 274.

13. Ibid p. 276.

14. Siollun SOF p. 140.

15. Agbese p. 370.

16. Siollun SOF p. 121.

17. Ibid.

18. Ibid pp. 122-123.

CHAPTER 13

The Fifth Military Government: Shaken and Stirred

Dictators ride to and fro upon tigers from which they dare not dismount.
And the tigers are getting hungry.

— **Winston Churchill, 1937**

In the early hours of 22 April 1990, Dodan Barracks, seat of the federal military government and Babangida's official residence, was rocked by heavy fire from small arms and support weapons. Possibly the most unusual, and definitely the bloodiest, coup in Nigeria's history was under way. Almost exclusively involving officers from the Niger Delta states, carried out largely by ex-servicemen, and funded and equipped by civilian friends of the plotters, the coup caught the security-conscious regime entirely by surprise. The usual intelligence chatter that would have been generated by attempts to enlist recruits, or to obtain access to transport and weaponry from mainstream military units, was absent. Whilst the plotters had the element of surprise on their side, the need for secrecy in an oppressive security environment also meant that numbers were not on their side, and that they were therefore dangerously overstretched. Speed in isolating the key command figures in the regime from the rest of the army was therefore essential to success; failure to do so would enable the regime to overcome the conspirators' initial advantage of surprise and ensure the failure of the coup, which is exactly what happened.

The conspirators were motivated by what the man widely regarded as the driving force behind the coup, Major Saliba Mukoro, described thus:

> After extensive consultation with bright-minded military officers and civilians, we agreed, beyond reasonable doubts, that Babangida was fastly [sic] digging in and if allowed to complete the digging-in scheme, even the strongest army in the world would not be able to dig him out, and thus we would have a Mobutu on our hands... we concluded then that Babangida has crossed the line of sanity and that, indeed, the totality of his activities now constituted an internal aggression against the Nigerian state and must, therefore, be checked by all means necessary. And as such, on April 22 1990 we launched a counter-offensive on Babangida and his junta...[1] (author's emphasis)

The attempts by the plotters to seize power led to heavy fighting at various army barracks in and around Lagos, especially at Bonny Camp and the Ikeja and Ojo Cantonments. The heaviest fighting, involving the use of armoured vehicles was at Dodan Barracks itself; Babangida and his family barely escaped with their lives, but his ADC, Lieutenant-Colonel UK Bello, was not so lucky. The plotters, crucially, also failed to eliminate the regime's strongman, the Army Chief of Staff, Lieutenant-General Sani Abacha, nor did they disrupt the communication networks, an omission that greatly eased the regime's task in rallying opposition to the coup. The plotters did not do themselves any favours either by their announcement read on broadcast by Major Gideon Orkar (whose name is now synonymous with the coup, but who was in fact a late recruit to it), that they were excising Bauchi, Borno, Kano, Katsina, and Sokoto states from the federation, which had the immediate effect of rallying soldiers from those states against the plotters. As General Bali succinctly put it:

> The manner in which the coup was executed was extremely amateurish, and in fact, irresponsible to say the least. I still insist that one of the main features of a serious coup is the ability to tamper with the nation's communication system and probably the Army's internal signal system. But when you leave the communication system intact, you give the impression that you are not serious....The greatest mistake on their part however, was the excisement [sic] of some parts of the country. It was the height of tactlessness.[2]

Abacha became the focus of rallying opposition to the coup, and it is interesting to speculate whether Nigeria's history would have taken a different course had the plotters succeeded in eliminating him. What is not in doubt is that Abacha played the central role in suppressing the coup, a fact that left Babangida indebted to him going forward. By midday, the coup was to all effects and purposes over. A bloody reckoning was to follow.

More than 800 people, both military personnel and civilians (including family members of suspects at large) were arrested. The regime followed the timeworn pattern of setting up a special investigation panel (this one headed by Brigadier Rufus Kupolati), from which suspects would be sent for trial by the Special Military Tribunal (SMT) (now headed by Major-General Ike Nwachukwu). The tribunal tried eighty-two persons, of which forty-two were convicted and sentenced to death by firing squad, nine convicted and given jail terms of various lengths, and thirty-one acquitted. The AFRC confirmed the sentences on 26 July 1990, and those condemned were executed by firing squad the following day. With breathtaking contempt for the most basic principles of the law, the AFRC directed the retrial by a second SMT (headed by Major-General Yohanna Kure) of the thirty-one people acquitted by the first SMT (plus seven new defendants); of the thirty-eight defendants before it, the second SMT convicted thirty-five and sentenced twenty-seven of these to death by firing squad, with those sentences being carried out on 13 September 1990. With this, the Babangida regime had earned the dubious distinction of being the most bloodthirsty regime in Nigerian history, carrying out two-thirds of all the executions for coup plotting in the country's history.[3] That said, it should also be pointed out that several of the core plotters of the April 1990 coup were able to make good their escape, including Lieutenant-Colonel Nyiam, Major Mukoro, Major Obahor, and Captain Tolofari.

As mentioned earlier, the April 1990 coup marked a turning point in the history of Nigeria and of its army. First, the nature of the coup itself. The plotters made clear their grievances about the fact that the region that produced the country's main source of wealth, the Niger Delta, was marginalised when it came to sharing in the common wealth; worse, those principally benefitting from it were the small clique of Northern military officers running the country, as well as their favoured (Northern) acolytes, whilst officers and men from the South were regularly and repeatedly passed over for promotion and choice appointments. As Orkar said in his broadcast, the objective of the plotters was to free the marginalized, oppressed and enslaved peoples of the Middle Belt and the South (and their) children yet unborn from eternal slavery and colonization by a clique of this country [who thought it was] their birthright to dominate till eternity the political and economic privileges of this great country to the exclusion of the people of the Middle Belt and the South.[4]

Somewhat belatedly, Babangida tacitly acknowledged this after the coup.[5] The resentment and frustration thus generated were responsible for the unprecedented decision to excise some Northern states from the country.

Second, the fact that the plotters had come so close to killing him and his family was a sharp reminder to Babangida of his own mortality, and meant that the regime became even more paranoid in its security consciousness; the result was both the paralysis of the army's operational effectiveness (such as there was of it) and the shrinkage of the inner core of government decision making to very few Babangida loyalists — which in turn meant that the government became increasingly isolated from the people and the country it was meant to be running.

Third, the bloody nature of the coup hastened Babangida's relocation of the seat of the federal government to the more easily defensible Aso Rock in Abuja the following year.

Fourth, Babangida conducted a purge of the armed forces in August 1990, in which over 100 senior officers across all three services were retired. Whilst it is true that some of these (such as Major-Generals Nwachukwu, Kure, Nasko, and Kontagora) were retained in the government as civilians, this nonetheless represented a huge loss to the military in terms of experience, training, and skill. At the same time, Babangida retired Aikhomu from the navy, promoting him to full Admiral and re-designating him Vice-President. Finally, and perhaps with the greatest consequences for both the army and the nation, Abacha's role in suppressing the coup cemented his position as the heir-apparent to Babangida, the transition programme notwithstanding. Although Babangida eased Abacha out from his position as Chief of Army Staff, he sweetened this by promoting him to General, and by ceding the position of Defence Minister to him. Abacha thus became the first serving officer to attain the same rank as the head of the government, and also the first serving four-star General who was not also the Head of the Government. (He also became the first four-star General to reach that exalted rank without skipping any rank along the way up from Second-Lieutenant.) Abacha wasted no time in demonstrating that he was fully aware of his status. He declined to vacate the official residence of the Chief of Army Staff and pointedly stayed behind in Lagos when Babangida moved the seat of government to Abuja.[6] Abacha's replacement as Chief of Army Staff, Major-General Salihu Ibrahim, one of the few widely respected and apolitical senior officers left in the service, perhaps delivered the best summary of what the Nigerian Army became under Babangida's regime:

> This political interest group [within the army, i.e., the IBB Boys], who though very small in number, constituted themselves into a very powerful pressure group, unfortunately to the detriment of the service, and, of course, their colleagues. The end result of the collective action of this pressure group was the very visible decline in professionalism, morale and discipline in the Nigerian army. For example, we suddenly found ourselves operating the Nigerian army with disregard to the existing rules and regulations....we became an army where subordinate officers would not only be contemptuous of their superiors, but would exhibit total disregard to legitimate instructions by such superiors...we created a situation whereby we were operating mini-armies within the larger Nigerian Army.[7]

Once the immediate crisis of the April 1990 attempted coup, and the fallout from it was done, it was back to the business of the transition programme. After the regime had designed, established, and funded the two political parties (the SDP and the NRC), it continued its manipulation of the transition programme in several ways. It decreed that, henceforth, the previously used election method where the electorate cast their votes in a secret ballot would be abandoned, and that the so-called open ballot system, where voters openly lined up behind the symbol of their preferred party/candidate, and cast their votes into a ballot box only for him/her/the party, would be adopted as the new electoral method. Having earlier said that it would fund both parties, the government changed course, with Babangida declaring in his budget speech of 1 January 1991 that "They [the parties] are now on their own and must fend for themselves"[8] — only to later reverse itself again and resume the funding of the parties. In order to stand for election to high office, prospective candidates had to secure the approval of the NEC Chairman, who was not permitted to delegate this authority. Whilst the NEC was in the midst of preparing for elections based on the twenty-one state structure, Babangida, out of the blue, announced, on 27 August 1991, the formation of an additional nine states (Adamawa, Delta, Enugu, Jigawa, Kebbi, Kogi, Osun, Taraba, and Yobe); an additional 136 local government areas were also created at the same time. All of this threw the election timetable in the transition programme out of kilter, as, all of a sudden, the NEC now had additional gubernatorial and state legislative elections to conduct. Given that Babangida had said at the time he created Katsina and Akwa Ibom States in 1987 that those would be the last states created in Nigeria, suspicions were soon voiced that the present state-creation exercise was a means of sabotaging the planned handover date of 1 October 1992 in order to perpetuate the military's (and Babangida's) stay in power. The situation was not helped by widespread irregularities when the parties held gubernatorial primary elections in October 1991; the results of some of these were cancelled, and the primary election rerun in early December, from which twelve of the previous contestants were barred from participating. Thirteen previously banned politicians (including Major-General Shehu Yar'Adua) were arrested and detained ahead of the state legislative and gubernatorial elections; four days afterwards, they were all released. At this point, Babangida again reversed himself and lifted the ban denying former public office holders from participating in elections. Around the same time, he signed Decree No. 51 of 1991, which formally made Abuja the capital of Nigeria.

It has to be said that, to his credit, Babangida then oversaw what has probably been Nigeria's best-conducted census to date. After setting up the National Population Commission in 1988, under the chairmanship of Alhaji Shehu Musa, Babangida invested time and resources in ensuring that the commission had all that was necessary to do its work properly. Following thorough preparatory groundwork (and a full dress rehearsal), the commission conducted the census in November 1991, with the results released in March 1992. These showed Nigeria's population to be significantly less, at 88 million, than the 100-120 million that was widely assumed. Although the North was still more populated than the South, the gap was much smaller (and therefore more credible to Nigerians) than indicated in previous census exercises.

The year 1992 began for Nigeria on a bright and optimistic note. This was the year that Nigeria would return to civilian rule. There had been a successful census, as well as governorship and legislative elections at state level. The newly elected governors were sworn in to office in January 1992, and the state legislators inaugurated shortly thereafter. All that remained was the election of the National Assembly and of the new president; by 1 October, as it was widely assumed, military rule would be over. Those who made such an assumption, however, had not reckoned with the range of

> shadowy groups [that] emerged on the political scene to campaign for an extension of military rule beyond the fourth quarter of 1992…. [they] argued that the country was not yet ready for civil rule. The most prominent and vociferous [of these groups] called itself, rather tongue in cheek, the Association for Better Nigeria (ABN). [It] said that "the military must not hand over a poisoned chalice to a rag-tag civilian administration under the guise of a transition to democracy".[9]

Babangida, who had not hesitated in the past to ban, arrest, and detain those — such as trade unionists, academics and politicians — whose actions were deemed inimical to the interests of the government, was strangely reticent to move against those who were so clearly flouting, with astonishing sang-froid, the spirit, if not the letter of the government's own laws regarding the transition programme. This reticence on his part fuelled suspicions in the minds of a public growing increasingly skeptical of Babangida's bona-fides regarding the transition programme; that the regime was sponsoring the ABN and the like in an attempt to scuttle the transition and perpetuate itself in power. The fact that the ABN leader, Arthur Nzeribe, was known to be a friend of Babangida's only strengthened these suspicions.

In the midst of all of this, Babangida announced that the handover date would not be 1 October 1992, as widely expected, but would now be on 2 January 1993, with the presidential elections taking place in early December 1992; the National Assembly elections, however, would go ahead on the original July 1992 date. No sooner had these been completed than the two parties held primary elections to decide who their presidential candidates would be. Amid widespread allegations of bribery and vote-rigging, the government voided both primaries and ordered that they be rerun, which duly took place in September 1992. From these rerun elections, Alhaji Adamu Ciroma for the NRC and Major-General Shehu Yar'Adua for the SDP were declared the winners. In what was now becoming a predictable, if somewhat tiresome ritual, on 16 October 1992 the government not only voided the result, but banned all twenty-three candidates in the primaries of both parties from any further participation in the transition process; it went further and dissolved the executive councils of both parties at national, state and local government levels, appointing caretaker committees in their place.

It did not require the brains of an archbishop to work out that the proposed presidential election date of 5 December 1992 and by extension the proposed handover date of 2 January 1993 were now unlikely in the extreme. One of Babangida's predecessors, Obasanjo, voiced publicly on 13 November 1992 what many Nigerians thought privately:

> In the name of political engineering, the country has been converted to a political laboratory for trying out all kinds of silly experiments and gimmicks. Principle has been abandoned for expediency. All kinds of booby traps were instituted into the transition process. The result is the crisis we now face.[10]

Babangida, to nobody's surprise, announced that the handover date had been pushed back yet again, this time to 27 August 1993, the eighth anniversary of his accession to power. Presidential candidates would be selected by March 1993, with the elections in June. At the same time, and in another surprise, Babangida inaugurated the members of the National Assembly who had been elected in July 1992 and had presumably been twiddling their thumbs since.

In possibly the biggest surprise thus far, on 2 January 1993, Babangida dissolved the AFRC, and created in its place the National Defence and Security Council (NDSC), which had fewer members than the AFRC it replaced, but exercised all the powers of that body. It had four civilian members, including Ernest Shonekan, the Chairman of the Transitional Council, which Babangida had created to replace the National Council of Ministers (NCM). Of the military members of the NDSC, other than Babangida himself, only Aikhomu, Abacha, Nyako, and Dogonyaro remained of the original AFRC of August

1985. The establishment of the aforementioned Transitional Council was another surprise, with the ministers now being designated as secretaries of their respective ministries. Described as part of the attempt to "civilianize" the government, whilst the NDSC ceded some powers to the Transitional Council, it retained for itself the executive authority over the transition programme.

The stage was now set for the finale of the transition programme. In March 1993, both parties held conventions to nominate their candidates for the presidency. The SDP nominated Moshood Abiola, whilst the NRC went for Bashir Tofa. Both men were known to be Babangida's friends. Babangida subsequently claimed that, whilst he tried to dissuade Tofa from running, he supported Abiola's candidacy, and "supported him a lot morally and financially in the campaign".[11] Interestingly, Babangida claimed subsequently that he had intended to make Abiola, and not Shonekan, the Chairman of the Transitional Council, but had been forced to backtrack by some members of the AFRC who opposed Abiola being Chairman of the council (although not to his being a member of it). Babangida then suggested to Abiola that he appoint him (Abiola) as a member of the council, and thereafter ensure that the council would elect him Chairman. Abiola, according to Babangida, declined, insisting that he be appointed Chairman from the beginning, on the basis (vaguely presciently, as it turned out) that his (Abiola's) family "feared that the president might change his mind once he made him an ordinary member".[12]

Several elements within the military were uneasy about *both* candidates for the presidency, but probably more so about Abiola than Tofa. The NDSC reportedly came close, on several occasions, to disqualifying both men, but, in the end, chose, in Babangida's own subsequent words, "to let the bloody thing [the election] go on....we [believed] that we would have an inconclusive election. We thought it would be fair to let it run, and when it became inconclusive, then we would take whatever action we deemed necessary over a re-run or a re-election or something like that".[13] This was a remarkable tacit admission that the military were expecting, indeed hoping for, the failure of the most critical part of their own much-vaunted transition programme. Even more remarkably, Babangida subsequently also admitted that "if Bashir [Tofa] had won that election, honestly, we would not have given it to him".[14] What, then, was the purpose of the eight-year long transition programme, if, as Major-General Ishola Williams put it, the army had assumed the function of negating the will of the Nigerian people?

The regime's gamble on an inconclusive election failed. As the campaign wore on, it became clear that Abiola was a much smarter and more widely accepted candidate than his detractors and enemies within the regime had bargained for, and all indications were that he would win, and win handily at that. Nzeribe's ABN now reentered the fray. Two days before the election, on 10 June, they sought, and obtained (at the unusual hour of 9.30 pm) from an Abuja High Court under Justice Bassey Ita Ikpeme, an order restraining the NEC from conducting the election on the spurious grounds that Abiola had corruptly used money to induce delegates at the SDP convention to support his nomination as the party's presidential candidate. That this order was in flagrant contravention of Section 19(1) of Decree No. 13 of 1993, which explicitly ousted the jurisdiction of any court or tribunal over the date or time of holding the election, did not apparently trouble His Lordship. Nor, it appeared, did it trouble the Attorney General, Clement Akpamgbo, who opposed Nwosu's passionate appeal to the NDSC on June 11 to ignore Justice Ikpeme's order and proceed with the election. No action was taken against Nzeribe and his ABN, despite the clear violation of Decree 13. Babangida sided with the NEC Chairman, and ordered the election to go ahead, against the wishes of several of his military colleagues in the NDSC, notably Abacha and Dogonyaro. It did so the following day, in what is still widely regarded as the freest and fairest election in Nigerian history. As the results started trickling in, and announced by the NEC, Abiola's enemies' worst fears were being realized: he appeared to be firmly on course for victory. Enter again the ABN, turning to another Abuja High Court on 15 June to seek an order restraining the NEC from releasing any further results on the basis that the election had been conducted unlawfully in violation of Justice Ikpeme's dubious order. Unbelievably, Mr. Justice Dahiru Saleh agreed, and granted the ABN the order it sought. The NDSC met again the following day to discuss the crisis, with Nwosu again in attendance. His subsequent account indicates that, with the exception of Aikhomu, most members of the NDSC were against the release of further results. When Nwosu suggested that Abiola be declared the winner of the election, Abacha shouted him down.[15]

Over the next few days, those elements of the military who were both opposed to the military leaving power, and to Abiola's accession to the top job, put Babangida under significant pressure. Rumours swirled around that if Babangida announced that he was handing over power to Abiola as the winner of the election, there would be an immediate coup, with Babangida himself reported as saying "they will kill me, they will kill the President-elect, Chief MKO Abiola, if I went ahead with the election and announced the winner...which we all know to be Bashorun, Chief MKO Abiola..."[16] Tellingly, Babangida is also reported to have singled out Abacha as the fount of the anti-Abiola movement in the army, saying:

> Sani [Abacha] is opposed to a return to civilian rule. Sani cannot stand the idea of Chief Abiola...becoming his Commander-in-Chief at all.....Where do I go from here?...Without Sani, I will not be alive today...he saw to my coming to office in 1985, and to my protection in the many coups I faced in the past, especially the Orkar coup of 1990 where he saved me and my family including my infant daughter...if he says he does not want Chief Abiola, I will not force Chief Abiola on him. I have just to end the whole matter and go back to the place of my birth....I cannot kill myself for the sake of what the country wants. I am sorry.[17]

In February 1976, Babangida had displayed a degree of physical courage in confronting an intoxicated and armed Dimka at the studios of the radio station; now in June 1993, what was on display was a significant failure of moral courage on his part. As his friend, Omo Omoruyi put it: "He was now at the sharp point of a dilemma: it was either his life or his honour as an officer and a gentleman. He was inclined to settle for the former and to let go of the latter".[18]

On 23 June 1993, Babangida caved in to the pressure and annulled the freest and fairest election in the history of Nigeria.

For what was one of the most momentous (and arguably *the* most momentous) statement in Nigeria's history, the announcement that the 12 June election had been annulled came in the most casually innocuous form and manner: an unsigned, undated statement, on a plain piece of paper with no official adornment, issued by the Press Secretary to the Vice President, Augustus Aikhomu.[19] The country's response was anything but innocuous and casual. Civil societies called for nationwide protests. Labour announced a general strike.

The international community made token gestures of protest such as withdrawing military attachés and suspending aid packages and military assistance; none of them went as far as taking the sorts of steps that might have given the regime something to really worry about, such as an embargo on oil purchases from Nigeria. Those elements of the military who still had any sense of honour and professionalism were outraged; indeed, one officer, the archetypal IBB Boy, Colonel Abubakar Umar, resigned his commission in protest (Babangida refused to accept it). Umar's boss, the Army Chief of Staff, Lieutenant-General Salihu Ibrahim, a member of the NDSC, was not even aware of the annulment until it was announced. Nor was the Vice-President, Aikhomu, whose Press Secretary issued the annulment statement. The politicians, on the other hand, uttered very little by way of protest.

Having failed the moral courage test, Babangida now had to pick up the pieces. In a broadcast on 26 June 1993, three days after the election had been annulled, Babangida tried to defend the indefensible. He claimed that both candidates had indulged in what he described as the "tremendous negative use of money" (bribes, in simple language) to rig the elections. He also blamed a potential conflict between the interests of both candidates and those of the government had either of them been elected, and the less-than-stellar performance of the judiciary. All of this was almost certainly true, but none of it provided an explanation for why the government had turned a blind eye before the election to these complaints, only to later use them as *ex post facto* reasons (and unconvincing ones at that) for the annulment. In the same speech, Babangida announced that there would be a new presidential election, and asked the two parties to put forward candidates under new rules that appeared carefully crafted to exclude Abiola. The candidates for the fresh election were to have been members of their party for at least a year, and were not to have personal, corporate, or business interests that conflicted with the national interest. Babangida also announced the lifting of the ban on those, such as Yar'Adua and Adamu Ciroma, who had been banned in October 1992. On 4 July, the SDP confirmed that it would not participate in a new election and claimed victory in the 12 June election; the NRC, grateful for another bite at the electoral apple, indicated that it would take part. Babangida responded with a forty-eight-hour ultimatum to both parties to accept fresh elections, failing which he would dissolve *all* the structures created during the transition, e.g., federal and state legislatures and the civilian state governors. As was easily predictable, this concentrated minds, especially within the SDP; the reemergence of the previously banned Yar'Adua, who was no fan of Abiola's, significantly shifted the calculus of interests within the party away from insisting on standing on 12 June (to Abiola's advantage) and towards a pragmatic solution that would favour a wider cross section of the party.

On 7 July, Babangida met with the chairmen of both parties at the Presidential Villa in Abuja. A statement was jointly released by the two parties declaring that they both resolved to "cooperate fully" with the regime to resolve the impasse, and that they had "accepted in principle the second option of a national government proposed by the Federal Military Government..."[20] A committee was set up to work out the mechanics of setting up what became known as the Interim National Government (ING). The committee was made up of representatives from both parties and from the government comprised several of the IBB Boys (Joshua Dogonyaro, Aliyu Mohammed Gusau, David Mark, and John Shagaya). The committee recommended, amongst other things, that the ING would be mainly composed of civilians, as well as be headed by a civilian, that it would commence on or before 27 August 1993, and that it would be in existence no later than 31 December 1993 (later moved to March 1994). Crucially, Babangida, Aikhomu, and all the Service Chiefs were to go, with the exception of Abacha. This would turn out to be a fatal mistake. On 17 August, Babangida announced that he would, "as a personal sacrifice", step aside from the presidency on 27 August. Shonekan, the Chairman of the Transitional Council, would head the ING. Although Babangida was leaving Abacha behind as the Secretary of Defence in the ING, he attempted to also leave behind his own people as the new Service Chiefs to replace those retiring with him and Aikhomu. Dogonyaro and Aliyu Mohammed were appointed Chief of Defence Staff and Chief of Army Staff, respectively.

On the morning of 27 August 1993, Babangida signed into law Decree No. 61 which brought the ING into being and brought the curtain down on his eight years in power. With the sole exception of Gowon, he had been in power longer than any other previous head of state. Babangida was undoubtedly the first military ruler who had actively prepared for and sought the position, and he appeared to have a clear idea of what he wanted to achieve in power. He did not leave office, as he hoped, with the adulation and acclaim of a grateful nation ringing in his ears. Rather, he departed under a cloud, with neither the nation nor the army sad to see him go. The Nigeria he left behind was one in which official corruption had been transformed into a policy of government, and one in which the people had never before felt quite so alienated from their leaders. Never the most forgiving of people at the best of times, Babangida's Nigeria was a more bitter and cynical place at his departure from office than it had been at his accession to it. The state's preparation to use lethal force against those with whom it differed took root and started to blossom under his leadership, and the bitter harvest would be reaped under his successor. The army was fragmented and divided against itself — no regime had suffered as many overthrow attempts as Babangida's, and none was more bloody than the events of April 1990. It is difficult, even with the benefit of hindsight, to single out one way in which the Nigeria of August 1993 was better off than the Nigeria of August 1985, when he was made president, and that is a damning indictment of Ibrahim Babangida.

There has been much speculation about the real reasons why the election was annulled, but the best (and most simple) explanation this author has read was provided by Siollun:

> The Transition commenced as a legitimate project, but as military officers became accustomed to power, they got cold feet and became reluctant to leave office. Thus they sought to manipulate and elongate the process, and provoke crises that would justify the Transition's abortion (sic).[21]

Whilst Babangida may not have been the prime architect of all of the crises, he undoubtedly was for some of them; so, also, was Abacha, who was definitely the prime architect of the biggest crisis of them all, the annulment of the 12 June election. Babangida himself acknowledged this after he left office (see chapter 8). He had survived in office since 1985 partly by "looking after" the IBB Boys who had executed the coup that brought him to power. This cabal of officers, led by Abacha and Dogonyaro, had form for pressuring Babangida into decisions such as the retirements of Ukiwe in 1986 and Bali in 1990. The annulment was their biggest — and last — success.

Interim National Government

The Interim National Government was, bluntly put, a bastard child that was not greatly loved by its parents — if, indeed, it knew for sure who its parents were. A largely toothless and ineffective government, it was put out of its misery after just over two and a half months of its inception, on 17 November 1993, when Abacha announced the resignation of Shonekan, and the dissolution of the ING (and all the structures of Babangida's transitional programme such as the National and State Assemblies, both political parties, and the sacking of all the civilian state governors and their commissioners, as well as the sacking of the federal secretaries/ministers). Sani Abacha also announced that he had taken over as Head of State and Commander in Chief of the Armed Forces. The ship of the Nigerian state and its army was venturing into uncharted waters.

NOTES

1. Siollun SOF p. 144.

2. Ibid p. 159.

3. Ibid p. 165.

4. Agbese p. 372.

5. Ibid p. 374.

6. Siollun SOF p. 166.

7. Ibid p. 202.

8. Agbese p. 289.

9. Ibid p. 378.

10. Ibid pp. 384-385.

11. Ibid p. 389.

12. Ibid.
13. Ibid p. 390.

14. Ibid p. 393.

15. Siollun SOF p. 240.

16. Ibid p. 242.

17. Ibid p. 244.

18. Ibid pp. 242-243.

19. Ibid p. 246.

20. Ibid p. 265.

21. Ibid p. 255.

CHAPTER 14

The Sixth Military Government: Descent into the Abyss

When government fears the people, there is liberty. When the people fear the government, there is tyranny.

— **Unknown**

The Nigerian public had, by this time, become used to hearing Sani Abacha's voice in relation to coups and coup attempts; he had first come to the nation's attention a decade earlier when he announced Shagari's removal from office, and had subsequently made broadcasts in relation to the coups of April 1990, August 1985, and now November 1993. But who was he?

Sani Abacha was born in Kano in September 1943; although widely believed to be an indigene of that ancient city, he was in fact of Kanuri origin. One of several siblings, his came from a fairly well-to-do family, with interests in transport and bakery businesses. He attended both primary and secondary schools in Kano, and was perhaps more noted for truancy than for any academic prowess during the course of his academic career. Like many other young Northern men of his age, he enlisted in the Nigerian Army in 1962, aged nineteen, and attended the Nigerian Military Training College (NMTC) for his basic training. He was sent to Mons Officer Training School in Aldershot, and was commissioned Second-Lieutenant in 1963. Upon his return to Nigeria, he was posted to the Third Battalion in Kaduna, where he was an active participant in the July 1966 coup that removed Ironsi from office. The previous year, he had married Maryam Jidah, and they went on to have ten children. Promoted Lieutenant in 1966, he attended courses at the British Army School of Infantry in Warminster in 1966 and 1971; in between he fought in the Civil War, and was promoted Captain in 1967 and Major in 1969. After the war, he commanded the training depot of the army's Second Division and served as Chief Instructor at the Nigerian Army School of Infantry. Promoted Lieutenant-Colonel in 1972 and Colonel in 1975, he attended the Army Command and Staff College in Jaji in 1976 and, following promotion to Brigadier in 1980, the Nigerian Institute for Policy and Strategic Studies (NIPSS) in Kuru in 1981. The following year, 1982, he attended the Senior International Defence Management Course at the US Naval Postgraduate School in Monterey, California. He was appointed Commander of Ninth Mechanised Brigade in Ikeja (in which post he announced Shagari's overthrow), and was then appointed GOC Second Division and promoted Major-General in 1984. After announcing the overthrow of Buhari in August 1985, he succeeded Babangida as Chief of Army Staff upon the latter's accession to the presidency. Promoted Lieutenant-General in 1987, he became Chairman of the Joint Chiefs of Staff in 1989 after Bali's removal, and, following his key role in suppressing the April 1990 coup that came within an ace of killing Babangida, was promoted four-star General as well as becoming Defence Minister (again, in succession to Babangida). He thereby became the first person ever to reach four-star status without skipping a rank along the way, and also without simultaneously being the Head of State. The only service chief to have been left in post when Babangida "stepped aside" in August 1993, he had now become the country's Head of State.

Abacha wasted no time in setting his imprint firmly on the new regime. Babangida's attempt to retain some residual influence at the highest levels of government and the armed forces was swiftly swatted aside. Abacha retired all the Service Chiefs appointed by Babangida, with the exception of AVM Femi John Femi of the Air Force. The others retired include: Lieutenant-General Dogonyaro as CDS, Lieutenant-General Aliyu Mohammed Gusau of the army, and Rear Admiral Suleiman Saidu of the navy. In their place Abacha appointed Major-General MC Alli (army) and Rear Admiral Allison Madueke (navy). He also appointed Lieutenant-General Oladipo Diya as Chief of the General Staff (CGS) whilst Major-General Abdulsalami Abubakar, a schoolmate of Babangida's, as Chief of Defence Staff (CDS). All the structures of Babangida's transition process were swept away — the Council of Ministers, all the legislative bodies at federal and state levels, political parties, the NEC, civilian state governors and their executive councils, local governments — all abolished and their leaders sacked. All forms of political assembly or activity were banned. The Provisional Ruling Council was established as the nation's highest decision-making body in the manner of the Supreme Military Council/Armed Forces Ruling Council of old. The Provisional Ruling Council would consist of Abacha himself as Chairman, Diya as Vice-Chairman, and the CDS, the Service Chiefs, the Inspector-General of Police (Ibrahim Coomassie); and the ministers of defence, foreign affairs, internal affairs; and the attorney general. Within days, several of the so-called IBB Boys — Akilu, Mark, Shagaya, Rasaki, Dasuki, Olurin, and Aminu — were retired.

A separate Federal Executive Council was appointed. In a shrewd political move (or possibly an act of perfidy on the part of the appointee, depending on one's point of view), Abacha appointed Abiola's running mate, Babagana Kingibe, as Foreign Minister. Several of the members of the new cabinet were from the South-west, Abiola's home region (including the Attorney General, Olu Onagoruwa; Lateef Jakande; and Ebenezer Babatope — the last two, associates of the late Obafemi Awolowo). Only two members of the Executive Council were members of the armed forces — the Minister for the Federal Capital Territory, Lieutenant-General Jeremiah Useni; and the Minister of Commerce, Rear Admiral Jubril Ayinla.

The new government, whilst sweeping away all the structures of Babangida's programme of transition to civilian rule, also tried to give the impression that it regarded itself as a temporary regime by describing its highest decision-making body as the Provisional Ruling Council, and by appointing only two military personnel to the Federal Executive Council. Beyond Abacha's statement in his speech of November 1993 announcing Shonekan's "resignation" and the dissolution of the ING that it would set up a constitutional conference, the regime had said virtually nothing for more than six months about its plans for a return to civilian rule, and then only in response to an accusation made in a magazine interview by one of the recently retired IBB Boys (David Mark); that it had no political programme and intended to remain in power until the turn of the century. Then on 22 April 1994, the regime announced that it would hold elections the following month into what it termed a National

Constitutional Conference to determine the country's constitutional and political future. A couple of weeks later, the formation of the National Democratic Coalition (NADECO) was announced; amongst its members were former politicians like Anthony Enahoro and Balarabe Musa, as well as retired military officers like Lieutenant-General Alani Akinrinade, a former Chief of Army Staff and Chief of Defence Staff; and Commodore Ebitu Ukiwe, a former Chief of General Staff. Insisting that the government should abide by the 12 June election, widely believed to have been won by Abiola, NADECO called for the 23 May elections into the Constitutional Conference to be boycotted, a call that was widely heeded, especially in the Southwest. The government's response, on 31 May, through the Inspector General of Police, was to declare NADECO illegal. Two weeks later, on the eve of the first anniversary of the 12 June election, Abiola declared himself the President and Commander-in-Chief of the Armed Forces. Correctly concluding that Abacha would not condone such a flagrant challenge to his authority, Abiola promptly went into hiding in an ultimately futile attempt to avoid arrest; he was arrested in Lagos on 23 June on charges of fomenting an insurrection against the government with the aim of deposing it. He never regained his freedom.

Early the following month, two key unions in the oil and gas sector — the Nigerian Union of Petroleum and Natural Gas Workers (NUPENG) and the Petroleum and Natural Gas Senior Staff Association (PENGASSAN) — began a strike in protest at the annulled elections (and presumably to pressure the government into reversing the annulment); a month later, they were joined by the National Labour Congress, which called a general strike. In the meantime, the country was paralysed by extensive fuel shortages and by riots that broke out, mainly in the Southwest. By mid-August, Abacha had had enough. In a TV broadcast on 18 August, he announced the dissolution of the executive committees of both NUPENG and PENGASSAN, as well as that of the NLC; shut down of three national newspapers (*Punch*, *The Guardian*, and *Concord Press*, the last of these owned by Abiola). Over the next few days, several NADECO leaders (including Enahoro and Akinrinade) as well as union leaders like Frank Kokori, General Secretary of NUPENG, were arrested. At the same time, the government promulgated decrees that put its actions beyond the purview of the courts. At the end of August, the government promulgated the Constitutional Conference, despite widespread opposition to its legitimacy.

Abacha now moved to cement his authority and the primacy of the armed forces in governance. In September 1994, the membership of the PRC was increased to twenty-five and all the civilian ministers, who had initially been members, were removed from the council, which was now almost exclusively military (with Coomassie, the Inspector-General of Police, as the only nonmilitary officer). The Constitutional Conference continued its deliberations, unperturbed by its perceived lack of legitimacy, and, in its final report submitted in June 1995, produced a number of recommendations such as a multiparty system, a rotational presidency between the North and the South, three vice-presidents, and an exit date for the Abacha government of 1 January 1996.

The country now received its first clear indication of Abacha's ruthless approach to dealing with those perceived to be threats to his authority. The regime announced in March 1995 that the former military Head of State, Obasanjo, and his former Deputy, Yar'Adua, had been arrested, along with several serving army officers (and some of the recently retired IBB Boys like Lawan Gwadabe). The dragnet was extended to include several civilians, particularly journalists who were perceived to be antagonistic or hostile to the regime, and critics and prodemocracy activists like Dr. Beko Ransome-Kuti. Accounts subsequently emerged (particularly at the Oputa-led Truth and Reconciliation Commission set up by Obasanjo after the return to civilian rule in 1999) of the torture some of those arrested were subjected to in an attempt to get them to "confess" and implicate themselves and others. A military tribunal was set up under the chairmanship of Major-General Patrick Aziza, and it duly returned, in June 1995, guilty verdicts and death sentences on several of the accused (including both Obasanjo and Yar'Adua); others were sentenced to long terms of imprisonment. All the sentences were later commuted or reduced.

Others, however, were not so lucky. Ken Saro-Wiwa was a prominent author and playwright, and was also a vociferous and prominent advocate for his people in Ogoniland, a key oil-producing area in the Niger Delta. Saro-Wiwa's ire was directed against what he saw as an unholy alliance between successive governments, the oil companies, and some of the more unscrupulous Ogoni chiefs to extract oil, pollute farmland and fishing creeks, and then fail to clean up the mess or pay compensation. When some chiefs who were perceived to be in league with the oil companies were set upon and killed by irate youths, Saro-Wiwa and eight others were arrested and tried by a special military court, convicted, and sentenced to death on 31 October 1995. The PRC, despite widespread concerns about the fairness of the trial and several pleas for clemency, confirmed the sentences, which were carried out on 10 November. Nigeria was immediately suspended from the British Commonwealth. Unfazed, the regime carried on along its merry way, appointing a new National Election Commission (NECON) and a Transition Implementation Committee (TIC) in December 1995.

Nigeria, and the Nigerian Army, entered 1996 under a heavy cloud of uncertainty and in a climate of fear and foreboding. Those fears proved, sadly, to be well founded. Starting in January 1996, the country witnessed a seemingly unending succession of bomb blasts and assassinations/assassination attempts in places as diverse as Kaduna, Kano, Ilorin, and Lagos; at hotels, police stations, and airports. Among the victims were the *Guardian* publisher, Alex Ibru and one of Abiola's wives, Kudirat. In the midst of this chaos and carnage, Abacha found time to depose Ibrahim Dasuki as the Sultan of Sokoto, replacing him with Muhammed Maccido (allegedly the original choice of the kingmakers but ultimately supplanted by Dasuki after Babangida intervened to force through the appointment of the latter).

At the end of September, it was announced that NECON had registered five political parties: Committee for National Consensus (CNC), United Nigeria People's Convention (UNPC), National Centre Party of Nigeria (NCPN), Democratic Party of Nigeria (DPN), and Grassroots Democratic Movement (GDM). The following day, 1 October 1996, the creation of six additional states was announced: Bayelsa (out of Rivers State), Ebonyi (out of Abia and Enugu States), Ekiti (out of Ondo State), Gombe (out of Bauchi State), Nassarawa (out of Plateau State), and Zamfara (out of Sokoto State). Three of these states were in the South and three in the North, bringing the total number of states to thirty-six, with nineteen in the North and seventeen in the South.

The spate of bombings continued into the new year of 1997, with further incidents in Ibadan, Lagos, and Ondo; the military administrators of Lagos and Ekiti states appeared to be the targets of some of these blasts. Meanwhile, the "transition" to civilian rule proceeded apace. Following a voter-registration exercise in February, elections were held in March for local government chairmen, triggering riots in some parts of the country. In June, the TIC announced the dates for elections for the individual state Assemblies (December 1997), the National Assembly (April 1998), and the Gubernatorial and presidential elections (August 1998). Shortly after the first of these elections took place in December 1997, it was announced that the former Chief of Staff, Supreme Headquarters in the Obasanjo regime, Major-General Shehu Yar'Adua, who had been convicted alongside Obasanjo in 1995 of plotting to overthrow the Abacha regime, and whose death sentence had similarly been commuted to imprisonment, had died in custody at Abakaliki Prison. As was to become familiar over the next few months, rumours swirled that he had been poisoned by the regime's agents. [One of those accused, Lieutenant-Colonel Ibrahim Yakassai, subsequently revealed how the regime had dragged its feet in authorizing Yar'Adua's transfer to a hospital for medical treatment; according to him, he arranged on his own initiative for Yar'Adua's body to be flown to his home state of Katsina for burial, which may have been the reason for his own subsequent fall from grace (see below).]

Whatever the truth about Yar'Adua's death, within days the regime dropped another bombshell. It announced that it had uncovered a coup plot against it, and that several of the alleged plotters had been arrested. However, this was not the bombshell; it was the identities of those arrested, the most prominent among them was the regime's number two man, the Chief of the General Staff, Lieutenant-General Oladipo Diya. Also arrested were Major-Generals Adisa and Olanrewaju, as well as a number of more junior officers such as Major Fadipe, Diya's Chief Security Officer (of whom more later), and civilians such as Diya's Political Adviser, Prof Femi Odekunle. At their arraignment before a military tribunal chaired by Major-General Victor Malu, Diya claimed that he had been set up by the Army Chief of Staff, Lieutenant-General Ishaya Bamaiyi, whom he swore had approached him for support for a plot by the army's most senior commanders to remove Abacha from power. Once more, subsequent revelations emerged of the arrested officers being subjected to physical violence in detention. At the Oputa Truth and Reconciliation Panel hearings, video footage emerged of Diya on his knees before Abacha, weeping and pleading for his life; he at least had the grace to do so before an officer senior to him. Adisa, a Major-General, was also shown behaving in a similar manner in front of Abacha's Chief Security Officer, Hamza al-Mustapha, a Major who was much more junior to Adisa. This craven behaviour on the part of the two Generals was in stark contrast to the fortitude shown by Major Fadipe, who had the courage to say that there had, in fact, been a coup plot, that he had been involved in it on the orders of his boss, Diya, and that he was fully aware of the consequences of his actions. Diya and Adisa's groveling did them no good; they, along with Olanrewaju and Fadipe and others were convicted and sentenced to death at the end of April 1998. (Malu, impressed by Fadipe's "candour and display of courage and integrity",[1] subsequently stated publicly, before the Oputa Panel, that he would have been happy to reabsorb Fadipe into the Nigerian Army.)

Whilst all of this drama was being played out, the so-called transition programme rumbled on. In April, all five of the registered political parties had nominated Abacha as their sole candidate in the forthcoming presidential election scheduled for August 1998. This represented a level of audacious cynicism never before seen in the Nigerian context — not even Babangida, the master manipulator, had been quite so brazen — and prompted the famous description by the former civilian Governor of Oyo State, Bola Ige, of the parties as "five fingers of the same leprous hand".[2] And still the violence continued, with bomb blasts in Lagos and Ife and riots in Ibadan, with heavy fatalities.

And then everything changed, quite literally overnight. In the early hours of 8 June 1998, Abacha died suddenly, in mysterious circumstances, which have not been fully explained to this day. All sorts of rumours abounded — he had expired in the company of foreign prostitutes after strenuous sexual activity fuelled by aphrodisiacs, he had been poisoned by his fellow officers or by the aforementioned prostitutes or by a security operative who accompanied Palestinian leader Yasir Arafat to a meeting with Abacha the previous day, or simply, according to the government, of a sudden heart attack. Since Abacha was buried later the same day without an autopsy, the truth may never be known. What is known, however, is that news of Abacha's death was initially held very tightly, until the internal manoeuvering within the regime to decide his successor was completed, resulting in the appointment of the Chief of Defence Staff, Major-General Abdulsalami Abubakar, to take Abacha's place. When the news of Abacha's death was made public, there was widespread jubilation in several parts of the country, but particularly in the Southwest.

The jubilation in the Southwest was short-lived. A month after Abacha's demise, it was announced on 7 July that Abiola had been taken ill during a meeting with visiting US officials, and had subsequently died. Like his arch nemesis Abacha, rumours swirled that Abiola had also been poisoned by hardliners within the military; these rumours persisted notwithstanding the release of the autopsy results (conducted by both Nigerian and foreign pathologists) that Abiola had died of long-standing heart disease. Whatever the cause of death, Abiola's demise triggered further unrest in the Southwest of the country, and a curfew was imposed in his home state of Ogun in response to the unrest. Possibly (at least partially) in an attempt to assuage the perceived grievances of Abiola's kinsmen, the PRC met on 9 July to review the sentences passed by the Special Military Tribunal on Diya and his colleagues, and the death sentences were commuted to terms of imprisonment. (Abubakar had earlier announced the release of several people from prison, prominent among them Obasanjo, Dasuki, Ransome-Kuti, Kokori, Bola Ige, and Chris Anyanwu.)

Sani Abacha had been in power for just under five years. In that time, it is not overly fanciful to say that Nigeria was gripped by an atmosphere of terror such as it had never seen before or since. Reference has been made already to the wave of bomb blasts and assassinations that swept across the country, mainly targeted at the regime's opponents (or those perceived as such); beyond these were several unsuccessful attempts on activists such as Abraham Adesanya, and the exile of several others in fear of their lives like Wole Soyinka and retired Lieutenant-General Alani Akinrinade. Within the armed forces, the fear of being perceived as an opponent of the regime was widespread, and paralysed what little residual operational effectiveness there might have been. Those unfortunate enough to have been identified as regime opponents were arrested on often-spurious coup plotting allegations, then brutally tortured in an attempt to extract confessions from them and force them to implicate others. Those who had previously been seen as in the regime's good books were not immune from this either. The erstwhile leader of Abacha's notorious Strike Force, an obstetrician and gynaecologist turned security operative, Lieutenant-Colonel Ibrahim Yakassai, who had been involved in the Yar'Adua death, found himself arrested and jailed by the regime.

Only his rapacious plundering of the nation's coffers exceeded Abacha's ruthlessness against those he regarded as threats to his security. It is estimated that Abacha alone stole in excess of *four billion dollars* from Nigeria's coffers whilst in office — much of it unaccounted for.[3] A story emerged following his death that huge amounts of money had been stashed away in banks in the UK, Switzerland, Liechtenstein, and the British Virgin Islands, amongst other places, by Abacha and members of his family and inner circle. Barely believable accounts of nocturnal visits to the Central Bank for the purpose of carting away huge amounts of foreign currency for "national security" expenses became commonplace. Whatever the true story is of the methods by which or the extent to which the nation's treasury was looted, the reality is that only a fraction of those funds were ever recovered. Perhaps only Babangida exceeded Abacha in terms of the extent to which he corruptly enriched himself, but even he was no match for Abacha when it came to the sheer audacity and cynicism with which the so-called transition to civil rule was manipulated — after all, even at his worst (or best, depending on one's point of view), Babangida never got as far as ensuring that he became the sole presidential candidate of five political parties in the way that Abacha did.

What was it about Sani Abacha that made him such a feared and fearful despot? Once famously described by Babangida as being "not very bright upstairs,"[4] he was an easy man to underestimate, and he repeatedly outmanoeuvered those who were considered more intelligent than he was (as well as those who just thought they were). He appeared to have worked out — quicker than any of his rivals — Babangida's vulnerabilities, and then successfully exploited them in order to make himself indispensable to him. It is no coincidence that he outlasted the likes of Bali and Aikhomu in the corridors of power; nor is it a coincidence that he remains the only man to attain four-star rank, equal to that of the Head of State, in a military regime without being the top man himself. Once in the saddle, he knew better than most how he had conspired to remove others from power (Ironsi, Shagari, Buhari) as well as how to keep them in power (Babangida), and, therefore, as some found to their cost, removing him was not going to be a walk in the park. He has often been described as soft-spoken, rarely raising his voice or even speaking in meetings, preferring to let others do the talking; at times he would even apparently appear to be asleep.[5]

Abacha was not often seen in public, and rarely ventured out of the fortress of the Aso Rock Presidential Villa; he ventured outside Nigeria even more rarely. He is reported to have frequently consulted various marabouts, diviners, and soothsayers from Nigeria and neighbouring West African countries like Mali, Senegal, and Niger. His engagements and movements were heavily influenced by what these soothsayers had to say about plots against him: for example, for several years, according to Vice Admiral Jubril Ayinla, Abacha refused to attend the graduation ceremony of the nation's premier military institution, the National War College.

Whatever the truth of the circumstances in which Abacha's regime came to an end, the country was now in the hands of another military leader, Major-General Abdulsalami Abubakar. The country waited to see what direction the new government would take.

NOTES

1. Malu, Lt. Gen. SVL. *In The Name of Victor: Confronting Errors With the Truth*. Author House, 2014, p. 63.

2. www.edureasourcecenter.blogspot.co.uk. Accessed 16/11/2017.

3. *The Guardian*, UK. 08 July 2000.

4. Siollun SOF p. 244

7. *Newswatch* 24/11/1997 & 01/02/1999.

CHAPTER 15

The Seventh Military Government: A Partial Redemption

It is even better to act quickly and err, than to hesitate until the time for action is past.

— **Carl von Clausewitz**

Even before Abacha was in his grave, intrigues had already began about whom his successor would be. According to Major Hamza al Mustapha, Abacha's much feared security officer, the Army Chief of Staff, Lieutenant-General Ishaya Bamaiyi (Diya's nemesis in the previous year's coup plot), had made a move to get himself appointed as the new Head of State after al Mustapha had quietly notified him of Abacha's death. Al Mustapha claims that a few hot-headed junior officers, enraged by this, had advocated shooting all the members of the PRC who had been summoned to a meeting by al Mustapha, ostensibly at Abacha's request. Al Mustapha said he sought the advice of Brigadiers Buba Marwa and Ibrahim Sabo, both staunch Abacha loyalists, who counseled against any bloodshed and suggested that al Mustapha seek Babangida's counsel. Al Mustapha did so, and Babangida also strongly advised against any bloodshed, suggesting that the next most senior officer in the PRC take over. Ordinarily, this would have meant the accession to power of Lieutenant-General Jeremiah Useni, who was known to be very close to Abacha; so close, in fact, that al Mustapha was aware that some members of Abacha's family, especially his wife (now widow) Maryam, had complained about the closeness of the relationship in the past. Bamaiyi then further poisoned the well by reminding al Mustapha that Useni had been the last officer to see Abacha prior to his becoming unwell the previous night, and that Useni would have been well aware of the fact that, with Diya now out of the equation, he was now the next most senior officer, and therefore next in the line of succession should Abacha no longer be on the scene. The barely veiled insinuation was that Useni had in some way played a role in bringing about Abacha's demise.

Al Mustapha relates that his first instinct was to storm Useni's residence with "almost a battalion of soldiers" in order to arrest him, but, again, cooler heads prevailed, and the plan was shelved. Support now switched to Abubakar, the Chief of Defence Staff, who was eventually appointed to take over from Abacha.[1]

Nigeria's latest military leader, was born to Alhaji Abubakar Jibrin and Hajiya Fati Kande Mohammed on 13 June 1942 in Minna, the capital of present-day Niger State. The second of ten children in a polygamous home, he attended Minna Native Authority Primary School between 1950 and 1956, and went on to the Provincial Secondary School in Bida between 1957 and 1962, where his classmates included his future fellow army officers: Ibrahim Babangida, Mohammed Magoro, Mamman Vatsa, Garba Duba, Gado Nasko, and Sani Bello. Whereas the others entered the army straightaway, Abdulsalami attended Kaduna Technical College from January to October 1963, before joining the nascent Nigerian Air Force on 3 October 1963 as an Officer Cadet. He was sent to West Germany the following year for flying training, but did not appear to have made the grade; he transferred to the army upon the outbreak of the Civil War in July 1967 and, after attending the Emergency Short Service Combatant Course No. 2, was commissioned second Lieutenant on 20 October 1967 and posted to the infantry, where he was now junior to his former classmates at school, all of them commissioned in 1963.

He served regimental and staff duty at the battalion, brigade and divisional levels over the next few years, before being posted to command the 145th Infantry Battalion, part of the Nigerian contribution to the United Nations Interim Force in Lebanon (UNIFIL) between 1978 and 1979. Upon his return, he was posted to the Third Armoured Division as Assistant Adjutant General, after which he became the Chief Instructor at the Nigerian Defence Academy between 1980 and 1982. Following another divisional level staff job, he was appointed to command a mechanized brigade in 1985, and, the following year was appointed Military Secretary. In 1988, as a Brigadier, he was appointed to his first divisional command, as GOC Eighty-Second Division in Enugu, after which he became GOC First Division in Kaduna between 1990 and 1991. He returned to Army HQ as Chief of Policy and Plans between 1991 and 1993 and then appointed by Abacha to succeed Lieutenant-General Joshua Dogonyaro as Chief of Defence Staff in December 1993. In his role as CDS, he convened the military tribunal presided over by Major-General Victor Malu that tried and condemned Diya and his fellow defendants. He was serving as CDS at the time that Abacha's unexpected demise catapulted him into the first and only political post in the course of his thirty-two-year military career.

The first order of business was to consolidate his grip on power. In order to resolve any lingering issues about seniority, Abdulsalami was promoted in fairly short order to four-star rank, thereby becoming the most senior officer in the armed forces. He appointed the Chief of Naval Staff, Vice Admiral Mike Akhigbe, to the vacant post of Chief of the General Staff; Rear Admiral (promoted to Vice Admiral on appointment) Jubril Ayinla to succeed Akhigbe as CNS; and Air Vice Marshal Al-Amin Daggash to succeed himself as Chief of Defence Staff, thus ensuring that all three services were represented at the top echelon of the government. Bamaiyi remained as the head of the army and Air Marshal Nsikak Eduok as the head of the air force. Rightly understanding that he needed to tread a fine line between keeping the army quiescent and at the same time reassuring the country that the Abacha years were over, he announced a one-month long period of national mourning for the late, largely unlamented Abacha; at the same time, he announced the release of several people who had been detained and imprisoned on dubious grounds, such as Obasanjo, Beko Ransome-Kuti, Lawan Gwadabe, and Frank Kokori. The death sentences passed on Diya and his fellow convicts were commuted to terms of imprisonment. Barely one month into his regime, Abdulsalami was forced to deal with the potentially explosive issue of Abiola's death in custody, and he proved himself up to the task. Immediately announcing that a team of local and international pathologists would conduct an autopsy, and that the results would be released, he managed to mitigate (at least to some degree) any suggestion of a government cover up of its having a hand in Abiola's demise; this did not, however, entirely quell the rumours (see chapter 9).

In a speech on 20 July 1998, Abdulsalami set out his programme for returning the country to civil rule. He announced the cancellation of all the elections conducted under Abacha, the dissolution of NECON and the five parties registered by it (Bola Ige's "leprous fingers"), the release of all detainees and the dismissal of all pending charges against those opposition activists who had gone into exile, and, most importantly, that his government would hand over to an elected civilian government on 29 May 1999. The following month, he inaugurated a fourteen-member Independent National Electoral Commission (INEC), under the chairmanship of a retired Judge, Mr. Justice Ephraim Akpata; on the same day, the abrogation of the decrees that had dissolved the Executive Councils of the NLC, NUPENG, and PENGASSAN was announced. Two weeks after being inaugurated, the INEC announced election dates: local government elections would take place on 5 December 1998, state elections on 9 January 1999, and federal elections the following month, with the presidential elections fixed for 27 February. On the international front, Nigeria slowly started shedding its pariah status. In October, the Commonwealth lifted the sanctions imposed on Nigeria following the execution of Saro-Wiwa and his colleagues in 1995; however, the suspension from the Commonwealth remained in place pending the successful conclusion of the transition programme. The leaders of the United States, United Kingdom, and France received Abdulsalami when it became clear to them that he was serious about handing over power, and lent their support. In the same month, the INEC announced that it had granted provisional registration to nine political associations, which included the People's Democratic Movement (PDM), the All Peoples Congress (APC), and the United People's Party (UPP).

The following month, on 11 November 1998, the government inaugurated the Constitution Debate Coordinating Committee (CDCC), under the chairmanship of Mr. Justice Niki Tobi. The CDCC was asked to "pilot the debate, co-ordinate and collate views and recommendations canvassed by individuals and groups" on the 1995 draft constitution that had been created under Abacha, and was tasked with submitting a report no later than the end of the year. The CDCC was asked to provide, in particular, fresh views on a number of specific provisions of the 1995 draft, such as whether to enshrine the principles of zoning and rotation in the Constitution (and if so, for what offices and for how long), the idea of multiple vice presidents, the legislative powers at federal, state, and local government levels; the perennial and thorny derivation issue, the independence of the judiciary, the creation of a specific constitutional court, proportional representation of ministers from different political parties in the federal cabinet and the concept of simultaneous membership of the legislature and the executive branches by ministers. Just over a month later, the CDCC submitted their report. It was striking in two ways: first, it unequivocally stated that the members of the committee had decided to reflect the views of the Nigerian people transmitted to them via memoranda and debates, and that they had agreed not to express their own views; and second, it was clear to the CDCC that the overwhelming opinion of the Nigerian people was a desire to return to the 1979 Constitution, with a few amendments taken from the 1995 draft.

The regime demonstrated that it meant to see this transition programme through, by conducting the elections as scheduled by the INEC. Three main parties emerged from the nine political associations; the Peoples' Democratic Party (PDP), the Alliance for Democracy (AD), and the All Peoples Party (APP). The climax was the presidential election held on 27 February 1999. For the first and only time in Nigeria's history, both candidates (Obasanjo for the PDP and Olu Falae on a joint AD/APP ticket) were Yorubas from the Southwest — there was a clear sentiment abroad in the land that, after twenty years of uninterrupted rule by Northerners, military and civilian, it was the Southerner's turn, and given the Abiola situation, the next president should be a Yoruba from the Southwest. Obasanjo won the election by a clear and convincing plurality of the votes, despite losing heavily in his native Southwest (for in many political circles, he was seen as the candidate of the Northern military oligarchy, having, of course, been a military Head of State in the past himself). An attempt by Falae to challenge the validity of the election in the courts was dismissed, and Obasanjo was confirmed as president-elect. It was a remarkable transformation from coup convict under sentence of death to president-elect in four short years.

Meanwhile, Abdulsalami continued to underline the fact that, whilst he might have been a key member of the Abacha regime, his was a completely different regime. In March 1999, several military officers and civilians imprisoned for their alleged roles in the 1995 and 1997 coups were released; in the same month, other officers who had been in prison since the Orkar coup of April 1990 were granted clemency and released from jail. In May 1999, just prior to the hand over, the PRC promulgated Decree No. 53 of 1999, which ordered the forfeiture to the federal government of all assets illegally held by Abacha, members of his family, and several of his key aides (such as National Security Adviser Ismaila Gwarzo and Finance Minister Anthony Ani). Those who had held sway under the regime, such as al Mustapha and Gwarzo, had been swiftly removed from positions of influence. The Abacha era was truly over.

On 29 May 1999, as promised, General Abdulsalami Alhaji Abubakar handed over the leadership of the Federal Republic of Nigeria to President Olusegun Obasanjo. The Nigerian Army's frontline role in Nigeria's politics was at an end.

NOTE

1. www.naij.com/368971. Accessed 19/9/16

CHAPTER 16

The Legacy of Hubris

All political lives, unless they are cut off in midstream at a happy juncture, end in failure....

— **Enoch Powell**

As General Abdulsalami Abubakar handed over the reins of power to the newly re-minted President Obasanjo on 29 May 1999 at the Eagle Square in Abuja, it was tempting for the discerning to mark the number of very interesting parallels between the two men. They were both four-star generals, both had been military heads of state who had come into office as a result of the sudden deaths of their predecessors in office, and both had become the only two military rulers in Nigeria's history to voluntarily relinquish power to an elected civilian government. Amid the celebrations that day, it was easy to overlook the salient question of how the involvement of Nigeria's armed forces (and particularly its army) in the politics of the country for twenty-nine of the thirty-nine years since Independence had impacted on both the country and its army. In this author's opinion, both country and army have suffered as a result of the latter's involvement in politics, and there is plenty of evidence to back this up, both before 1999 and the years since.

There can be little doubt that the professionalism of the army was significantly eroded once it overtly intruded into the political arena. The first clear signs of this came in the way in which the Civil War was ineptly fought, tactically and strategically, on both sides. The attrition in the army's officer and senior NCO Corps as a result of the events of 1966 meant that there was little experience or expertise available to prosecute the war on any sort of sound military footing, thus prolonging the conflict and the attendant loss of life, both military and civilian. Indeed, there is a very strong case for suggesting that the war would never have been fought *at all* if not for the army's intervention in politics.

Once the war was over, the army remained in power for almost another decade. In this period, it became used to the trappings and perks of political power, and also to the tremendous material wealth (for those who wished or were able to accumulate it) that accompanied unfettered power. Whilst this was going on, the army had become a bloated bureaucracy, gulping huge proportions of the national wealth, with little operational effectiveness to show for it. And, ominously, there was a growing population of army officers who had developed a taste for coup plotting — the subalterns and senior NCOs of July 1966 became the majors and lieutenant-colonels of July 1975, the colonels and brigadiers of 1983 and the brigadiers and major-generals of 1985 — and they had more junior officers who had been groomed in their image and likeness following on behind them.

It was a pity (although, perhaps, not a complete surprise) that the 1979-1983 civilian government of Shehu Shagari provided the army's coup merchants with abundant excuse to justify another intervention in politics at the end of 1983. Gowon's 1974 lament that the politicians had not learned any lessons from the First Republic had been proved correct (again, unsurprisingly, given that it was largely the same group of people in 1979-83 as it had been in 1960-66). The return of the army to power ushered in an era of factionalism, graft, cynicism and, quite frankly, terror that the country had not witnessed hitherto. The army became, as Lieutenant-General Salihu Ibrahim put it, one where "anything goes", where you got on not so much on the basis of how good you were, but on the basis of whom you knew, whose "boy" you were, or which part of the country you came from. Those deemed unreliable, or who had crossed those who were now at the centre of power were prematurely retired, irrespective of how professionally capable they were. Others were got rid of in order to create room for the advancement of those in favour, again irrespective of merit. The inevitable resentments burst forth in the April 1990 coup, which in turn added to the bloodshed of 1986, and fuelled the paranoid mistrust within the armed forces throughout the 1990s. The armed forces that Obasanjo inherited on 29 May 1999 was a thoroughly politicized, operationally ineffective and, in the eyes of the citizenry, totally discredited institution. Perhaps Obasanjo, as someone who was not only a previous military ruler but had also suffered humiliation and imprisonment at the hands of his erstwhile comrades in arms, understood this better than most. One of his first acts in office was to appoint Theophilus Danjuma, one of his closest associates in his time as military head of state, as Minister of Defence. His subsequent purge of all officers of field rank and above who had held political posts under previous military regimes showed he was fully alive to the potential threat to the new regime from these officers, among other strategies, (firing all the service chiefs of the Abdulsalami era). The rot, unfortunately, ran very deep, and the evil legacy of a loss of operational effectiveness was sadly manifest in the inept and ham-fisted response to the Boko Haram insurgency in North Eastern Nigeria between 2009 and 2015. Any hopes that the leadership of the armed forces during this period, which was made up of those who had ostensibly not been poisoned by previous exposure to political power, would boldly speak truth to power, and discharge their professional duties effectively and efficiently were dashed.

And what of the country? Military rule may not have been a *totally* unmitigated disaster for Nigeria...but it was not far from being just that. Although the nation had witnessed some mayhem under the civilian government of the First Republic (the Tiv riots and the unrest following the rigged Western Region elections of late 1965 being two immediate examples), at least the nation had not been plunged into a civil war, which the soldiers managed to achieve within a year and a half of coming to power. This is not to mention the pogrom against the Igbos and other Southerners in the North in May and October 1966. Even the most conservative estimates reckon that at least a million Nigerians lost their lives between January 1966 and January 1970.

Several aspects of present-day Nigeria, for good or for ill, are legacies of the several years of military rule. In the seventeen years since the return of civilian rule in 1999, two of the four elected presidents are retired generals who were also military heads of state. There have been more retired military officers in the legislature (especially the Senate) than one can shake a stick at. On the subject of the legislative arm of government, it is no coincidence, in the opinion of this author, that it has been the weakest and least effective arm of government since 1999, mainly because it was the only one which did not exist under military regimes (at least not in any meaningful way); whereas there has always been an executive and a judiciary, irrespective of whether the government is military or civilian. The old saying that power corrupts, and absolute power corrupts absolutely, was never truer than in Nigeria under military rule. The absence of strong institutions in present-day Nigeria can be, to a large degree, laid at the feet of several years of military rule — the civil service after the purges of 1975 being but one example.

The structure of present-day Nigeria, and the weaknesses inherent in that structure, are also directly attributable to military rule. There can be little doubt that the regional structure bequeathed by the departing British colonial masters was flawed, and in need of reform, and that Gowon's creation of twelve states in May 1967, with parity in numbers of states between North and South, was not only a deft solution to the political problems of the time, but also addressed the long-standing issue of ethnic minorities which the old regional structure did not do. That said, the same Gowon regime began the process of moving powers away from the states to the centre, which every successive military regime has continued, whether in terms of revenue allocation or exclusive/residual legislative lists. This centralization of power has made Nigeria a federal republic in name only, and has resulted in a do-or-die approach to the gaining of power at the federal level. Successor regimes have created more states, but in a lopsided manner, entrenching the current situation where there are more states in the North than in the South. This, in and of itself, would not necessarily be that big a deal in a more politically mature society, which Nigeria, at least as of 2016, sadly is not. In any event, there remain serious questions about whether Nigeria needs, or can afford, so many states, many of which are far from being economically viable, with the resultant multiplication of the already bloated costs of governance.

As stated earlier, military rule has not *quite* been a totally unmitigated disaster — one can point to the establishment of the National Youth Service Corps (NYSC) under Gowon, or to Babangida's conduct of probably the most accurate census in Nigeria's history as examples. In the final analysis, however, the balance sheet has far more entries in the debit column than in the credit column, and that is a lesson that the politicians and soldiers in the Nigeria of today would be wise to heed.

Appendix

APPENDIX 1: The Welby-Everard Top-Secret Memo to the Permanent Secretary of the Ministry of Defence

TOP SECRET

PERSONAL

NA/GOC/20

Permanent Secretary

    I attach a memorandum which discusses the problem of the next GOC.

2.   I suggest that this matter should be discussed by the Army Council unless HMD would prefer to discuss it with me personally.

Major-General,
G.O.C.

14 September, 1964.

TOP SECRET

Copy of memo with GOC 14/9

TOP SECRET

THE PROBLEM OF THE NEXT G.O.C.

(Memorandum by the GOC)

It would appear that there are three contenders for the post of GOC when I leave. In order of seniority they are:-

Brigadier J. T. U. AGUIYI-IRONSI
Brigadier S. A. ADEMULEGUN
Brigadier B. O. A. OGUNDIPE.

I have not included Brigadier MAIMALARI as I consider him to be too young at present and not sufficiently mature.

2.   My personal observations on these three officers follow:-

a.   IRONSI has been away from Nigeria and consequently out of direct contact with the Army for the past 3 years, first as Military Adviser in London, then as a student at the Imperial Defence College and finally for the first 6 months of this year as Commander of the United Nations Force in the Congo.
He has never commanded a Brigade in Nigeria and has only been a Battalion Commander for about 6 months in 1960/61. He has therefore been out of direct touch with recent developments and is not as familiar with the careers of officers in the Army as are other senior officers.
As he has never served under my command it is difficult for me to assess accurately his professional ability but I have not been impressed by his military knowledge on the occasions when he has attended the GOC's Conference and other meetings.
It is also my duty to point out that there is a record against him of financial instability.
My personal opinion is that I doubt whether he has either the professional military knowledge or the personal characteristics to make a good GOC.

b.   ADEMULEGUN has served continuously in the Army except for the year 1963 when he was a student at the Imperial Defence College. He has commanded a Battalion for over a year and has commanded both Brigades in Nigeria.
He therefore has a wide and up to date knowledge of the Army and its current problems and his professional military knowledge is good.
He is a forceful leader but somewhat intolerant in his opinions and hasty in his judgment. For this reason he has a good many critics, not to say enemies, in the Army.
There is no doubt in my opinion that he has the professional ability to make a good GOC and also has the necessary leadership qualities, but I fear that he might not command the unswerving loyalty of all the officers. This would not apply to the same extent if IRONSI was Chief of Defence Staff.

TOP SECRET   ....../2.

c. OGUNDIPE has also served continuously with the Nigerian Army except for a period of 6 months in 1963 when he was Chief of Staff to the United Nations Force in the Congo. He has commanded a Battalion for nearly a year. He has also commanded the Nigerian Brigade in the Congo as well as currently commanding 2 Brigade in Lagos. Whilst Chief of Staff in the Congo he earned high praise for his military ability, fine character and powers of organisation. His professional knowledge is good and he possesses a sound and well balanced judgment. He has an equitable temperament and is universally respected by all ranks in the Army.

He has the military ability, leadership qualities and the personal characteristics to make a good GOC.

3. After very careful consideration of all the military and personal factors involved my opinion is that OGUNDIPE would make the best GOC, because I consider that he would be more likely to command the loyalty of the whole Army than either of the other two, and there would be less likelihood of opposing factions springing up within the Officer Corps.

4. I will now make my recommendations regarding Senior Officer appointments in the various circumstances. These must be regarded as provisional recommendations as the views of the new GOC, whoever he is to be, will have to be taken into account.

The second tour of my own contract terminates on 11th February, 1965 and I have made plans to leave Nigeria on 16th February. I consider therefore that I should finally handover command to the new GOC on 12th February, 1965.

5. If OGUNDIPE is to be GOC

a. If it is decided to appoint a Chief of Defence Staff, either IRONSI or ADEMULEGUN could fill this post but it must be remembered that neither the Navy nor the Air Force would be able to contribute officers for a Defence Staff until 1966 at the earliest. This does not however necessarily rule out the appointment of a Chief of Defence Staff in 1965. If IRONSI were selected for this he could be Deputy GOC until I leave.

b. If it is decided NOT to appoint a Chief of Defence Staff in 1965 then:-

(i) IRONSI would have to leave the Army and be found other employment.

(ii) ADEMULEGUN could remain in the Army but would have to be found a post outside Nigeria e.g. Military Adviser in London or Washington, or possibly employment with OAU.

³ TOP SECRET

c. The two Brigade Commanders would be:-

    1 Brigade KADUNA   -   MAIMALARI
    2 Brigade LAGOS   -   ADEBAYO

d. OGUNDIPE would not be able to attend the IDC course in 1965 but MUHAMMED could take his place.

e. NJOKU would be suitable to take MUHAMMED's place as Deputy Commandant of the Defence Academy.

f. There would have to be a new Chief of Staff. PAM would be very suitable.

6. If ADEMULEGUN is to be GOC

a. IRONSI would either have to be Chief of Defence Staff or he would have to leave the Army and be found other employment.

b. OGUNDIPE would attend the IDC in 1965.

c. The two Brigade Commanders would be:-

    1 Brigade KADUNA   -   MAIMALARI
    2 Brigade LAGOS   -   ADEBAYO

d. NJOKU or PAM could be Chief of Staff.

7. If IRONSI is to be GOC

a. There would be no Chief of Defence Staff.

b. OGUNDIPE would attend the IDC.

c. The two Brigade Commanders would be:-

    1 Brigade KADUNA   -   MAIMALARI
    2 Brigade LAGOS   -   ADEMULEGUN

d. It would be essential for ADEBAYO to remain as Chief of Staff in order to retain continuity of policy.

e. As IRONSI has no appointment at present the question would arise of his employment until I leave. There are the following alternatives:-

(i) As IRONSI has not commanded a Brigade in Nigeria, OGUNDIPE, who has had no leave for 3 years, could go on leave until he goes to the IDC and IRONSI could command 2 Bde from October to December. The experience would be of great value to him and would in my opinion benefit the Army when he became GOC.
He could become Deputy GOC in January for the last few weeks before taking over.
The fact that he would, to start with, be a Brigadier and not a Major-General would not matter because his appointment as GOC designate would have been announced, and when he held the Acting rank of Major-General he was employed with the United Nations in the Congo and not with the Nigerian Army.

TOP SECRET   ..../4

(ii) IRONSI could become Deputy GOC in October. I could delegate some duties to him and in any case I would be away a good deal on tour making my farewell visits. In this capacity he could if considered desirable be promoted to Major-General and one of us could be held supernumerary to establishment until I leave.

In order to enable IRONSI to gain more experience in command in view of his long absence from service with the Nigerian Army I would strongly recommend alternative (i).

(f) It has been suggested that IRONSI might take over from me in October and that I should become a Training Adviser until I leave. I most emphatically do NOT recommend this suggestion for the following reasons:-

(i) After having been GOC for $2\frac{1}{2}$ years my position as an Adviser would be very embarrassing both to the Army and to myself. There cannot be two GOCs at the same time.

(ii) I could hardly carry out my farewell visits as GOC and receive the customary honours and ceremonial if I had already lost the executive authority of the appointment. It would be an intense disappointment to me to leave without carrying out a full tour of farewell visits.

(iii) There would also be the anomaly of IRONSI paying his initial visits as the new GOC before I paid my farewell visits.

(iv) The amount of training taking place during that period will inevitably be strictly limited because of the Army's Federal Election commitments. In any case the amount of bush training for the rest of the current financial year is greatly restricted by shortage of funds.

BIBLIOGRAPHY

Ademoyega, Adewale. *Why We Struck: The Story of the First Nigerian Coup.* Evans Brothers, 1981.

Agbese, Dan. Ibrahim Babangida: *The Military, Politics and Power in Nigeria.* Adonis and Abbey Publishers, 2012.

Akpan, Ntieyong. *The Struggle for Secession 1966-1970: A Personal Account of the Nigerian Civil War.* Routledge, 1972.

Clark, Trevor. *A Right Honourable Gentleman: Abubakar From the Black Rock.* Edward Arnold, 1991.

Dannatt, General the Lord Richard. *Boots on the Ground: Britain and Her Army Since 1945.* Profile Books, 2016.

De St. Jorre, John. *The Brothers War: Biafra and Nigeria.* Houghton Mifflin, 1972.

Effiong, Philip. *Nigeria and Biafra: My Story.* African Tree Press, 2007.

Elaigwu, Isawa J. *Gowon: The Biography of a Soldier-Statesman.* West Books Publisher, 1985.

Enahoro, Chief Anthony. *Fugitive Offender: An Autobiography.* Casell, 1965.

Kirk-Greene, A.H.M. *Crisis and Conflict in Nigeria: A Documentary Sourcebook, 1966-1970.* Vol. 1: January 1966-July 1967. London: Oxford University Press, 1971.

Luckham, Robin. *The Nigerian Military: A Sociological Analysis of Authority and Revolt, 1960-67.* Cambridge University Press, 1971.

Madiebo, Alexander A. *The Nigerian Revolution and the Biafran War.* Fourth Dimension Publishing, 1980.

Malu, Lt. Gen. S.V.L. *In the Name of Victor: Confronting Errors with the Truth.* Author House, 2014.

Miners, N J. *The Nigerian Army: 1956-1966.* Methuen & Co., 1971.

Nigerian Army Education Corps and School. *History of the Nigerian Army: 1863-1992.* Nigerian Army Headquarters, 1992.

Ojiako, James. *Thirteen Years of Military Rule (1966-79).* Daily Times of Nigeria.

Omoigui, Nowamagbe. : www.segun.bizland.com/omoigui13

Onukaba, Adinoyi. *Olusegun Obasanjo: In the Eyes of Time.* Spectrum Books, 2007.

Personal and confidential communication to the author, October 2016.

Siollun, Max. *Oil, Politics and Violence: Nigeria's Military Coup Culture (1966-1976)*. Algora Publishing, 2009.

Siollun, Max. *Soldiers of Fortune: Nigerian Politics under Buhari and Babangida (1983-1993)*. Cassava Republic Press, 2013.

Tamuno, Tekena N. *Proceedings of the National Conference on Nigeria Since Independence*. Vol. 3 The Panel on Nigeria Since Independence History Project, 1984 (Jemibewon/Haruna).

www.Buhari2015.wordpress.com

www.naij.com/368971

INDEX

Petroleum and Natural
  Resources, 155
fifth military leader, 154
First Chairman of NNPC, 155
Foray into the army, 154-155
Hajia Zulaihatu Musa (mother),
  154
Hardo Adamu (father), 154
Head of State, appointed, 153
Platoon Commander, 155
played key roles in coups, 155
Promotions in the army, 155
retired from the army, 162
Burkina Faso, 32
Burma, 4

Calabar, 2, 12, 63, 82
Cameroon Army, 76
Cameroon, 3
Canada, 20
Census
  1952, 13
  1963, 113
  1973, 97-98, 107
  1991, 188
Census Data Review Committee, 98
Central African Republic, 32
Central Bank of Nigeria, 96, 208
China, 63
Christians, 174
Chude-Sokei, 48, 76
Chukwuka, Humphrey, 28, 33, 141
Church Missionary Society (CMS),
  56
Ciroma, Alhaji Adamu, 190, 194
Civil service, purges in the, 111
Civil societies, 193
Civil War, the (Nigeria), xxii, 1, 6,
  28, 52, 55, 75-84, 142, 146, 155,
  167, 173, 200, 217
  a uniting factor, 84

"police action", viewed as, 78
Civilian government, 149-152
  military intervention, 151
  Overthrown, 150, 152
Clark, JP, 172
Clausewitz, Carl von, 29
CMS Grammar School, Lagos, 64
cocoa, 97
Code of Conduct Bureau, 112, 178
Colonial government, 9
Committee for National Consensus
  (CNC), 204
Commonwealth, 5
Concord Group newspapers, 150
Concord Press, 202
Congo, 21, 22, 107, 141
Constituent Assembly, 180
Constitution Debate Coordinating
  Committee (CDCC), 214
Constitution Drafting Committee
  (CDC), 112, 143
Constitution Review Committee
  (CRC), 177, 180
Constitutional Conference (1957),
  15
Constitutional Review Study
  Group, 49
Cookey, Dr. Samuel J., 176
Coomassie, Ibrahim, 201
Corruption, 89, 92-93, 150, 154, 156,
  162
Coups
  April 1990 (Orkar coup), 187,
    193, 216, 218
  August 1985 coup, 161, 170, 180
  Coup plots, 31-41, 50, 100, 105,
    116, 118, 151, 160-161, 169,
    183-187, 218
  December 1983 coup, 152
  December 1985 (attempted)
    coup, 172
  Enugu coup, 34

9 780998 479675